C000083983

great dishes of spain

Photographs by Robert Carrier

GREAT DISHES OF
SPAIN

ROBERT CARRIER

B⊞XTREE

To Mari Roberts, my editor, and to
Roger Hammond, my art editor, my
heartfelt thanks: they brought order –
and beauty – out of chaos.

First published 1999 by Boxtree, an imprint of Macmillan
Publishers Ltd,
25 Eccleston Place, London SW1W 9NF
and Basingstoke

Associated companies throughout the world

ISBN 07522 24921

9 8 7 6 5 4 3 2 1

Designed by Roger Hammond
Edited by Mari Roberts
Index by Dorothy Frame
Spanish language consultant: María Jesús Vence Lodeiro

A CIP catalogue record for this book is available from the British
Library

Typeset by SX Composing DTP, Rayleigh, Essex
Printed and bound in Great Britain by Bath Press, Bath

Contents

Introduction 6

Olives and olive oil 10

Chapter 1 Simple tapas 12

Chapter 2 Hot tapas 16

Chapter 3 Salads 36

Chapter 4 Bacalao 54

Chapter 5 Tortilla and other egg dishes 64

Chapter 6 Gazpacho and other soups 76

Chapter 7 Sauces and marinades 86

Chapter 8 Paella and other rice dishes 96

Chapter 9 Fish and shellfish 112

Chapter 10 Cocido and other meats 131

Chapter 11 Vegetables 162

Chapter 12 Crema catalana and other postres 186

Index 212

Acknowledgements 216

Introduction

From gypsy Sevilla, the birthplace of *tapas*, to the rice fields around Valencia, home of Spain's greatest *paella* – Spain is a country of contrasts, not the least of which is its food. Once one of the world's most powerful countries, discoverer for Europe of the Americas, home of the *conquistadores*, rich in art and architecture, full of the resonance of its colourful history, Spain still lives on a sensual, very human scale.

It was in Sevilla, during the full swing of the *feria* – the spring fertility festival – that I first discovered the enduring magic of Spain. The crowded, sun-splashed streets were full of handsome men and beautiful women on horseback. People I met were talking about pilgrimages to El Rocío and Santiago de Compostela, about the closed mule-drawn carriages in holy processions, the perfect miniature bullring at Ronda, the beautiful haciendas lost in the mountains behind Marbella. I was lost.

Spain became one long pleasure for me. It was *tapas* in the crowded bars of Sevilla and *pinchos* in San Sebastián. I visited the splendiferous market of La Boqueria in Barcelona's Ramblas district, and enjoyed visits to famous restaurants, wonderful meals in bougainvillea-scented patios, fabulous street treats at country fairs. It was Spain with its colourful, laid-back lifestyle and healthy informal cuisine – so right for today.

Over the past few years I have made five extensive trips through Spain: from the foothills of the Pyrenees to the sun-baked expanses of Andalusia; from the rocky shores of the Costa Brava to the rich green countryside of Galicia, north of Portugal. Here, in addition to the famed dishes that have become the glamorous passwords of Spanish cooking all around the world – *gazpacho, paella, zarzuela, cocido, bacalao, chuletas, albóndigas, pisto, churros,* and that grandiose custard cream of all time, *crema catalana* – I discovered Spain's hidden *cocina*, passionately regional to this day, rich, immediate and intensely colourful, completely in key with our modern health-obsessed way of life.

And along the way, of course, I fell in love with the snow-capped mountains of the Sierra Nevada, the regimented olive groves, the bullrings and the bullfighter bars, the flamenco dancers, the sherry growers of

Jerez de la Frontera and Sanlúcar de Barrameda and the curers of ham in the high-up mountain villages, absorbing to the full their free and easy lifestyles. But perhaps the most evocative and instructive of my journeys started out in the ancient Arab strongholds of Granada and Córdoba and Sevilla, and finished in the little white Arab villages of the Alpujarras. It was on these visits that I discovered the ancient Iberian, Roman and Arabian roots of Spanish cuisine. *Great Dishes of Spain* is my ardent compilation of all these adventures. Enjoy this book. Trust your instincts. Discover the new smoothness of emulsions made with virgin olive oil, the unexpected savour of dishes cooked with pure pork fat, the delights of foods dry-seared *a la plancha*. And above all, open your heart and your mind **to the dazzling, full flavours of new and old Spain**.

Spain has a rich culinary history. In the following chapters we celebrate the many wonderful dishes of Spain's ancient cuisine (the fabled *cocina del país*), going back to its early Arab and Andalusian precedents, to begin to understand where the luscious orange salads come from; how preserved lemons entered Spain's southern, Arabo-Andaluz cuisine; and to attempt to decide at last whether Catalan *allioli* or Provence's *aïoli* came first, and how Spanish *pisto* compared with Provençal ratatouille.

One thing we do know for certain: it was Spain who first brought the fruits of Columbus's early voyages to the cooking of Italy, France, North Africa, and Spain itself. What did the world do before the importation and subsequent production of tomatoes and peppers and potatoes and maize, and before it experienced the rich heady warmth of Aztec chocolate? Remember it was Eugénie de Montijo from Granada, Napoleon III's empress, who first made chocolate elegant at the French court, and thence the world. She alone changed, with her fashion sense, her sophistication and her daring, life at the French court, and thus all the other courts of Europe.

The world owes Spain a lot. And perhaps we have forgotten it. *Great Dishes of Spain* sets out to redress this *oubli*. It is time to set Spanish cooking once again among the great cuisines of the world and to trumpet forth the dazzling modern *cocina* of the talented new lights of Spanish cooking: Ferran Adrià of El Bulli at Roses near Girona, and Juan Mari Arzak of Arzak, who first banded together to create modern Spanish cooking and who currently lead Spain's truly exciting new cuisine. Add to these Martin Berasategui of El Amparo in Madrid, the Albacar brothers Tito and Salvador in Valencia, and José Luis Capo of Maricel in Sitges, and you will get a small idea of what modern Spanish cooking is all about.

Great Dishes of Spain is a loving tribute in words and pictures and received memories of meals spent with friends enjoying the wonderful rice-based dishes of Spain: such as *arroz a banda* (golden saffron rice with a deep sea flavour), and the sumptuous *paellas*, truly one of the world's greatest dishes when made with a fantastically rich stock as they do in Spain, and especially the famous *paella* of rabbit and chicken and greens (and sometimes snails) served in the age-old fashion by Don Rafael Vidal in his popular restaurant at Benissanó, near Valencia. I love, too, the wonderful flavours of

seventeenth-century Spanish stews, *cocido* and *caldereta*, and the sizzling little dishes of *angulas* (baby eels) and *gambas al ajillo* (prawns with garlic), the ever more rare *percebes* (primeval-looking goose barnacles), and the great classic dishes of baby kid, baby lamb and suckling pig cooked *al horno* (in wood-fired ovens) or spit-roasted over embers.

It was in Spain, too, that I made a study of the joys of *alioli* (in Catalan, its true home, *allioli*), that sumptuous, demanding, surrealistic sauce that makes such a simple thing as garlic, olive oil, egg yolks and salt a work of art, to serve with roast quarters of lamb cooked *al horno* or with casseroles of roasted rabbit, half heads of garlic and preserved lemon, or (most exciting of all perhaps) to fork-streak through a golden-tinted seafood *paella* or an arrogant *arroz negro*. It is a poem, a majestic entity. Let its magic impregnate your cooking.

Rich, old-fashioned puddings abound: *tarta de Santiago*, a delicious, sugar-dusted almond cake, served with cream and purple figs; *leche frita* (fried cream); *torrija antequerana* (honey-dipped fried bread), and *torta de naranja*, Spain's famous orange tart, with its richly orange-flavoured *crema catalana* filling (Spain's most famous egg-custard dessert). And of course *crema catalana* itself, individual portions of delicious custard cream served in flat saucers, the tops beautifully blistered and coloured by a special kitchen implement once kept hot over the embers of the fire in the Spanish kitchen.

OLIVES AND OLIVE OIL

Spaniards love olives. They eat them every day. And I understand why. The olive tree is the oldest tree in the world, the most profoundly rooted in the earth and in the Mediterranean tradition. For centuries, olive oil has reigned supreme over all the table oils of the Mediterranean basin. There is evidence that the first olives were cultivated on Crete as early as 3500 years before the birth of Christ, making this probably the oldest cultivated fruit tree in the world. It was the Romans who brought the first olive trees to southern Spain. And from the eighth century to the fifteenth, when the country was under Arab rule, the cultivation of olive trees flourished. Today as one drives from Andalusia in the south and up through Cervantes country in Castille–La Mancha in central Spain – even as far north as Toledo and Madrid – the countryside is dotted with geometric rows of carefully tended olive trees. Today, Spain is perhaps the biggest producer of olives and olive oil in the world.

Like fine wines, extra virgin olive oils in Spain have their crus, which depend on the provenance of the olives and the manner in which they are pressed. They can be sweet-flavoured or fruity, and the colours can go from a sharp clear green to pale gold. There are three qualities available: extra virgin olive oil with its irreproachable

flavour, whose count of oleic acid cannot exceed 1 gram per 100; virgin olive oil, where the acidity cannot exceed 2 grams per 100; and finally more commercial olive oils, produced by blending less expensive refined olive oils with a percentage of virgin olive oil to make smooth comfortable blends.

Spanish olive oil was most important to the early Romans. Production in Baetica (as what is now Andalusia was known) began to rise steeply, rapidly overtaking the traditional sources in Greece and Italy. From Spain they could send it north to meet the huge demand in Gaul, Britain and Germany, as well as dispatch it direct to Rome. Fortunes were made with what became a star product.

In the early days of the first century the Romans were shipping thousands of amphorae of the golden oil from Spain to the whole of Italy, to Africa, and as far as Egypt. They soon supplied Dalmatia, Crete, Syria and – because of the superior mellow flavour of the Spanish oil – even Greece, who had been oil producers for centuries before this time.

Olive oil was used by the early Romans in Spain to improve the health of their livers, stop rust on their iron pots and preserve food; the wood from the olive trees was used, as now, to make bowls, small platters, salad servers and kitchen tools, even mortars and pestles for grinding peppercorns, garlic, almonds and spices and herbs. And the oil was also used by the rich to provide odourless oil lamps to light their houses.

The finest olive oil was produced in the area stretching from Gades (Cádiz) to Hispalia (Sevilla), Corduba (Córdoba), and Malaca (Málaga) on the southern coast. Málaga was also famed for the production of garum salarum, the top flavouring of the ancient world, made

from the fermented entrails and trimmings of sardines and grey mullet, much as the Thais and Vietnamese use fermented fish today to produce Thai nam pla and Vietnamese nuoc mam, the top flavour accents of oriental cooking now so popular in the western world. Spain should research the old ways of making garum with sun-dried fish or with fermented grains and use it today as they did in the time of the early Roman empire.

But back to Roman Baetica, the rich, hot treasure house of southern Spain where the world's greatest olive oil was produced, with its golden colour and fabulous flavour full of warmth and sunshine: liquid gold as it was known to the ancients. From the early days, the Spanish provincials – ahead of those of Gaul and Britain (ever since their admission to Roman society) – had packed the Roman Senate, plucked the plum salaried jobs in the equestrian ranks, conquered literary life with a galaxy of world-famous poets and rhetoricians, and produced vast quantities of silver and deliciously cured sausages and hams.

Olive oil was a staple of cultured life, the master ingredient, lighting the best houses and public buildings, giving a steady clear light, with no disagreeable odour. It was used as a base for perfumes and medicines, and the oil-based unguents that were used in the ancient world's wondrous bath houses and gymnasiums. It was golden olive oil that made the people from southern Spain rich.

Chapter 1

SIMPLE TAPAS

Tapas **are almost a way of life in Spanish cities.** People like to gather for a drink and a small plate or two of *tapas* with friends before going on to a late lunch or dinner. More recently *tapas* have crossed the borders of Spain to be much appreciated in France, Britain and America. At their simplest they might be just a plate of olives, some salted almonds, cubes of *manchego* cheese drizzled with extra virgin olive oil, or perhaps a slice of country bread rubbed with garlic and tomato, sprinkled with olive oil and topped by a thin slice of *serrano* ham. The more filling, hot *tapas* are for the most part popular descendants of country cuisine: a fat cube of cooked tripe on a toothpick, batter-fried spring onions or squares of salt cod, tiny dishes of favourite Andalusian and Catalonian stews, a mini dish of hot clams in a spicy green sauce or of snails in a paprika- and tomato-infused broth, a wedge of *tortilla*, or a plate of fried whitebait, grilled sardines or garlic prawns. *Tapas* have come to define, for many of us, a new style of carefree entertaining.

On my many visits to Spain researching this book, I caught the *tapas* habit. All Spain loves nothing better than to talk, be it poetry or politics, and the *tapas* bar is the primary place to do it. It is such an agreeable pastime to wander with good companions from bar to bar to indulge in a glass of wine, sherry or beer, here with a fine fat olive stuffed with *pimiento* or an almond, there with a wedge of *tortilla*, or even a glass of *cava* (Spain's own champagne) and a *banderilla* of grilled sweet prawns speared on long wooden toothpicks, dressed with chopped hard-boiled egg white, parsley, *serrano* ham and red pepper.

Some cold *tapas* suggestions:
olives
salted almonds
caper berries in vinegar
manchego cheese squares with olive oil

Bread and oil-based *tapas*:
thumb-sized calamari or baby rougets marinated in extra virgin olive oil, sherry vinegar, salt, pepper and oregano, char-grilled and served on oil-drizzled bread with lemon wedges and *alioli* (page 93)

cooked fat white beans (*pochas*), drizzled with olive oil and served on garlic-rubbed bread with grilled vegetables and strips of juicy seared pork

a quick salad of canned drained chickpeas and strips of pimiento tossed in pungent *alioli* (page 93), served on garlic-rubbed bread with strips of pan-seared tuna

thin spears of grilled baby asparagus, brushed with extra virgin olive oil and served on garlic-rubbed bread, or on a bed of *piparrada* (page 71)

Pa amb tomàquet
Garlic and tomato toasts

By far the favourite *tapa* (or informal starting point to a restaurant meal) in Barcelona is *pa amb tomàquet* (garlic- and tomato-rubbed toast), whether served in a stall in the bustling Boqueria market, in a crowded *tapas* bar, or at Barcelona's trendiest port restaurant, El Barceloneta. You'll find these lightly toasted rounds of bread, brushed with crushed-garlic-flavoured oil and rubbed with a super ripe tomato, addictive. This is sunshine food, to be enjoyed when tomatoes are at their juicy best. Don't try it in the depths of a British winter.

6 tablespoons extra virgin olive oil

4 cloves garlic, mashed to a paste

juice of ¼ lemon

4–6 slices coarse-textured bread: in this country, I use a large French country loaf, or an Italian ciabatta

1 large very ripe tomato, cut in half

In a small bowl, combine the olive oil and crushed garlic. Add the lemon juice and mix well. Toast the bread slices slightly in a hot oven until they just begin to turn golden. Remove from the oven and brush with the oil and garlic mixture. Then rub them with the cut tomato halves, using all the tomato pulp and juices. Serve immediately.

Makes 4 to 6

Variations on the pa amb tomàquet theme

1. Top the garlic- and tomato-rubbed toasts with paper-thin slices of *serrano* ham – the thinner the better so that you can ruffle up the tender ham attractively on each slice of garlic and tomato toast.

2. Top the ruffled-up ham on each garlic- and tomato-rubbed toast with a small hot pickled green pepper or anchovy.

3. Top each garlic- and tomato-rubbed toast with ¼ roasted and peeled green pepper and an anchovy fillet.

4. Top each garlic- and tomato-rubbed toast with a little piped *brandada* (page 128) and an anchovy fillet.

5. And while you're at it, use this flavour-filled toast as a base for ruffled-up paper-thin slices of chilled smoked salmon or smoked sturgeon. Make sure you add a squeeze of lemon and the tiniest pinch of crushed dried chillies to bring out the full flavour of the smoked fish.

Migas
Pan-browned bread with garlic

Migas has always been one of the unexplained mysteries of Spanish cooking for me. After all, it was famous in the old days as a hunger-quenching breakfast dish served on its own or with fried eggs, or served sometimes as a sort of hot *tapa* or *entremés* as the humble beginning to a country meal in a local inn. In its classic version it consists of bread cubes, moistened with a little cold water before being pan-browned in oil with garlic and diced bacon, and flavoured and coloured with *pimentón*. Interesting, but unprepossessing.

Unprepossessing, that is, until I met the fabulous *nueva cocina* version of the brothers Albacar at their restaurant in Valencia. Their more sophisticated version is served with a brilliantly conceived dish of roast lamb with a brandy and honey sauce; the *migas*, crisp golden cubes of bread wrapped in a round (or ribbon) of grilled bacon, is topped with a fat slice of pan-seared fresh foie gras. Sublime. I give you both versions. Here is the classic one. The brothers' treatment can be found on page 142 in the *Cocido* chapter.

450 g / 1 lb stale bread, cut into slices, crusts removed, and then diced
salted water
6 tablespoons olive oil

2 slices unsmoked back bacon (or 2 thin slices of pork fillet, or even *serrano* ham), diced
4 cloves garlic, peeled but kept whole
2 teaspoons *pimentón* (Spanish sweet paprika)

Moisten the cubed stale bread with a little cold salted water (the classic recipe soaks it overnight in enough salted water to cover and drains it before cooking).

When ready to cook the *migas*, heat the olive oil in a large thick-bottomed frying pan. Add the diced bacon (or pork fillet or *serrano* ham) and fry until golden. With a slotted spoon, transfer the diced meat to a plate and reserve. Add the whole garlic cloves to the oil and cook, stirring, until golden. Remove from the pan and reserve. Stir the *pimentón* into the pan; add the drained bread and sauté over a medium heat for 2 to 3 minutes. Return the diced meat and garlic to the pan and continue to cook, stirring constantly with a wooden spoon, until the bread is golden and begins (a little like choux pastry) to come away from the sides of the pan. Serve immediately.

Serves 4

Chorizo a la plancha
Frazzled chorizo

Many a *tapas* bar or simple *venta* in Spain serves a small plate of what I like to call frazzled *chorizo*: thinly sliced *chorizo*, with the skin peeled off, pan-grilled for seconds only in a very hot metal pan until the sliced *chorizo* is soft, hot and slightly coloured, with its own red juices just beginning to run free. This simple *tapas* must be eaten piping hot. Eat as it is, or use to garnish slices of garlic tomato bread, to add interest and colour to a green salad, or to stir into hot saffron rice (virgin *paella*: see page 111), scrambled eggs or pan-braised potatoes. Simple, but simply delicious.

2 *chorizo* sausages

With a small sharp knife, trim the ends from the *chorizo* and carefully remove the skin. Cut the sausages crosswise into the thinnest slices possible.

When ready to serve, heat a non-stick frying pan over a high heat. Add the sliced *chorizo*, spreading it out in a thin layer on the bottom of the pan. Reduce the heat and 'frazzle' (sauté) the *chorizo* slices, turning them over in the pan, for 1 to 2 minutes, just until the *chorizo* begins to crisp and the red paprika-stained juices begin to seep out into the pan. Remove from the heat and serve immediately.

Serves 4 as a *tapa*, or as a garnish for a tossed green salad, scrambled eggs, saffron rice or pan-braised potatoes

***Jamón serrano* – the world's finest cured raw ham** – is so special, so fine, so richly flavoured that it can cost up to £50 per pound. And worth it. Every penny. Why? Because the hams are taken from special black-legged, dark-skinned Iberian pigs raised in the oak forests of south-western Spain. Before their last care-free months spent rooting through the loamy undergrowths of the oak forests, they are hand-reared on small farms in the mountain regions around Jabugo, Trevélez and Montánchez on a diet of grasses and grains such as corn and rye. From November to January, the pigs roam the forests feeding to their heart's content on acorns, consuming as much as 7 kilos in a single day.

The hams are cured and then matured for a year to 18 months. They are first wind-dried; then salted, and finally washed of their salt and hung in airy cold storage for months before being air-dried again. Then in winter when the temperature drops, the hams are cellar-stored so that the texture of the fat can begin to stabilize.

The acorn-raised pigs give ham that is a pale pink to deep burgundy red in colour bordered with a band of melt-in-your-mouth fat. The ham is at its best when served in paper-thin, near-transparent slices of great tenderness and flavour.

Chapter 2

HOT TAPAS

When *tapas* move from simple snacks and finger food to little hot dishes, the distinction blurs, from little brochettes of grilled prawns or mussels, or cubes of meat and poultry, to crisp beignets of chicken, sweetbreads, *chorizo* and *bacalao* (dried salt cod). From there we move on into the richer realm of slow-simmered dried beans with pig's ears, pig's tails and *tocino de cerdo* (an aged flavoursome slab of cured pork fat, very popular in Spain), or dishes of tripe cooked *a la madrileña* with long-simmered tomato, onion, red pepper, breadcrumbs and olive oil. The dish of snow-white tripe and its orange-red sauce is studded with tasty bits of *chorizo* sausage.

These are little tastes of whatever main dishes are on the menu and can be served as intriguing hot *tapas*, in slightly larger portions as first courses ... or as a delicious hot main course on their own. *Cazuelitas* (special little dishes), served with small forks, are used for more important hot *tapas* served in a sauce: *pochas* (large beans in tomato sauce with diced ham or salt pork), *gambas al ajillo* (prawns fried with garlic), *bacalao al pil-pil* (salt cod with fried garlic and chilli), *albóndigas* (meatballs in tomato sauce), clams in green sauce ... to mention just a few.

Calamares a la plancha
Grilled baby squid

Looking for an elegant and quick first course for a special lunch party? Try one (or both) of these delicious *tapas* recipes from Spain: succulent, tender and highly flavoured pan-grilled baby squid.

First of all, make sure that the squid are no longer than 7 to 10cm / 3 to 4in. If not already cleaned by your fishmonger (or the fresh fish counter in your local supermarket), see the directions on page 116. This recipe takes only 3 to 5 minutes' grilling on a very hot ridged grill pan.

Calamares a la plancha I
Grilled baby squid I

4 tablespoons olive oil

12–16 baby squid, cleaned

sea salt and crushed dried chillies

2 tablespoons finely chopped flat-leaf parsley

2 cloves garlic, finely chopped

finely grated rind of ½ orange

Garnish

mixed salad leaves, or sprigs of watercress and leaves of young spinach or red-stemmed chard

Place a ridged grill pan over a high heat. Brush the pan with a little of the olive oil. When the oil is sizzling hot, add the baby squid; season with salt and a pinch of crushed dried chillies, to taste, and cook over a high heat for 2 minutes. Turn the squid and continue cooking for another 1 or 2 minutes, adding a little more olive oil if necessary.

Transfer the grilled squid to a heated serving dish; sprinkle with finely chopped parsley and garlic and finely grated orange rind. Drizzle the squid with the remaining hot olive oil, garnish the dish with mixed leaves and serve immediately.

Serves 4

Calamares a la plancha II
Grilled baby squid II

12–16 baby squid, cleaned

4–6 tablespoons olive oil

sea salt and crushed dried chillies

2 tablespoons finely chopped flat-leaf parsley

2 cloves garlic, finely chopped

finely grated rind and juice of 1 large lime

Garnish

mixed salad leaves

alioli (page 93) or crème fraîche and crushed dried
     chillies

Cut each squid lengthwise into 6 even strips. In a medium-sized bowl, combine the squid strips with 1 tablespoon of the olive oil; season with sea salt and crushed dried chillies, to taste, and toss well. Reserve.

When ready to grill the squid strips, brush the heated ridged grill pan with a little of the remaining olive oil, add the squid strips and cook over a high heat for 2 minutes. Turn the squid and continue cooking for another 1 to 2 minutes.

Transfer the grilled squid to a heated serving dish and sprinkle with the finely chopped parsley and garlic and finely grated lime rind. Drizzle with the lime juice and remaining olive oil and season with a little sea salt and a pinch of crushed dried chillies. Garnish the dish with mixed salad leaves and serve immediately with an accompanying bowl of *alioli* (page 93), or crème fraîche with the tiniest pinch of chillies.

Calamares al pil-pil
Baby squid with chilli and garlic

In Spain and the Maghreb countries of North Africa you often come across the culinary term *pil-pil*: a chilli-hot, garlicky oil for sizzling seafood in little heatproof earthenware dishes – baby squid strips (in this case); prawns; poached *bacalao* (salt cod), the classic option; clams; fillets of hake or halibut, or even close-cap mushrooms. You'll soon claim cooking *al pil-pil* as your own.

12 baby squid, cleaned (see page 116) and cut into
    lengthwise strips
150 ml / 5 fl oz olive oil
2 cloves garlic, thinly sliced
1 small hot red chilli pepper, cut into thin rings
sea salt and crushed dried chillies

Garnish
sprigs of flat-leaf parsley

In a frying pan, combine the olive oil, garlic and chilli pepper. Place the pan over a medium heat and sauté the garlic and chilli for a few minutes or until the garlic begins to turn pale gold.

Remove the pan from the heat and remove the garlic and chilli with a slotted spoon (or strain the hot oil through a small sieve into a heatproof bowl). Reserve the garlic and chilli for later use.

Return the hot oil to the frying pan over a medium to high heat. Add the squid strips and sauté for 3 to 4 minutes, shaking the pan as you cook. Return the garlic and chilli to the pan to heat through.

To serve, transfer the contents of the pan to 4 individual earthenware dishes (which you have kept hot in a medium oven) and garnish each dish with sprigs of flat-leaf parsley. Serve immediately.

Serves 4

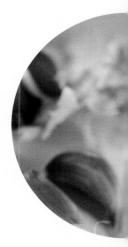

Albóndigas de cordero
Lamb meatballs

Little lamb meatballs called *albóndigas* are served the length and breadth of Spain. I particularly like the rustic version I first enjoyed in Valencia. Served in a tomato- and-paprika-flavoured wine sauce with diced carrot and peas, the lamb meatballs are made tender with minced fat pork and moistened breadcrumbs. A great idea for any meatballs.

400 g / 14 oz meat cut from a shoulder of lamb, minced

100 g / 4 oz fat pork, minced

100 g / 4 oz fresh breadcrumbs, soaked in 4 tablespoons of dry white wine and 2 of water

1 clove garlic, finely chopped

1 hard-boiled egg, finely chopped

sea salt and crushed dried chillies

sifted flour and olive oil, for frying the meatballs

Garnish

2 tablespoons chopped flat-leaf parsley

6 tablespoons fresh peas

6 tablespoons blanched, diced carrot

Sherry Tomato Sauce for Albóndigas

2 tablespoons lard (traditional), or the same amount of olive oil (for a lighter sauce), or a combination of the two

1 clove garlic, finely chopped

4 tablespoons finely chopped onion

about 1 tablespoon flour

½–¾ teaspoon *pimentón* (Spanish sweet paprika)

300 ml / ½ pint well-flavoured beef stock

3 tablespoons tomato purée, dissolved in 6 tablespoons dry sherry

sea salt and crushed dried chillies

To make the meatballs: In a medium-sized bowl, combine the lamb, fat pork, moistened breadcrumbs, garlic and hard-boiled egg. Season with salt and crushed dried chillies, to taste, and set in the refrigerator to mature for about 2 hours. Remove the lamb mixture from the refrigerator and roll into small balls the size of a walnut. Refrigerate again until ready to cook.

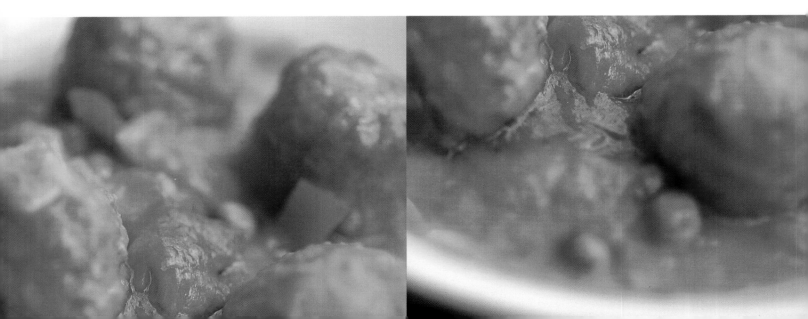

In the meantime prepare the sherry tomato sauce for the *albóndigas* (see the directions below).

When ready to cook the *albóndigas*, roll them in sifted flour. Heat enough olive oil in a large frying pan and sauté half the meatballs quickly on all sides until golden brown. Remove with a slotted spoon and allow to drain on folded kitchen paper while you sauté the remaining meatballs.

To make the sherry tomato sauce: In a saucepan, heat the lard (or olive oil, or a combination of the two), add the garlic and onion and sauté until soft. Then add the flour and continue to cook, stirring constantly, until a roux has formed. Add the *pimentón* and beef stock and bring the sauce gently to the boil, then stir in the tomato purée (dissolved in sherry). Lower the heat and simmer the sauce gently for 10 to 15 minutes. Season with sea salt and crushed dried chillies, to taste.

To serve, pour the prepared sauce over the *albóndigas* in a pan, add the peas and blanched carrots and simmer over a very low heat for 20 minutes. Sprinkle with chopped flat-leaf parsley and serve immediately.

Serves 4 to 6

Cerdo con salsa de pimentón
Pork strips in paprika sauce

This Cádiz *tapa* recipe, served in *cazuelitas*, is one of my favourites. Floured strips of roast pork are sautéed briefly in lard, then simmered in dry white wine with paprika and oregano, and served hot or cold.

2 tablespoons lard

4 slices cold roast pork, cut into 2.5-cm / 1-inch wide strips

4 tablespoons plain flour, seasoned with a little salt and freshly ground pepper

1 tablespoon *pimentón* (Spanish sweet paprika)

1 tablespoon fresh marjoram, or oregano leaves

300 ml / 10 fl oz dry white wine

Melt the lard in a small frying pan. Dip the pork strips in the seasoned flour and then sauté until the meat is well coloured. Add the *pimentón* and fresh herbs and stir for 1 minute more. Then stir in the dry white wine, lower the heat and simmer gently, stirring from time to time, until the meat is tender and the wine has reduced to sauce consistency.

Skim off any excess fat. Correct the seasoning and serve hot in *cazuelitas* or *tapas* dishes or allow to cool and serve cold.

Serves 4

Banderillas de gambas y jamón con vinagreta

Banderillas (picador's sticks) of grilled prawns and ham in a sherry vinegar dressing

The city of Logroño, in the heart of the Spanish wine country, boasts a street that is lined with *tapas* bars. Every other doorway in the calle del Laurel opens into another bar and at the busy *tapas* hours the bars as well as the street are filled with happy people enjoying *pinchos* and *tapas* , like this recipe for grilled prawn *banderillas* dressed with thin squares of *serrano* ham, chopped hard-boiled egg white and parsley, in a sherry, garlic and onion dressing. Delicious.

12 lightly poached tiger prawns
8 paper-thin squares (cut postage-stamp size) *serrano*
    ham
coarsely chopped white of 1 hard-boiled egg
4 pinches coarsely chopped flat-leaf parsley

sherry *vinagreta* (below)

Garnish
curly endive and Spanish black olives (optional)

Thread 3 poached prawns on each of 4 short bamboo skewers. On a flat plate, in separate piles, arrange ham squares, chopped hard-boiled egg white and chopped flat-leaf parsley. Make the sherry *vinagreta* (below).

    When ready to grill, brush the prawns lightly on both sides with a little of the *vinagreta* and grill on a hot ridged grill pan (or in a hinged electric grill) until heated through and slightly browned.

    To serve, place 1 prawn skewer on each of 4 *tapas* plates (or use small saucers, or bread and butter plates). Garnish each skewer with 2 postage-stamp sized squares of *serrano* ham, a sprinkling of chopped hard-boiled egg white and flat-leaf parsley and a teaspoon of sherry *vinagreta*. Decorate each plate, if desired, with a sprig of curly endive and a large Spanish black olive. Serve immediately while the prawns are still hot … and get ready to make more.

Makes 4 *banderillas*

Sherry Vinagreta

4 tablespoons extra-virgin olive oil
2–3 teaspoons sherry vinegar
1 teaspoon finely chopped onion
¼ clove garlic, finely chopped
sea salt and crushed dried chillies

In a small bowl, combine the olive oil, sherry vinegar and the finely chopped onion and garlic. Season with sea salt and crushed dried chillies (just a hint) and mix well.

Potaje de alubias blancas
Braised white beans

Hearty stews of lentils, white beans, or the famous red beans of Tolosa make wonderful *tapas* when served hot, or at room temperature, in small portions, or let these hearty vegetable stews serve as a traditional first course for an informal Spanish meal which might continue with *chuletas* of lamb or a chicken *chilindrón*. I like to serve them on their own, too, as a vegetable hotpot full of fabulous flavour. But don't make the mistake of thinking these are vegetarian dishes: they contain bits of fresh pork, salt pork, ham, *chorizo* and *morcilla*. This is Spanish rustic fare at its greatest. And most delicious.

450 g / 1 lb dried white beans

2 medium onions, cut into quarters

2 cloves garlic, cut into quarters

100 g / 4 oz salt pork, cut into 'fingers'

1 *chorizo* sausage, sliced into rounds

1 *morcilla* sausage, sliced into rounds

2 tablespoons *pimentón* (Spanish sweet paprika)

4 tablespoons olive oil

1 bay leaf

2 sprigs fresh thyme

4 medium potatoes, cut into quarters

4 medium carrots, cut into quarters

4 tablespoons olive oil

4 medium tomatoes, skinned and cut into quarters

2 tablespoons chopped flat-leaf parsley

Place the dried beans in a large bowl and add enough boiling water to cover them by 5 cm / 2 in. Allow beans to soak for at least 4 hours, or overnight.

When ready to cook the beans, drain them and place them in a medium-sized casserole. Add enough fresh cold water to cover, then add the quartered onions and garlic and bring to the boil. Then add the salt pork, *chorizo* and *morcilla*. Bring to the boil again, skim off any froth and impurities, lower the heat, cover the casserole and simmer the contents for 1 hour, adding a little more water as necessary.

Mix the *pimentón* with a ladleful of the bean stock and return it to the pan with the olive oil, bay leaf, thyme, quartered potatoes, carrots and tomatoes. Simmer for 20 to 30 minutes, or until the carrots and potatoes are tender. Season with salt and crushed dried chillies, to taste; add the chopped parsley and serve from the casserole.

Serves 6

Atún escabeche
Tuna in chilli-lime dressing

This is one of my favourite hot *tapas* dishes: individual snacks of grilled tuna, dressed just before serving with a spoonful or two of three-pepper *escabeche* dressing. For best effect, serve each *tapa* – with its thin lemon round and its basil – in a little *tapa* dish or porcelain (or real) scallop shell, and accent the sizzling hot tuna with its singing lime- and chilli-flavoured *escabeche* and its colourful garnish of crisp red and green pepper strips. You'll need 2 or 3 strips of each pepper colour for each dish … so start counting.

4 red tuna steaks (about 1½ cm / ½ inch thick)
8 tablespoons extra virgin olive oil
2–3 tablespoons fresh lime juice
24–36 thin strips of green pepper
24–36 thin strips of red pepper
2–3 tiny hot red chillies, seeded, cut into thin rings
salt and freshly ground pepper

Garnish
12 thin rounds of lemon
12 fresh basil sprigs

Cut each tuna steak into 3 even-sized rectangles.

In a small bowl, combine the olive oil, lime juice, pepper strips and chilli rings. Season generously with salt and pepper, to taste. Mix well and allow the flavours to amalgamate for at least 1 hour.

When ready to grill the tuna, heat a ridged grill pan until a drop of water sizzles on contact with the hot metal. Then place the tuna rectangles on the pan and grill for 2 minutes on each side until well-marked. Transfer the tuna sections to a gratin dish large enough to hold them in 1 layer (or make individual servings as suggested above). Spoon the cold marinade over the hot tuna and served immediately, each tuna section garnished with a lemon round and a sprig of basil.

Makes 12 tapas

Almejas finas en salsa verde
Small clams in spicy green sauce

Salsa verde **is one of the most popular sauces (more a broth really) in Spain,** used to add flavour and colour to clams, mussels, prawns or hake. The ingredients are so simple that it is almost impossible to believe how delicious the final dish can be, especially if a pinch of finely chopped garlic and a tablespoon or two of fish or vegetable stock is used to add savour. Some recipes include a tablespoon or two of fresh peas added at the last minute just before serving. Try it.

Clams and palourdes are now available in many fish markets, if not in supermarkets as yet. So if your local fish market has them in stock, try this recipe. Otherwise, substitute mussels for the clams. Serve chilled, or at room temperature.

36 small clams (palourdes), scrubbed
extra virgin olive oil
½ Spanish onion, finely chopped
600 ml / 1 pint dry white wine
4 cloves garlic, finely chopped

1 bunch (or, failing this, substitute 2–3 supermarket packets) flat-leaf parsley, finely chopped
sea salt and freshly ground pepper
pinch of crushed dried chillies
lemon wedges

Steam the clams open in a covered saucepan over a medium to high heat (shaking the pan once or twice) with 2 tablespoons of olive oil, the onion and dry white wine for 3 to 5 minutes.

Remove the clams from the poaching liquid, discarding any that do not open. Strain the poaching liquid through a fine sieve lined with muslin or kitchen paper. Reserve the opened clams and the strained liquid in separate bowls until ready to use.

Heat 4 tablespoons of olive oil in a large, thick-bottomed frying pan. Add the garlic and cook over a medium heat, stirring constantly, until the garlic just begins to change colour, then add the reserved poaching liquid and 4 tablespoons of the finely chopped parsley. Cover the pan and simmer for 15 minutes. Season the sauce generously with salt, freshly ground pepper and a pinch of crushed dried chillies. Stir in the remaining chopped parsley. Allow the sauce to cool to room temperature.

Place the opened clams in a serving dish or bowl. Spoon over the green sauce and serve with lemon wedges.

Makes 6 to 8 *tapas* or serves 4 as a first course

Patatas al alioli
Potatoes with alioli

Alioli, the rich, fiery-tasting, pure gold sauce of Catalan cuisine, made simply enough from crushed garlic, egg yolks and olive oil, makes a fabulous *tapa* out of simple boiled potatoes. Even better, I find, when served separately as a dip with grilled potato quarters with their skins left on. I give you both versions.

4–6 red waxy potatoes
¼ vegetable stock cube, crumbled
lightly salted water

alioli sauce (page 93)
2 tablespoons finely chopped flat-leaf parsley (or chives)

Wash but don't peel the potatoes. In a medium-sized saucepan, combine the vegetable stock cube and enough lightly salted water to cover the potatoes and bring to the boil. Add the potatoes and cook for 20 minutes, or until the potatoes are just tender. Drain the potatoes. Allow them to cool enough to hold them without burning your hand, and peel them.

Cut the potatoes into bite-sized pieces and, while they are still a little warm, fold them into the bowl of *alioli*. Keep at room temperature for about 20 minutes before serving scattered with parsley (or chives).

Serves 4

Patatas a la plancha con alioli
Grilled potatoes with alioli

4–6 red waxy potatoes
¼ vegetable stock cube, crumbled
lightly salted water

extra virgin olive oil
sea salt and crushed dried chillies
alioli sauce (page 93)

Wash but don't peel the potatoes. In a medium-sized saucepan, combine the vegetable stock cube and enough lightly salted water to cover the potatoes, and bring to the boil. Add the potatoes and gently boil for 10 minutes. Drain the potatoes and reserve them.

When ready to grill, cut each potato into 4 or 6 segments lengthwise, leaving the skins on.

Toss the potato segments in a little olive oil, season with sea salt and crushed dried chillies (just a hint) and grill on a preheated ridged grill pan, or under an electric or gas grill, turning the segments from time to time until the potatoes are crisp and golden. Serve with a bowl of *alioli* as a dip.

Serves 4

Champiñones al horno
Baked mushrooms

I first came across these hot baked mushrooms as a *tapa* at a party in Seville. I liked them so much I have been serving them ever since. Whole small button mushrooms, quartered oyster mushrooms, thick-sliced open-cap mushrooms, or a combination of the three, all fit the bill.

2 slices *serrano* ham, finely chopped

2 tablespoons finely chopped flat-leaf parsley

2 tablespoons fresh breadcrumbs

2 tablespoons freshly grated *manchego* cheese

600 ml / 1 pint tomato sauce (shop-bought or see page 183)

1 tablespoon olive oil

2 anchovy fillets, finely chopped

sea salt and freshly ground pepper

225 g /8 oz button mushrooms

Preheat the oven to 190°C/375°F/gas 5.

In a large bowl combine the ham, parsley, breadcrumbs, cheese, tomato sauce, olive oil and anchovy fillets and season with salt and freshly ground pepper, to taste.

Wipe the button mushrooms with a damp cloth, trim the stems and stir the mushrooms into the sauce. Pour the mushrooms and sauce into a shallow ovenproof baking dish and bake in the preheated oven for 30 minutes until the mushrooms are tender and the top golden brown. Serve hot or cold as a delicious *tapa* or as a first course.

Serves 8 as a *tapa*, 4 as a first course

Champiñones al ajillo con jamón
Mushrooms with garlic and ham

Pan-seared button mushrooms, ceps or chanterelles make a wonderful hot *tapa* to serve in little dishes or bowls with a glass of *fino*, or on garlic-rubbed squares of oven-toasted bread as a first course for an informal outdoor lunch. Small dice of thinly sliced *serrano* ham (or *chorizo*) add substance and flavour.

1 kilo / 2 lb mushrooms	**salt and freshly ground pepper**
4 tablespoons olive oil	**cayenne pepper**
4 thin slices *serrano* ham (or 1 small *chorizo* sausage), diced	**4 tablespoons finely chopped flat-leaf parsley**
2 cloves garlic, finely chopped	**1–2 tablespoons lemon juice**

Wipe the mushrooms with a damp cloth and trim the stems.

Heat the oil in a thick-bottomed frying pan. Add the diced ham, or *chorizo*, and sauté for 5 minutes or until lightly golden, stirring with a wooden spoon. Stir in the garlic and the mushroom caps. Stir to coat the mushrooms in the oil and season with salt, freshly ground pepper and cayenne, to taste. Stir in the parsley. Cover and simmer the mushrooms over a low to medium heat for about 8 minutes or until tender, shaking the pan occasionally.

Correct the seasoning and stir in the lemon juice. Spoon the mushrooms into heated individual shallow bowls and serve immediately.

Serves 6 to 8

Sardinas a la plancha
Grilled sardines

Grill super-fresh sardines as the Spanish do: on a pre-heated sheet of flat metal over a charcoal fire, or, failing that, in a barbecue over charcoal (or even under a preheated grill). Wash and gut the sardines before cooking but leave on the scales.

12 to 16 fresh sardines, cleaned and gutted
olive oil
sea salt and freshly ground pepper
crushed dried chillies

Garnish
lemons, halved or quartered

Pat the sardines dry with kitchen paper. Brush with olive oil and season generously with sea salt, freshly ground pepper and a pinch of crushed dried chillies.

Grill the sardines *a la plancha*, over a barbecue, or under a hot grill, for 2 to 3 minutes on each side, sprinkling with a little more oil as they cook. Serve straight from the fire, with lemons.

Serves 4

Sardinas rellenas a la plancha
Grilled stuffed sardines

12 to 16 fresh sardines
lemon juice
sea salt
olive oil

Garnish
lemons, halved or quartered

Stuffing
½ Spanish onion, peeled and grated
1 bunch flat-leaf parsley, chopped
¼ teaspoon each crushed black pepper, paprika, cayenne and powdered cinnamon
½ teaspoon powdered cumin
salt

Clean and gut the sardines and remove the backbones and heads. Flatten out each sardine and sprinkle the insides with a little lemon juice and sea salt.

To make the stuffing, combine all the ingredients, including salt, to taste.

Place the opened sardines, skin-side down, on the work surface. Spread half of each sardine with the stuffing mixture. Press the halves together and fasten, if desired, with a cocktail stick.

Brush with olive oil and grill, as above. Serve straight from the fire, with lemons.

Serves 4

Cebollitas en adobo
Marinated button onions in a sweet and sour Andalusian sauce

These button onions are simmered in a sweet and sour Andalusian *adobo* sauce flavoured with a hint of honey and tomato. The Arab-inspired ingredient: sultanas.

2 carrots, coarsely chopped

4 tablespoons olive oil

700 g / 1½ lbs button onions, peeled

425 ml / ¾ pint water

150 ml / ¼ pint dry white wine

4 tablespoons lemon juice

1 tablespoon honey

50 g /2 oz sultanas

2 tablespoons tomato purée

2 bay leaves

2 sprigs fresh thyme

sea salt and freshly ground pepper

crushed dried chillies

Garnish

extra virgin olive oil

finely chopped flat-leaf parsley

In a frying pan, sauté the carrots in the oil until soft and golden. Combine in a saucepan with the whole onions, water, dry white wine, lemon juice, honey, sultanas, tomato purée, bay leaves and thyme, and add sea salt, freshly ground pepper and crushed dried chillies, to taste.

Simmer over a very low heat for about 1 hour, or until the onions are cooked through and the sauce has reduced a little. Pour into a bowl. Allow to cool and then chill in the refrigerator until ready to serve.

Just before serving, correct the seasoning, transfer to a serving dish, drizzle over a little olive oil and sprinkle with chopped parsley.

Serves 6

Cocas de verduras
Vegetable croustades

Flat croustades of combinations of vegetables, ham, sausage, duck and olives, and even seafood, called *cocas*, are the pizzas of Spain. I like to make them using a Catalan tart dough, or even – when in a hurry – split pitta bread, brushed with olive oil, sprinkled with salt and toasted in a 180°C/350°F/gas 4 oven for 5 minutes, or until crisp and golden.

Coca Filling

1 small red onion, thinly sliced

2 cloves garlic, finely chopped

extra virgin olive oil

½ large red pepper, thinly sliced

½ green pepper, thinly sliced

1–2 small courgettes, thinly sliced

6 button mushrooms, thinly sliced

2 sprigs fresh oregano, or marjoram (leaves only)

4 plum tomatoes, peeled, seeded and diced

salt and freshly ground pepper

pinch of crushed dried chillies

2–4 tablespoons freshly grated *manchego* cheese, or a
    mix of freshly grated Emmental and Parmesan

Catalan Coca Pastry

300 g / 10 oz plain flour

finely grated zest of 1 lemon

pinch of salt

150 g / 5 oz lard or butter (room temperature), diced

1 egg, beaten

iced water

To make the *coca* dough, combine the flour, lemon zest, salt and diced lard or butter in a mixing bowl. Cover the lard or butter well with the flour and then rub the mixture together lightly with your fingertips until the mixture resembles fine breadcrumbs. While rubbing, keep lifting the flour well up into the bowl, so that air may mix with it and the fat is not made too soft.

Combine the beaten egg yolk with an equal quantity of iced water and gradually mix it into the flour mixture with a fork. Shape the dough lightly into 4 flattened rounds, wrap in clingfilm and chill in the refrigerator for 30 minutes, while you make the filling.

Sauté the onion and garlic in 3 tablespoons of olive oil until the vegetables just begin to change colour. Add the peppers, and continue to cook, stirring from time to time, until softened. Then add the courgettes, mushrooms, oregano or marjoram, and stir over a medium heat for 3 to 5 more minutes. Spoon in the chopped tomatoes and season with salt, pepper and crushed dried chillies, to taste. Remove from the heat and reserve.

Roll the chilled pastry into 4 thin rounds (as you might for making a pizza) and place 2 rounds on each of 2 buttered baking trays. Spread with the *coca* filling, leaving 6 mm / ¼ inch uncovered around the edges. Cover with a clean tea towel (careful of the filling) and leave to rise in a warm place for about 1 hour. Meanwhile, preheat the oven to 190°C/375°F/gas 5. When ready to bake, sprinkle the *cocas* with a little olive oil and bake for 20 to 30 minutes until crisp and golden brown. Serve at once.

Serves 4

Buñuelos
Fritters

Spanish *buñuelos* are deep-fried fritters made with a kind of choux-pastry dough – the kind that combines water, butter, flour and eggs, salt and nutmeg – poured all at once into a saucepan and stirred over a medium heat until the dough leaves the sides of the pan and forms a ball. In French cookery this dough is used for *éclairs*, cream puffs and certain elegant cakes such as Gâteau St Honoré and delicate puff pastry sweets called *réligieuses*. In Burgundy, this dough is made (without sugar) and combined with Gruyère cheese to make a *gougère*. In Spain, the savoury version is used to make puffy golden *buñuelos* to encase a garlic, spinach and cheese filling, or a crisp fried slice of *chorizo* with *manchego* cheese.

Buñuelos de espinacas
Spinach fritters

225 g / 8 oz young spinach leaves, stems removed

1 small clove garlic, finely chopped

2 tablespoons olive oil

4 tablespoons freshly grated *manchego* cheese

2 tablespoons crème fraîche

sea salt and crushed dried chillies

buñuelo dough (facing page)

oil for deep-frying

Wash the spinach leaves and shake them dry.

In a medium-sized saucepan, sauté the garlic in the olive oil until just golden. Remove the pan from the heat and stir in the young spinach leaves until they wilt. Add the *manchego* and crème fraîche. Season with sea salt and a hint of crushed dried chillies. Turn into a small bowl and reserve.

Make the *buñuelo* dough as described at the bottom of the facing page and stir the spinach and cheese mixture into it.

To cook the spinach and cheese *buñuelos*, heat the cooking oil in a pan or an electric deep-frier to 190°C (380°F) and drop the dough by tablespoonfuls into the hot oil. Fry the *buñuelos*, turning them occasionally with a slotted spoon, until they are puffed and golden.

Drain the *buñuelos* on kitchen paper and serve immediately.

Makes about 24

Buñuelos de chorizo y queso manchego
Chorizo and cheese fritters

2 *chorizo* sausages, cut into 24 slices

1 tablespoon olive oil

24 squares of *manchego* cheese (cut to roughly the same size and thickness as the *chorizo*)

buñuelo dough (see below)

oil for deep-frying

In a large frying pan, sauté the *chorizo* slices in the olive oil until they start to tint the olive oil a reddish orange: a few minutes. Remove the pan from the heat and reserve.

Make the *buñuelo* dough as described below.

Remove 4 *chorizo* slices from the pan and pair each one with a square of *manchego* cheese. Wrap each *chorizo* and cheese pair in *buñuelo* dough. Heat the cooking oil in a pan or an electric deep-frier to 190°C (380°F) and drop the 4 *buñuelos* into hot oil. Deep-fry, turning occasionally with a slotted spoon, until they are puffed and golden. Drain on kitchen paper; keep warm in a preheated low oven while you prepare and deep-fry the remaining *buñuelos*.

Makes about 24

Masa para buñuelos
Fritter dough

225 ml / 8 fl oz water

4 tablespoons butter

¼ teaspoon freshly grated nutmeg

½ teaspoon salt

100 g / 4 oz plain flour, sifted

2 eggs

In a small saucepan (preferably with high sides), combine the water, butter, nutmeg and salt and bring to the boil, stirring, over a medium heat. When the butter has melted and the flavoured water is boiling briskly, add the flour, all at once, and stir with a wooden spoon over the heat until the dough leaves the sides of the pan and forms a ball. Continue cooking and stirring the dough for a minute or two longer. Then remove the pan from the heat and beat in the eggs, one by one. You will find that the dough separates as you beat in the eggs, but it will re-form as you continue the operation.

Chapter 3

S A L

Salads in Spain are not salads as we know them. The influences of Italy, France, Australia and the East are strangely missing in the markets and speciality shops. There is no radicchio, no baby ruby chard, no pak choy or choy sum, no rapini – but who needs them when we can use fresh watercress, endive, spinach, mint leaves, basil leaves, tarragon and flat-leaf parsley; finely sliced cabbage, celery and courgettes; some of the best asparagus in the world; and wild mushrooms of every description? My only real surprise when salad-tasting in Andalusia in the summer was that avocados were used so little, even though the *conquistadores* brought back knowledge of this exotic fruit (as well as trees) from Montezuma's court.

Salads in Spain are, to me, Californian in personality – and why not? California was once a Spanish colony. Like the Californians, Spaniards like to serve salads made of seafood or game with cooked or raw

vegetables and mixed greens, or sparkling combinations of red peppers, oranges and onion, or fresh-tasting blends of chilled melon, grapes and radishes. What is *gazpacho* but a staggeringly successful salad? As is that smoky blend of open-fire roasted strips of aubergine and peppers dressed with a garlic vinaigrette called *escalivada*.

Even more in keeping with California, salads in Spain are often served at the beginning of the meal. That is why I have devoted our salad chapter to wonderful and unusual combinations of fish, shellfish, rice and quail, of quince paste, *manchego* cheese and figs, to name but a few. And even if in Spain on requesting a salad you are served something simple, rest assured, for it will be dressed with finely chopped fresh herbs and the best olive oil you ever tasted.

Ensalada verde con cebolletas y aceitunas
Simple Spanish salad

Salads in Spain are usually served as first courses, a tradition inherited from the Moors, and are relatively simple: a few green leaves in a *vinagreta* dressing with quartered tomatoes, a few green olives stuffed with *pimiento* or lemon, a few spring onions or spears of poached asparagus and perhaps a hard-boiled egg. This is my favourite.

2 Little Gem lettuces
½ head frisee, inside yellow leaves only
16–24 sprigs of watercress
2 tomatoes, quartered

Garnish
16–24 stuffed green olives, drained
16–24 x 5-cm / 2-inch lengths of spring onion

Vinagreta
6–8 tablespoons extra virgin olive oil
2 tablespoons wine vinegar
1 tablespoon lemon juice
1–2 cloves garlic, finely chopped
2 tablespoons freshly chopped flat-leaf parsley
sea salt and freshly ground pepper

Remove the outer dark green leaves from the lettuces. Cut off the base of the Little Gem lettuces and wash the leaves in cold water. Drain and shake dry. Separate the leaves of the frisee and wash in cold water. Drain and shake dry. Trim the stems from the watercress sprigs. Drain and shake dry.

Fold the salad greens loosely in a clean tea towel and refrigerate until you are ready to make the salad.

To prepare the *vinagreta*, combine the first 5 ingredients in a bowl, mix well and season with salt and pepper to taste.

When ready to serve, arrange the salad greens attractively in a salad bowl, preferably a glass one. Pour over the *vinagreta* and toss gently until each leaf glistens. Add the quartered tomatoes and toss lightly, and garnish with stuffed olives and lengths of spring onion.

Serves 4

Ensalada andaluza de pimientos
Andalusian salad

A cold salad of roasted peppers and tomatoes in the Arab fashion, dressed with a simple garlic-flavoured *vinagreta*, is a southern salad I have enjoyed all around the Mediterranean. I make it for my Andalusian friends, who claim it as their own.

2 medium-sized red peppers, quartered lengthwise

2 medium-sized green peppers, quartered lengthwise

6 ripe plum tomatoes, halved lengthwise

2 cloves garlic, finely chopped

6–8 tablespoons extra virgin olive oil

1–2 tablespoons wine vinegar

sea salt and freshly ground pepper

pinch of crushed dried chillies

½ lemon or lime

Little Gem lettuce leaves and/or watercress sprigs, to serve (optional)

Preheat the grill. Place the pepper quarters, cut-side down, on the rack of the grill pan. Grill until the skins have charred and blistered. Transfer the peppers, while still hot, to a plastic bag and allow to sweat for 10 minutes. When cool, remove the pepper sections from the bag and carefully rub off the blistered skins under gently running cold water. Remove the stalks, seeds and thick membranes, and pat the pepper sections dry with a paper towel. Reserve.

Gently squeeze the seeds from the tomatoes and lay them, cut-side down, on a foil-lined baking tray. Cook them under the grill, as above, until the skins are black. With a small sharp kitchen knife, peel off the blackened skins, and reserve the tomato sections.

Combine the roasted red and green peppers (in a colander placed over a bowl) with the roasted tomato sections. Sprinkle with garlic and toss the vegetables gently to allow the flavours to blend. Chill until ready to serve. (The colander allows the juices to drain off.)

To serve, transfer the chilled vegetables to a glass salad bowl, spoon over the olive oil and wine vinegar, and season with salt, pepper and crushed dried chillies, to taste. Toss the salad gently and, immediately before serving, sprinkle with the juice of the lemon or lime half to perk up the flavours. Serve in a flat salad bowl as a first course salad; or line the bowl with Little Gem lettuce leaves and/or watercress sprigs and serve as a light luncheon dish or a colourful salad course.

Serves 4

Ensalada al gazpacho
Gazpacho salad

I was inspired by the traditional garnish for *gazpacho* to create this special salad one day when I was preparing outdoor lunch for friends at a *finca* just outside Ronda. The layered salad was served in a tall top-hat-shaped glass salad bowl and looked wonderful.

Now I am not suggesting that you have such a bowl in your kitchen cupboard, but I have served it since in this country in large-scale brandy snifters – one to each guest – the colourful layers of sliced tomatoes, white onion, unpeeled cucumber and crisp-dried breadcrumbs showing to splendid advantage through the fragile glass containers.

1½ large white onions

iced water

1½ cucumbers

12 ripe firm red tomatoes

6–8 tablespoons oven-toasted breadcrumbs (made from good country bread)

Vinagreta

150 ml / ¼ pint extra virgin olive oil

3 tablespoons sherry vinegar

2 cloves garlic, finely chopped

3–4 tablespoons chopped flat-leaf parsley

fresh lime juice

sea salt and freshly ground pepper

pinch of crushed dried chillies

Peel and slice the white onions thinly and soak for 20 minutes in iced water (to remove the onion's too pungent flavour). Drain well, and pat dry with kitchen paper. Wrap in clingfilm and chill. Slice the cucumbers thinly, but do not peel or seed. Wrap in clingfilm and chill. Slice the tomatoes. Wrap in clingfilm and chill. To prepare the *vinagreta*, combine the olive oil, sherry vinegar, garlic and parsley in a small bowl and flavour to taste with lime juice, sea salt, freshly ground pepper and a hint of crushed dried chillies. Chill.

When ready to serve, arrange the thinly sliced cucumber, tomato and onion, and the breadcrumbs, in alternate thin layers in the glass salad bowl of your choice. Pour over the well-flavoured *vinagreta*.

Serves 6

Ensalada mixta con foie gras
Mixed salad with sizzled fresh foie gras

Pan-flashed slices of fresh duck liver and a champagne *vinagreta* (made with *cava* vinegar) liven up a mixed greens and fresh herb appetizer salad, the perfect starter for a Spanish luncheon in the sun. If fresh *foie gras* is not available, substitute sautéed duck or chicken livers, but I am afraid the salad will not be as good as with the pan-flashed fresh *foie gras* version.

extra virgin olive oil

16 slices of fresh *foie gras*, or 4 fresh duck's livers, or 8 fresh chicken livers

sea salt and freshly ground pepper

crushed dried chillies

mixed salad greens: your choice of watercress, rocket, frisee, mâche and Little Gem

3–4 tablespoons Spanish *cava* vinegar (or sherry vinegar)

2 tablespoons finely chopped chives

4 tablespoons thinly sliced spring onion (both white and green parts)

Heat 2 tablespoons of olive oil to sizzling in a large heatproof nonstick frying pan. Add the sliced fresh foie gras (or slice and add the duck or chicken livers) and sauté over a high heat for 1 minute per side, or until the livers are golden brown on the outside, but still quite moist and pink on the inside. Season with salt, pepper and a pinch of crushed dried chillies, toss once in the pan, and then, with a slotted spoon, transfer the livers to a plate.

Arrange the mixed greens, cut or torn into bite-sized pieces, in a salad bowl. Top with the livers.

Add 3 tablespoons each of olive oil and *cava* vinegar to the pan, and heat over a low heat, stirring all the crusty bits from the bottom of the pan into the sauce. Season, to taste, and pour over the salad. Sprinkle with chives and spring onions and serve immediately.

Serves 4

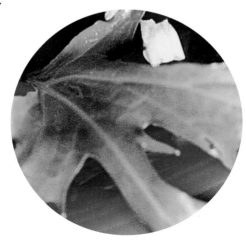

Ensalada de atún y alubias blancas
Tuna and white bean salad

Optimum amounts of finely chopped garlic and flat-leaf parsley make a wonderfully fresh-tasting *salsa verde* dressing for this Spanish bean and tuna salad. Make sure you use the large clove 'green' garlic now available in supermarkets. If at first you are timid about the amount of garlic used in the recipe, chop the 2 cloves as directed, then halve the quantity specified. Taste the marinated beans after the first half an hour and add a little more chopped garlic as desired. Serve as a *tapa* or a first course for an informal luncheon or dinner.

400 g / 14 oz can white beans in brine

4 tablespoons finely chopped flat-leaf parsley

2–4 tablespoons finely chopped onion

2 large cloves garlic, finely chopped

90 g / 3½ oz can tuna fish in olive oil, drained and
   broken into chunks

12 small onion rings

12 black olives

enough flat-leaf parsley sprigs, watercress or small
   inner Little Gem leaves to make a green border
   around the beans

juice of ½ lime

Green Dressing

8 tablespoons extra virgin olive oil

2 tablespoons sherry vinegar

½ teaspoon Dijon-style mustard

sea salt and freshly ground pepper

crushed dried chillies

Drain the beans and rinse well with cold running water. Drain again and toss gently in a salad bowl with the parsley, onion and garlic.

Beat the first three ingredients for the dressing together with a fork until they form an emulsion. Add sea salt, pepper and crushed dried chillies, to taste. Pour the dressing over the beans and toss gently. Allow the beans to marinate in this dressing for at least 1 hour, turning once or twice to ensure that the beans are well flavoured.

When ready to serve, transfer the beans (and dressing) to a serving bowl. Arrange the tuna chunks on the beans and garnish with the onion rings and black olives. Arrange the parsley sprigs, watercress or small lettuce leaves around the dish and sprinkle the leaves with lime juice.

Variation with Eggs (*Ensalada de Atún y Huevo Duro***):** For an interesting *tapas* variation, substitute 4 to 5 sliced hard-boiled eggs for the white beans in the above recipe. I like to use an egg slicer to slice the shelled eggs crosswise into uniform slices. Arrange the sliced eggs in a serving dish, pour the dressing over and, just before serving, garnish with tuna chunks, onion rings, black olives and green leaves (as above).

Serves 4 to 6

Ensalada de queso manchego y dulce de membrillo

Manchego cheese and quince paste salad

An interesting appetizer salad (and a variation on a classic Spanish dessert) serves rectangles of Spain's favourite *manchego* cheese and quince paste with dressed herbs and grilled figs or thin slices of *serrano* ham.

Ready-prepared quince paste (*dulce de membrillo*) is available in department-store food halls, such as the Fifth Floor at Harvey Nichols in London, or in Spanish provision stores.

8–12 slabs *manchego* cheese, about 2.5 cm / 1 inch thick

8 slabs quince paste, about 2.5 cm / 1 inch thick

12–16 sprigs each watercress, purslane (or green basil), flat-leaf parsley and tarragon

4 ripe figs, halved, brushed with olive oil and pan-grilled, or 4 thin slices of the best *serrano* ham you can find

Honey and Lime Dressing

8 tablespoons extra virgin olive oil

2–3 tablespoons lime juice

1–3 teaspoons lavender honey

1–2 cloves garlic, finely chopped

sea salt and freshly ground pepper

pinch of crushed dried chillies

In a small bowl, combine the first 4 ingredients for the dressing. Season with salt, pepper and a hint of crushed dried chillies.

To make the salad, arrange overlapping slabs of manchego cheese and quince paste on individual plates. Garnish each plate with sprigs of fresh herbs. Grill the halved figs until just slightly charred (if using) and arrange on the sides of the salad. Or drape each salad with a very thin slice of top quality *serrano* ham.

Drizzle over the dressing and serve at once.

Serves 4

Ensalada de arroz al azafrán con atún
Saffron rice and tuna salad

Sliced stuffed olives, red and green pepper threads and thin sticks of spicy *chorizo* sausage add colour, texture and flavour to this saffron rice salad. This is a very adaptable recipe: double the quantities for a great summer buffet centrepiece; halve the quantities for a delicious *tapa*; or serve it as it is for an easy-to-make dinner party first course.

1 recipe virgin *paella* (page 111)

1 red pepper, stem, seeds and pith removed, thinly sliced lengthwise

1 green pepper, stem, seeds and pith removed, thinly sliced lengthwise

1 cooked *chorizo*, thinly sliced and cut into sticks

12 stuffed olives, thinly sliced

½ Spanish onion, finely chopped

salt and freshly ground pepper

Saffron Vinagreta

6 tablespoons olive oil

3 tablespoons wine vinegar or lime juice

1 clove garlic, finely chopped

¼ teaspoon saffron threads

salt and freshly ground pepper

Garnish

1 tuna steak, lightly grilled and flaked while warm

2 tablespoons chopped flat-leaf parsley

Combine the saffron rice in a mixing bowl with the red and green peppers, *chorizo* and stuffed olives. Add the onion and season with salt and pepper, to taste. Fork gently until well mixed.

Make the saffron *vinagreta* by combining the olive oil, wine vinegar (or lime juice), garlic, saffron threads and salt and pepper, to taste, and pour over the salad. Toss gently and transfer to a salad bowl.

Top with flaked grilled tuna, sprinkle with chopped parsley and serve at once.

Serves 4 to 6

Ensalada de gambas, chorizo, patatas y roqueta
Prawn, chorizo, new potato and rocket salad

Ever since I toured through Spain photographing for this book, I have had the habit of keeping a *chorizo* sausage or two in the refrigerator. It's great for adding – with a piece or two of salt pork and a slice of blood sausage – to lovely rustic red bean stews . . . or 'frazzled' (i.e. sautéed for seconds only in a hot pan, as they do in Chinchón) to serve as a quick little hot *tapa* with drinks, to stir into sautéed potatoes or saffron rice, or, as here, to spark up a first-course salad.

1 salad bowlful of rocket (or watercress and
  baby spinach)
16–20 tiger prawns, poached
16–20 slices of skinned *chorizo*
4 boiled new potatoes, peeled

Herb Dressing
8 tablespoons extra virgin olive oil
2 tablespoons sherry vinegar
juice of ½ lime
½ small hot red chilli pepper, thinly sliced
2 cloves garlic, finely chopped
sea salt and freshly ground pepper
½ bunch chives, cut into snippets

To prepare the salad, wash and shake dry the salad leaves. Place them in a salad bowl and chill in the refrigerator until ready to serve.

To prepare the herb dressing, combine the first five ingredients in a small bowl and mix well. Season with sea salt and freshly ground pepper, to taste. Reserve.

In a large frying pan, heat the olive oil, add the *chorizo* and sauté until lightly 'frazzled' (lightly browned but still soft in texture). Reserve. Add the poached prawns to the pan and sauté in the hot fat for 1 or 2 minutes. Reserve.

When ready to serve the salad, toss the leaves with half the dressing and place the frazzled *chorizo* and the prawns on top. Sprinkle with chopped chives. Drizzle a little of the remaining dressing over the prawns and serve immediately.

Serves 4

Ensalada marinera
Seafood salad

Let fresh tuna – or fresh hake, haddock, monkfish or cod – play the central role in this seafood salad. Accompany it with sautéed prawns and mussels (or palourdes) and the game is won. The fish and shellfish are sautéed for minutes only in sizzling olive oil and then tossed, while still warm, in a Mediterranean dressing flavoured with red onion, garlic, parsley and chives. A treat.

4 tablespoons olive oil

350 g / 12 oz fresh haddock, cod or tuna fillets

salt and freshly ground pepper

225 g / 8 oz peeled tiger prawns

36 mussels or palourdes (clams), steamed open

pinch of crushed dried chillies

Mediterranean Dressing

300 ml / ½ pint extra virgin olive oil

4–6 tablespoons wine vinegar

4 tablespoons finely chopped red onion

2 garlic cloves, finely chopped

2 tablespoons finely chopped flat-leaf parsley

2 tablespoons finely chopped chives

salt and freshly ground pepper

crushed dried chillies

Garnish

crisp leaves of Little Gem lettuce and endive

sprigs of watercress

4–6 ripe tomatoes, cut into wedges

1 large yellow or orange pepper, stem, seeds and pith removed, cut into long strips

12 stuffed olives

2–3 tablespoons chopped flat-leaf parsley

In a heatproof frying pan, heat 2 tablespoons olive oil to a sizzle. Add the fish and pan sear for 2 to 3 minutes on each side. Season with salt and pepper, to taste. Remove the fish from the pan. Remove any skin or bones while the fish is still warm and flake the flesh. Put into a bowl and reserve.

Add the tiger prawns to the pan with the remaining 2 tablespoons olive oil and sauté them for 3 to 4 minutes. With a slotted spoon, transfer the sautéed prawns to a small bowl and reserve. Add the opened mussels or palourdes (clams) to the pan and sauté for a few minutes. Season and transfer to a small bowl.

Make the Mediterranean dressing: in a small bowl, combine the olive oil, wine vinegar, red onion, garlic and herbs. Season generously with salt, pepper and a pinch of crushed dried chillies. Pour 3 to 4 tablespoons of the dressing into each of the 3 bowls of seafood and toss the seafood and dressing carefully. Cover the bowls with clingfilm, place in the refrigerator and leave to marinate for at least 2 hours. Reserve the remaining dressing.

Trim, wash and thoroughly dry the lettuce, endive and watercress. Just before serving, arrange the salad greens in a large salad bowl. Place the marinated seafood in the centre and garnish the edges of the bowl with tomato wedges, pepper strips and olives. Pour over the remaining dressing, sprinkle with chopped parsley and serve.

Serves 6

Ensalada de naranja y pomelo con pimiento rojo
Orange and grapefruit salad with red peppers

Oranges and red peppers go together like love and marriage. Add the sharp taste of grapefruit and the marriage seems made in Heaven. The possibilities are almost limitless when you live on the southern coast of Spain with a few citrus trees in your garden – and perhaps an avocado tree at the kitchen door.

3–4 large juicy oranges

2 pink or yellow grapefruit

2 tablespoons lemon juice

4 tablespoons extra virgin olive oil

sea salt and freshly ground pepper

crushed dried chillies

1 red pepper

6 sprigs fresh mint

Prepare the oranges and grapefruit as follows, working over a shallow dish so that no juice is lost: using a sharp knife, slice off the top and bottom of each fruit, taking the pith and the outer membrane away with the peel. Stand the fruit on one (cut) end and, with downward strokes, whittle off slices of peel and membrane around the sides. Turn the fruit on its other end and repeat the process. Finally, slice off the ring of peel left around the centre. You should now have a slightly barrel-shaped fruit, completely free of pith as well as peel. With a little practice, and providing your cutting tool is really sharp, this method takes far less time than the more conventional one.

Now take the fruit in one hand and slip your knife between each segment and the membrane which holds it on either side. Cut the segment out, keeping it whole if possible. Remove any pips and drop the segment into the juice below. Proceed in this manner until all you have left is the central core and empty membranes, fanned out like the leaves of a book.

Squeeze out any remaining juice into the dish.

Toss the orange and grapefruit segments with the lemon juice and olive oil. Season with sea salt, freshly ground pepper and a pinch of crushed dried chillies. Toss again. Chill.

To prepare the red pepper, first cut it into quarters. Peel the skin from each quarter with a vegetable peeler. Remove the stem, seed and white pith. Cut each quarter lengthwise into thin strips. Add to the citrus fruit and toss well.

Serve in 6 individual glass dishes, each decorated with a sprig of fresh mint.

Note: If you *do* happen to have an avocado tree at the kitchen door, pale green slices of fresh avocado will not come amiss in this salad.

Serves 6

Rollitos de jamón rellenos de higos
Grilled figs wrapped in serrano ham strips

Savoury beef marrow and grated orange peel add their moistness and flavour to these grilled purple figs wrapped in strips of *serrano* ham. Garnish each plate with black olives and roasted rosemary sprigs. Memorable.

12 ripe purple figs
marrow from 2 cracked marrow bones (about 7.5 cm / 3in long)
finely grated peel of 1 large navel orange
sea salt and freshly ground pepper
pinch of crushed dried chillies
12 thin slices *serrano* ham
12 sprigs fresh rosemary
extra virgin olive oil
juice of 1 lemon

Garnish
green leaves (lettuce, rocket, watercress)
black olives

Preheat the oven to 190°C/375°F/gas 5.

With a sharp knife, cut each fig almost through to the bottom to make a four-petalled flower. Place a thin round of beef marrow in each fig 'flower'. Season the centre of each open fig generously with a pinch each of grated orange peel, sea salt, and dried chillies. Gently close the figs, wrap a strip of *serrano* ham around each one and fasten with a wet cocktail stick.

Arrange the fresh rosemary sprigs on an oiled baking tray. Arrange 1 ham-wrapped fig on each rosemary sprig, sprinkle with a little extra virgin olive oil and roast the figs in the preheated oven for 10 minutes, or until the ham strips are crisp and well coloured.

To serve, remove the cocktail sticks from the ham-wrapped figs. Place 3 roasted figs on each plate. Stir the lemon juice and a little olive oil into the juices on the baking tray; spoon over the figs and garnish each plate with a few green leaves, some black olives and the roasted rosemary sprigs.

Ensaladas de verano con picada
Summer salads with picada dressing

A choice of summer salads – peppers, tomatoes and red onion, and lettuce leaves, sprigs of green herbs and red onion – are dressed with a piquant Spanish dressing in which chopped gherkins, garlic, flat-leaf parsley and hard-boiled egg white play their part. The recipe for the dressing is enough for one salad. If you are going to serve both at an outdoor luncheon, double the picada recipe.

Ensalada de verano I
Summer salad I

2 red peppers, stems and seeds removed, cut into eighths
2 green peppers, stems and seeds removed, cut into eighths
4 ripe vine tomatoes, cut into eighths
1 small red onion, thinly sliced

In a salad bowl, combine the prepared vegetables, cover the bowl with clingfilm and chill in the refrigerator until ready to serve.

Ensalada de verano II
Summer salad II

2–3 Little Gem lettuces, inner leaves only
12–18 sprigs each of watercress, lamb's lettuce, green basil and rocket
1 small red onion, thinly sliced

In a salad bowl, combine the prepared vegetables, cover the bowl with clingfilm and chill in the refrigerator until ready to serve.

Picada con huevo
Picada salad dressing

3 tablespoons finely chopped flat-leaf parsley
2 cloves garlic, finely chopped
1 hard-boiled egg white, finely chopped
3 tablespoons finely chopped baby gherkin
8 tablespoons extra virgin olive oil
juice of 1 lemon or lime
sea salt and freshly ground pepper
pinch of crushed dried chillies

In a small bowl, combine the first 6 ingredients. Season with sea salt, freshly ground pepper and a hint of crushed dried chillies, to taste. Mix well. Chill until ready to serve the summer salad of your choice.

When ready to serve, take the prepared salad from the refrigerator, remove the clingfilm, pour over the picada dressing and serve at once.

Each salad serves 4 to 6

Escalivada
Charred vegetable salad

Is it a *tapa*? Is it a salad? Is it a vegetable dish? It's all of these things: it's *escalivada*. And you will find it in every restaurant you visit in Catalonia. I first met and enjoyed this charred vegetable mix (aubergines and peppers) at the chic, noisy, trendy Barceloneta restaurant, on Barcelona's newly remodelled seafront. The charred pepper permeates the oil and the other vegetables. You'll be an *aficionado*.

2 medium-sized aubergines

2 large red peppers

extra virgin olive oil

sea salt and freshly ground pepper

1 fat clove green garlic, finely chopped

1–2 tablespoons chopped flat-leaf parsley

The secret of a delicious *escalivada* is the wonderful smoky flavour a wood fire gives these thin strips of grilled vegetables, so it is important, especially when using a commercial electric or gas grill, to cook the vegetables on a baking tray that has a good 3 mm / ⅛ inch of olive oil on the bottom. The oil will absorb the smoky taste of the grilled peppers and when strained over the salad give it its traditional flavour.

Cut the aubergines and peppers in half lengthways and place the vegetables, cut-side down, on the oiled baking tray. Bake or grill them for about 12 minutes, or until their skins are charred and blackened. Remove from the oven or grill and allow to cool enough to handle. Then remove them from the oiled pan (reserving the oil) and transfer to a plastic bag. Allow the vegetables to 'steam' in the bag until cold. Then cut off the stems (and in the case of the peppers, their seeds and pith). Remove the charred skins with your fingers or with a small kitchen knife: I usually do this under cold running water.

Pat the vegetables dry with kitchen paper, cut them into long strips and lay on a small serving dish. Strain over the flavoured oil and season generously with salt and freshly ground pepper. Garnish with a little finely chopped garlic and flat-leaf parsley just before serving, if desired.

Variation I: Add strips of grilled, sliced courgettes, tossed in a little of the flavoured oil, to the aubergine and peppers.

Variation II: Swirl the grilled aubergine and red pepper strips in a pinwheel pattern in individual pre-baked pastry cases. Spoon over the flavoured oil, garnish with a sprig of flat-leaf parsley or basil, and serve as little *escalivada* tarts.

Serves 4 to 6

Ensalada de arroz al azafrán
Saffron rice salad

Serve this light salad as a glittering first course, double the quantities for a more substantial lunch or supper dish (summer entertaining at its best) or triple the quantities and make it the colourful centrepiece of a glamorous buffet party. To make a real dash, serve it surrounded with chilled langoustines and topped with a cold fresh lobster. Bowls of *alioli* then become a must.

1 recipe virgin *paella* (page 111)

½ red, ½ green and ½ yellow pepper, stem, seeds and
  pith removed

1 cooked *chorizo* sausage, peeled and sliced

½ Spanish onion, finely chopped

2 plum tomatoes, peeled, seeded and diced

12–16 tiger prawns, sautéed in olive oil

12–16 mussels, steamed open in dry white wine

12–16 black olives

2 tablespoons chopped flat-leaf parsley

Vinagreta

8 tablespoons olive oil

3 tablespoons lemon juice or sherry vinegar

1 clove garlic, finely chopped

1 packet saffron threads, moistened with
    1 tablespoon hot dry white wine or water

salt and freshly ground pepper

pinch of crushed dried chillies

Combine the cooked rice in a salad bowl with the peppers, *chorizo*, onion and tomato.

Make the dressing by combining, in a small bowl, the first 4 ingredients. Add salt, pepper and crushed dried chillies, to taste. Mix well and pour over the rice.

Drain the sautéed prawns and the steamed mussels and add, along with the black olives and the chopped parsley, to the rice. Toss well with a fork. Correct the seasoning, adding a little more olive oil, lemon juice or vinegar, and salt and pepper, if necessary.

Serves 6 as a first course, 4 as a main course and 8 or more as a *tapa*

Chapter 4

BACALAO

Bacalao is salted and dried cod. The fresh fish is caught in the North Atlantic waters off the coasts of Norway, Denmark, Newfoundland and Iceland, then salted and dried (or semi-dried), ready to be exported to Portugal and Spain, where it is much prized for traditional *bacalao*-based casserole dishes, as well as for lighter pan-seared or poached dishes of intense flavour and texture. I particularly like thicker cuts of *bacalao*, pan-seared in olive oil *al pil-pil* with golden slices of sautéed garlic and tiny hot red peppers, or pounded with alternate amounts of garlic, olive oil, double cream and lemon juice in the famous *brandada*. Sometimes the *brandada* mixture is 'softened' with a few beaten egg yolks and egg whites (like a soufflé) and baked into a deliciously light and creamy souffléd fish pudding.

In Spain you will find *bacalao* in all sort of qualities in every market. There are even special *bacalao* stores where true *aficionados* go for optimum choice. I find it at its best when sold in semi-moist slabs *sin espina* (without bones), ready to be taken home and made into something a true *bacalao* lover can only dream about. In this country you will find it dried (whole or in pieces) in Spanish, Greek and Italian speciality stores, or moist-packed in some supermarkets.

Trust me – and trust the Spanish – dried salt cod is something no self-respecting cook should be without. Yes, of course, it has to be soaked in cold water for up to 48 hours before using (with 3 or 4 changes of water), but we all have cold water, in abundance, and soaking the salt cod in a stainless-steel or glass bowl requires little attention. The result is delicious: use bits of your moistened desalted cod to flavour cooked vegetable salads, or scrambled eggs, or fold gently poached flaked salt cod into a creamy Sunday brunch omelette. Coat it in a saffron-flavoured batter and deep-fry it for a great hot *tapa*, or a star-of-the-show first course your friends and family will remember. Or feature it in any one of the recipes on the following pages.

Bacalao con pasas, buñuelos de queso y picata con tomate
Salt cod with raisins, cheese puffs and tomato picata sauce

There are certain Spanish recipes for *bacalao* which enchant me with their rustic simplicity: vivid planes of colour, texture and flavour on a plate. Crisp golden pieces of fried dried salt cod, set on a tomato red sauce, sprinkled with sherry-plumped raisins and accompanied by feather-light cheese puffs is a case in point. Serve it as a light first course, as a luncheon or supper dish, or double the recipe and make it the centrepiece of a Pantagruelian feast on its own.

Note: Classicists spoon the sauce over the *bacalao* and bake it for 10 to 15 minutes. I prefer to prepare the sauce and the batter before frying the cod and then to serve the golden cod pieces on a bed of the fragrant sauce, garnished with plumped-up raisins and cheese puffs.

8 rectangles presoaked (see page 54) dried salt cod

4 tablespoons plain flour, seasoned with 2 pinches each of salt, cinnamon, *pimentón* (Spanish sweet paprika) and powdered saffron

6–8 tablespoons olive oil

100 g / 4 oz raisins, plumped up in a little boiling-hot dry sherry

Tomato Picata Sauce

2 cloves garlic

2 tablespoons olive oil

50 g / 2 oz whole almonds

2 sprigs flat-leaf parsley, leaves only, finely chopped

1 tablespoon cinnamon

1 tablespoon *pimentón* (Spanish sweet paprika)

400 g / 14 fl oz can chopped plum tomatoes, with juices

150 ml / ¼ pint dry white wine

300 ml / ½ pint water

Cheese Puffs

225 g / 8 oz plain flour, sifted

5 tablespoons freshly grated *manchego* cheese

1 tablespoon olive oil

salt

2 egg whites

To prepare the sauce, sauté the garlic in the olive oil until golden. Remove and reserve. Add the almonds to the pan and sauté until golden. Remove and reserve. Add the flat-leaf parsley to the pan with the cinnamon and *pimentón* and stir for 1 minute. Then add the tomatoes, white wine and water and simmer over a low heat for 20 minutes. Remove from the heat and reserve.

To prepare the cheese puff batter, combine the flour, cheese, olive oil and salt in a medium-sized mixing bowl and whisk until the mixture is smooth. In a clean bowl, and with a clean whisk, beat the egg whites until stiff. Fold into the prepared batter.

To prepare the *bacalao*, first dredge the presoaked salt cod with the seasoned flour. Fry the rectangles in sizzling hot olive oil until golden brown on all sides. With a slotted spoon, transfer to a baking dish, sprinkle with sherry-plumped raisins and bake in a 200°C/400°F/gas 6 oven for 15 minutes.

In the meantime, reheat the tomato picata sauce over a low heat while you deep-fry the cheese puffs.

To serve, spread the hot sauce on the bottom of a heated serving dish; arrange the salt cod pieces on the sauce; sprinkle with the raisins and garnish with the cheese puffs.

Serves 6

Bacalao con ostras
Salt cod with fresh oysters

Along the Breton coast of France, in the little fishing villages where Gauguin, Van Gogh and the Nabis once painted, the fishermen combine chilled raw oysters with piping hot tiny sausages. Along the Spanish coast, the combination is crisp-fried *bacalao* served hot with the briny fresh oysters. An astounding combination.

1 recipe tomato picata sauce (facing page)

24 fresh oysters

600 g / 1¼ lb presoaked (see page 54) dried salt cod

4 tablespoons plain flour lightly seasoned with salt and *pimentón* (Spanish sweet paprika)

olive oil

2 tablespoons finely chopped flat-leaf parsley

½ teaspoon saffron threads, moistened with 2 tablespoons dry white wine

Prepare the tomato picata sauce as on the facing page. Reserve.

To prepare the oysters, open them, remove the top shell, cut the oysters free from the bottom shell with a small sharp knife, and chill the oysters 'on the half shell' in the refrigerator while you prepare the salt cod.

Cut the presoaked salt cod into 2.5-cm / 1-inch cubes. Dredge them with the seasoned flour. In a large frying pan, heat the olive oil until it is sizzling hot. Add the cubed salt cod and sauté, turning the pieces from time to time, until golden on all sides. With a slotted spoon, transfer the cod pieces to the tomato sauce. Add the parsley and saffron with wine and bring to the boil again.

Serve with the chilled oysters.

Serves 6

Esqueixada
Salt cod salad

One of the great Catalan appetizer salads of all time is *esqueixada*, a fresh-tasting marinated *bacalao* (dried salt cod) and vegetable salad. Whenever I see it on a Barcelona restaurant menu, I go for it.

Dried salt cod is available in this country in some supermarkets as well as Spanish food stores and speciality food markets. To enjoy this colourful salad at its optimum best, soak the dried salt cod in cold water (with at least four changes of water) for 48 hours to render the fish marvellously white and wonderfully tender. This is especially important as the cod is not cooked and so must be moisturized and tenderized as well as desalted.

450 g / 1 lb presoaked dried salt cod (see
    introduction above)
2 large roasted red peppers, charred skins, seeds and
    membranes removed
4 plum tomatoes, cut into thin wedges
12 large black olives, pitted

Vinagreta
6–8 tablespoons extra virgin olive oil
2 tablespoons sherry vinegar
1 clove garlic, finely chopped
1 tablespoon flat-leaf parsley, finely chopped
sea salt and freshly ground pepper, to taste
pinch of crushed dried chillies

Combine all of the dressing ingredients in a large bowl. Thinly slice the salt cod and add to the dressing in the bowl. Turn the cod over in the dressing and leave in the refrigerator to marinate for at least 2 hours.

Cut the roasted pepper into thin strips. In a salad bowl, combine the thin tomato wedges, pitted black olives and strips of roasted pepper. Drain the *vinagreta* from the bowl containing the marinated salt cod (now salt-cod flavoured), pour over the prepared vegetables and toss. Then arrange the marinated salt cod slices attractively on the salad and serve.

Variation I: Proceed as above, but substitute knife-thin slices of raw red and green pepper for the roasted red pepper, and add thin slices of red onion, which you have briefly soaked in iced water, along with the black olives. (See picture.)

Variation II: Proceed as in either of the two recipes above, and pile into individual pre-baked tart shells. Sprinkle with finely chopped parsley and serve immediately.

Serves 4 to 6

Croquetas de bacalao con azafrán
Salt cod and saffron fritters

Deep-fried fritters of flaked salt cod in a saffron-flavoured batter make one of the best *tapas* I know. They are usually served cold in *tapas* bars, but are a revelation when served hot. Easy to do – as all the preparation except the frying can be done the day before.

225 g / 8 oz presoaked dried salt cod (see page 54)

2 tablespoons olive oil

1 medium onion, finely chopped

100 g / 4 oz plain flour

1 teaspoon baking powder

½ teaspoon salt

1 egg, lightly beaten

120 ml / 4 fl oz milk

¼ teaspoon saffron threads, moistened with
    4 tablespoons of the milk

2 tablespoons olive oil

pinch of crushed dried chillies

vegetable oil (not palm), for frying

Rinse the salt cod well under cold running water and then put it into a large saucepan. Add cold water to cover, bring to the boil, then reduce the heat and simmer the cod for 20 minutes. Drain the water through a colander. Remove the skin and bones from the cod and flake the fish.

To make the batter, sift the flour, baking powder and salt into a mixing bowl. Add the beaten egg, milk, saffron in milk and olive oil and whisk until well blended. Add the flaked cod, season with a pinch or two of crushed dried chillies and mix again.

When ready to cook, pour the vegetable oil to a depth of 1cm / ½ inch in a large frying pan and heat until very hot. Drop the batter, a tablespoon at a time, into the hot oil and fry for 2–4 minutes, turning the *croquetas* over so they cook evenly on both sides. Drain on kitchen paper. These little *tapas* can be served hot or cold.

Makes 20 to 24

Bacalao vasco con pimientos choriceros

Basque salt cod with dried red peppers

Pimientos choriceros (**Spanish dried red peppers**, available in Spanish food stores) add a pleasantly tongue-tingling flavour to this dish of sautéed salt cod simmered in a red pepper and onion sauce. If you cannot find the dried peppers, substitute freshly roasted red peppers spiked with 2 to 3 hot red chilli peppers to achieve the necessary tingle.

600 g / 1¼ lb presoaked dried salt cod (see page 54), cut into rectangles about 6 x 8 cm (2½ x 3¼ inches)
2–3 tablespoons olive oil

Onion and Red Pepper Sauce
75 g / 3 oz lard
2 large Spanish onions, finely chopped
8 Spanish dried red peppers (*pimientos choriceros*) soaked for the same amount of time as the salt cod

To make the onion and red pepper sauce, heat the lard in a sauté pan, or large shallow casserole, until sizzling hot. Stir in the onions, reduce the heat to the gentlest simmer possible, and cook, stirring from time to time, until the onions are very soft, almost dissolved, adding a little water from time to time to keep the onions from browning as they simmer in the pan. After half an hour of cooking, add the presoaked red peppers to the pan and continue to cook, stirring occasionally, for another half hour, adding a little water if necessary.

Remove the pan from the heat. Transfer the onions and peppers to a food processor and process in short bursts until the sauce is well blended. Then, to ensure the sauce is smooth, press it through a fine sieve into a clean bowl. Reserve.

To cook the cod, heat the olive oil until sizzling in a large sauté pan, or shallow casserole. Drain the cod rectangles and place the pieces, skin-side down, in the pan. Sauté the cod for 2 to 3 minutes in the hot oil. With a spatula or fish knife, turn the cod pieces over. Spoon the sauce over the cod and simmer for about 20 minutes or until the fish is cooked through. Serve at once.

Serves 6

Bacalao al pil-pil
Poached dried salt cod with garlic and dried chillies

Pil-pil **recipes** – whether shrimp, baby squid rings or presoaked, poached dried salt cod – are to the Basques what fish and chips are to us: pure delight. This exuberant combination of golden garlic chips and thinly sliced dried hot red chilli peppers with presoaked cod (it must be best quality) is simmered in olive oil, with a little water. Shake the pan frequently during the last few minutes of cooking to create the famous Basque emulsion that gives the unique style and flavour to this classic dish.

350 g / 12 oz dried salt cod, cut into thin pieces with skin left on but bones removed

150 ml / 5 fl oz olive oil

3 cloves garlic, thinly sliced lengthwise

1 dried red chilli pepper, seeded and cut into long thin threads or thin rounds

Soak the cod in a bowl of cold water placed in the kitchen sink under a dribbling cold-water tap for 12 hours. On the following day, change the water, rinse the salt from the cod and resume the operation for another 12 to 18 hours. Drain well.

Pour the oil into a shallow heatproof earthenware (or stainless steel) casserole. Add the garlic and chilli pepper, and, over a very low heat, sauté until the garlic turns pale gold. With a slotted spoon, remove the garlic and chilli and reserve. The oil will remain garlic and chilli flavoured.

Place the cod, skin side down, in the garlic- and chilli-flavoured oil and cook, shaking the pan constantly, for 4 minutes. Turn the fish over and cook the other side for 2 to 3 minutes. Then add 2 tablespoons water (standing away from the pan as you do so), cover the pan and simmer the cod gently over the lowest of heats for about 15 minutes, shaking the pan often during this time.

To serve, remove the cod from the hot oil using a palette knife, cut it into *tapa*-sized squares or rectangles and return it to the hot oil. Garnish with the golden garlic and chilli pepper and serve immediately in the oil.

Serves 6 as a *tapa*

Chapter 5

TORTILLA AND OTHER EGG DISHES

The Spanish tend to eat later than other nationalities. It is not uncommon to have lunch as late as three or four in the afternoon, and dinner at ten. On my first evening out in Spain, we didn't sit down to dine until midnight because my hosts had decided to meet friends in a *tapas* bar first. And from one bar, where we tasted tiny hot clams fried with garlic and chillies, to another where we just had to try the *pochas* with *jamón*, we went on to the very best place to have *bacalao al pil-pil*. Then the conversation came round to *tortilla española*, and I just had to taste that. And fine it was. And so on to dinner at midnight.

From that moment on, *ir de tapeo*, the Spanish habit of going from bar to bar with friends to sample a chilled *manzanilla* or a cold beer and a selection of *tapas* before lunch or dinner, or, indeed, instead of lunch or dinner, became a habit for me. And each time I had to try the tantalizing *tortilla*, to discover for myself why it was Spain's most famous *tapa*.

It wasn't until dinner at El Churrasco restaurant in old Córdoba, near the Mezquita – perhaps the most original architectural work carried out under the Omayyads, and certainly one of the most beautiful buildings in Spain – that I first encountered a *tortilla* to live up to its glamorous reputation. Here at last was a *tortilla* with a difference: deep-baked in a special sloping-sided pan, its outside crisp, and as golden as the light in a Zuberon painting, its inside soft and moist and highly flavoured – a brilliant combination of the world's simplest ingredients: potatoes, onions and eggs. A *tortilla* to end all *tortillas*. Just look at the picture.

Other *tortillas* in Spain are legion: *tortillas* with courgettes, with *chorizo*, with saffron, with tomatoes and aubergines, with sweetbreads and ham, even with baby eels. But most famous of all – and perhaps the most maligned when served up in cold, grease-laden slabs as the real thing, the gen-u-ine *tapa* from Spain, in dingy, dusty, desolate cafés and bars around the world – is the *tortilla española*. Play with this recipe and make it your own.

Tortilla española
Spanish potato omelette

One of the simplest dishes in the Spanish culinary repertoire, *tortilla española* – when well made, its savoury insides of diced potato and creamy eggs, still a little runny, are encased in their light golden crust – is found everywhere in Spain. Served in wedges, hot or cold, as a *tapa*, as part of a buffet, or, more simply, as a lunch or supper dish on its own with a fresh-tasting salad, it is delicious.

Try this comforting flat omelette flavoured (at its most basic) with a little finely chopped onion and cooked in the best extra virgin Spanish olive oil you can find, as in the following recipe. And then, more adventurously, try one of the more glamorous tortilla variations that follow.

4–5 organic free-range eggs

4–5 tablespoons extra virgin olive oil

1 large potato, peeled and cut into large dice (1 cm / ½ inch)

2–3 tablespoons finely chopped onion

pinch of finely chopped garlic (optional)

salt and freshly ground pepper

1 tablespoon chilled butter, to glaze

Garnish

sprigs of fresh watercress or flat-leaf parsley

thin wedges of lemon

Break the eggs into a medium-sized bowl. Add 1 tablespoon of water and beat with a fork or wire whisk.

Heat 2 tablespoons of the olive oil in a small frying pan. Add the potato and onion (and the garlic, if using) and sauté, stirring constantly, for about 10 minutes, or until the potatoes are soft and beginning to change colour. Season with salt and pepper, to taste, then remove the potatoes and aromatics from the pan with a slotted spoon and add them to the bowl containing the beaten eggs.

Heat a small deep frying pan or omelette pan (15–18cm / 6 or 7 inches in diameter) over a medium heat. Add 2 tablespoons of the olive oil. When the oil sizzles, pour in the *tortilla* mixture and cook, lifting the edges of the *tortilla* from the bottom of the pan with a spatula to allow the still semi-liquid eggs to slip underneath. Be sure to shake the pan gently while cooking (and add a teaspoon or two of olive oil around the sides of the pan) to keep the *tortilla* from sticking to the bottom.

When the bottom edges of the *tortilla* turn golden (lift it up gently with a spatula to see), place a large plate over the pan and turn the *tortilla* out onto the plate. Wipe the bottom of the pan clean with a paper towel moistened with a little olive oil and slide the *tortilla* back into the pan to brown the other side.

Slide the *tortilla* onto a heated round serving dish. Garnish with sprigs of fresh watercress or flat-leaf parsley and thin wedges of lemon. As a last touch of perfection, glaze the top with a bit of chilled butter held on the point of a sharp kitchen knife.

Note: The *tortilla* should not be too cooked. At its succulent best, the surface of the *tortilla* should be golden and slightly crisp to the touch, but the eggy filling should remain almost runny in texture.

Serves 2 to 3

Tortilla de chorizo con azafrán
Spanish omelette with chorizo and saffron

Cook as in recipe on the previous page, but (1) add 1 to 2 pinches of saffron to the tablespoon of water before you add it to the eggs and (2) sauté 8 thin *chorizo* slices with the potatoes and aromatics.

Tortilla con chile y cebolla
Spanish omelette with chilli and onion

This variation on the *tortilla española* theme adds a small red onion, finely chopped with flat-leaf parsley and hot red chilli to the mix.

4–5 organic free-range eggs

4–5 tablespoons extra virgin olive oil

1 large potato, peeled and cut into large dice (1cm / ½ inch)

1 small red onion, diced

1 hot red chilli pepper, without the seeds, finely chopped

4 tablespoons finely chopped flat-leaf

parsley, leaves only

1 clove garlic, finely chopped

1 tablespoon chilled butter, to glaze

Garnish

sprigs of fresh watercress or flat-leaf parsley

thin wedges of lemon

Cook as in the recipe on page 66, adding the chilli pepper, parsley and garlic to the potato in the olive oil. Add to the beaten eggs and proceed to cook the flat omelette mixture as on page 66.

Serves 2 to 3

Tortilla de setas
Wild mushroom omelette

In the spring and autumn months, when wild mushrooms are in the markets, a friend of mine who lives in a *finca* in the hills outside San Sebastián (as she says, 'in full País Vasco'), loves to combine eggs and wild mushrooms. She's too shy to be named here, so we will have to know her as X. In the spring she briefly scrambles eggs with herbs and the tiny little Basque mushrooms (rare and expensive) called *perretxiko*. And last autumn she prepared a late supper for me when I arrived unexpectedly a day early for my yearly visit. This was a recipe for her own home-bottled ceps (pan-seared in olive oil with bay leaves and lemon rind, dried hot chillies and peppercorns; cooled; spooned into sterilized jars; filled to the top with boiling oil and pasteurized in boiling water). She wouldn't give me the recipe for the marinated ceps: said it was woman's work. So we shall have to make do with wild ceps, cooked with the aromatics above and spooned over a *tortilla* base. Fantastic country flavours and texture. Thank you, X.

6–7 large free-range eggs

2 tablespoons diced butter

sea salt and freshly ground pepper

1–2 tablespoons extra virgin olive oil

The Mushrooms

4 tablespoons olive oil

12 small to medium-sized fresh ceps (or other mushrooms of your choice), sliced or quartered according to size

4 tablespoons finely chopped shallots

1 clove garlic, finely chopped

chopped leaves of 1 sprig each fresh rosemary and thyme

1 strip lemon rind

6 black peppercorns, bruised with a rolling pin

1 small dried hot chilli pepper

sea salt

First, prepare the mushrooms. Heat the oil in a large frying pan until it just begins to sizzle. Add the ceps (or other mushrooms), shallots and garlic and briefly toss in the hot oil. Add the chopped herbs, lemon rind, peppercorns and chilli pepper, and salt to taste. Sauté until the mushrooms are well browned. Remove from the heat and reserve.

After you've had a drink of your best Spanish red wine, break the eggs in a bowl and, with a wire balloon whisk, beat until they are frothy. Add the butter and season with salt and pepper.

Heat olive oil in a 20-cm / 8-inch omelette pan. When the oil begins to sizzle, pour in the beaten eggs and allow them to set slightly. Then stir them constantly with a wooden spoon, running the edge of the spoon round the pan and drawing the eggs into the centre. Cook until creamy. With a slotted spoon, spoon the mushrooms (leaving their oil behind) on to this golden egg bed and serve immediately from the pan on to hot plates.

Serves 2, 3 at a pinch

Tortilla española de azafrán
Potato saffron omelette

I often notice saffron-coloured and saffron-flavoured *tortillas* in *tapas* bars in Andalusia. And as I am a devotee of this most expensive of all spices, I couldn't resist. If you want to go the whole hog, another of my favourite variations on the *tortilla* theme crumbles 2 or 3 tablespoons of peeled chopped *chorizo* in the potato, onion and saffron mixture. It is as simple as that. I make this slightly differently to the classic *tortilla española* on page 66, in that I first cook the potatoes in water until just tender.

6 organic free-range eggs
salt and freshly ground pepper
pinch of crushed dried chillies
4–6 tablespoons extra virgin olive oil
2 medium-sized onions, finely chopped

600 g / 1½ lb baking potatoes, peeled, cut into
**   6mm / ½ inch cubes, and cooked in boiling salted**
**   water until just tender**
¼ teaspoon saffron threads, soaked in 4 tablespoons
**   hot vegetable stock (made with 2 pinches of**
**   crumbled vegetable stock cube)**

Beat the eggs in a bowl until frothy. Season with salt, pepper and crushed dried chillies, to taste. Reserve. Heat 2 tablespoons of the olive oil in a large frying pan. Sauté the onions until they just begin to turn golden. With a slotted spoon, transfer the sautéed onions to the bowl of beaten eggs. Add the drained boiled potato cubes to the pan and toss them over a medium heat in the oil to take on the oil flavour. Season as above and add the potatoes to the onion and egg mixture.

Stir the saffron stock into the *tortilla* mixture.

When ready to cook the *tortilla*, heat the remaining oil in a 25–30 cm / 10–12 inch frying pan. Add the *tortilla* mixture, spreading the potatoes and onions evenly over the pan. Lower the heat to moderate and cook the *tortilla*, stirring, for about 1½ minutes or until the eggs just begin to set. With a spatula, lift the sides of the *tortilla* free from the sides of the pan, adding a teaspoon of olive oil around the edges of the pan to keep the *tortilla* 'slipping' free. When the eggs are almost set, place a large plate over the pan, and turn the *tortilla* out onto the plate. Wipe the pan clean and slide the *tortilla* back in to cook for a minute of two or the other side.

Serve the *tortilla* cut into wedges, hot or, more traditionally, at room temperature.

Serves 2 to 3 as a luncheon or supper dish

Piparrada
Basque piperade

This vegetarian version of Basque piperade is delicious hot or cold. When serving it hot, sprinkle it with chopped flat-leaf parsley and garnish with crisp-fried croûtons. If you are serving it cold, turn it out into a shallow bowl to cool. Use it to fill hollowed-out small rolls which you have brushed (inside and out) with paprika-flavoured butter and crisped in the oven.

Piparrada is also a great way to have eggs for breakfast. For company, serve it in individual *paella* pans, or in crispy filo pastry cups for a New Spain touch. Or, serve the *piparrada* (hot or cold) on tiny plates and garnish the eggs with thin strips of festive red and green peppers … and (for non-vegetarians) thin strips of *serrano* ham for a *tapa* that your guests will love.

2–4 tablespoons extra virgin olive oil

1 large Spanish onion, chopped

2 cloves garlic, finely chopped

2 medium-sized roasted green peppers, peeled, seeded and diced

4 plum tomatoes, peeled, seeded and diced

salt and freshly ground pepper

8 organic free-range eggs, lightly beaten

Garnish

8 triangles country bread (e.g. ciabatta), brushed with olive oil and crisp-fried

2 tablespoons freshly chopped flat-leaf parsley

Heat the olive oil in a large thick-bottomed frying pan. Add the onion and garlic and sauté, stirring constantly, until the onion is soft. Stir in the roasted peppers and the tomatoes and cook for 2 or 3 minutes more, or until the vegetable mixture is soft but not watery. Season generously with salt and pepper.

When ready to finish the *piparrada*, stir in the beaten eggs and simmer over a low heat, stirring constantly, until the eggs are just set and the mixture is thick and creamy. Serve at once.

Serves 4 to 6

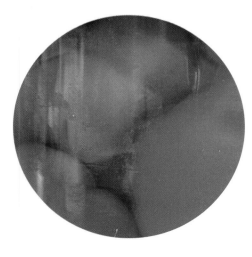

Huevos a la flamenca
Andalusian baked eggs

This celebrated Andalusian recipe for eggs baked in a savoury tomato-based *sofrito* makes an attractive light lunch or supper dish, or it can be served in individual ramekins, or egg dishes, as a delicious hot appetizer for a Spanish meal. The first time I met baked eggs *a la flamenca* it was served in individual *paella* pans and came sizzling hot to the table, the eggs glistening and golden, surrounded by a colourful garnish of asparagus tips, *pimiento* strips and thin slices of spicy *chorizo*.

I like, too, to serve this dish in individual shallow heatproof dishes with the spicy *sofrito* sauce as a base and the eggs set in hollows in the richly flavoured sauce, as in the recipe below. I also serve it in a large *paella* pan in the same way. Accompany with crusty country bread and a bottle of red wine

8 organic free-range eggs

The Sofrito

3 tablespoons extra virgin olive oil

1 Spanish onion, finely chopped

1 clove garlic, finely chopped

1 *chorizo* sausage, skinned and diced

2 canned *pimientos*, diced

6 plum tomatoes, peeled, seeded and diced

2 thin slices *serrano* ham, diced

2 tablespoons finely chopped flat-leaf parsley

½ teaspoon *pimentón* (Spanish sweet paprika)

sea salt and crushed dried chillies

water, dry white wine or vegetable stock

Garnish

8 lightly cooked small asparagus spears, drained (or 8 canned white asparagus spears or celery fronds)

1 canned *pimiento*, drained and cut into long strips

8–12 thin slices *chorizo* sausage

First make the *sofrito*. Preheat the oven to 220°C/425°F/gas 7. In a large frying pan, heat the olive oil until it sizzles. Add the onion and garlic and cook over a low heat, stirring constantly, until the vegetables just begin to turn pale gold. Add the *chorizo* and *pimientos* and cook, stirring, for 3 more minutes.

Then add the tomatoes, ham and half the parsley. Season with the *pimentón*, and salt and crushed dried chillies, to taste. Stir the mixture well and simmer, covered, for about 10 minutes, adding a little water, dry white wine or vegetable stock, if the mixture becomes too dry. The sauce should remain quite thick.

Meanwhile, brush 4 shallow heatproof baking dishes (eared porcelain egg dishes are good for this) with olive oil.

When you are ready to bake the eggs, reheat the sauce and then spread the mixture evenly in the bottom of the baking dishes. Make 2 hollows in the *sofrito* mixture in each of the dishes with the back of a spoon. Break an egg into a saucer and slide the egg into one of the hollows. Repeat with the remaining eggs.

Garnish the dishes by arranging the asparagus tips (or celery fronds), *pimiento* strips and *chorizo* slices around the eggs. Put the dishes into the preheated oven for about 5 minutes, or until the whites of the eggs are just set and the yolks are still soft. Remove the dishes from the oven, sprinkle with the remaining parsley and serve immediately.

Serves 4

Huevos revueltos con chorizo
Scrambled eggs with chorizo

Chorizo – the red-tinted, paprika-flavoured sausage of Spain – is a Spanish cook's cupboard staple, used to lend flavour, texture and colour to soups, stews, salads, rice and vegetable dishes … and to serve on its own, either raw or cooked, as a most satisfactory *tapa* or garnish. Here, *chorizo* lends its own distinctive savour to scrambled eggs.

2 tablespoons extra virgin olive oil

2 fat *chorizo* sausages, skinned and diced

1 teaspoon *pimentón* (Spanish sweet paprika)

pinch of crushed dried chillies

6 or 7 organic free-range eggs, lightly beaten

salt and freshly ground pepper

2 slices coarse-textured country bread (e.g. ciabatta), diced and sautéed until crisp in a tablespoon of olive oil to which you have added half a clove of garlic

Heat the oil in a medium-sized frying pan. Add the diced *chorizo* and sauté, stirring constantly, until the *chorizo* begins to 'frazzle' at the edges. Stir in the *pimentón* and crushed dried chillies and stir for one minute.

Add the beaten eggs to the pan, and lightly combine them with the *chorizo* as you would for scrambled eggs. As soon as the eggs begin to set, remove from the heat and spoon onto heated plates. Toss the garlic croûtons in the paprika-coloured oil remaining in the pan in which you scrambled the eggs, and, when they have warmed through, spoon over the eggs and serve immediately.

Serves 4

Huevos revueltos con atún
Sea scramble of grilled tuna and eggs

On a blustery March day, on the Costa Brava, I watched three hardy Spanish fishermen, tightly wrapped against the storm, launch their boat straight off the beach into the sea to catch me some lunch. The water frothed in tiny clipped wavelets against the prow as the boat set off from shore driven by the sharp wind. I was sure that unless they were visiting their nets for tiny red mullet, *chanquetes* or a lucky catch of baby *bonito*, lunch for me that day would be limited to thin-sliced *escalopes* of milk-fed veal, pan-seared with baby artichokes – not a bad thing, but the boys had promised me fish.

I was in luck: the boat soon came back and I had tuna, lightly grilled, then flaked and 'scrambled' with eggs whipped to a froth, cooked in 2 tablespoons of olive oil with a tablespoon or two of finely chopped onion, garlic and diced roasted red pepper.

1 fresh tuna steak

extra virgin olive oil

sea salt and freshly ground pepper

1 tablespoon finely chopped onion

½ clove garlic, finely chopped

2 tablespoons diced roasted red pepper

pinch of finely chopped fresh red chilli pepper

6 large organic free-range eggs, beaten

finely chopped fresh flat-leaf parsley or coriander

Brush the tuna steak with olive oil on both sides and pan-grill for 2–3 minutes. Season with sea salt and pepper and turn over to grill until coloured on the other side (about 1 minute). Remove from the heat and flake with a fork.

In a small frying pan, sauté the onion and garlic in 1 tablespoon olive oil until the onion becomes transparent. Add the red pepper and hot red chilli; season with salt and pepper and sauté for 1 minute more. Remove from the heat.

In another, slightly larger frying pan, sauté the beaten eggs in 2 tablespoons of olive oil, stirring constantly until cooked through but still a little liquid. Lightly stir in the flaked tuna and the red pepper and chilli mix, correct the seasoning, divide between 2 or 3 heated plates and sprinkle with finely chopped parsley or coriander. Serve immediately.

Serves 2 to 3

Chapter 6

GAZPA

AND OTHER SOUPS

Southern Spain's favourite soup, *gazpacho*, is one of the world's most magical summer starters. This combination of everyday ingredients – uncooked tomatoes, water, yesterday's bread and olive oil – can create a chilled summer soup that is almost unreal in texture and flavour. The secret here is, first of all, the quality of the tomatoes and the quality (and quantity) of the olive oil. This is a soup of summer and early autumn, when tomatoes are at their freshest and their best. And the tomatoes must be ripe, ripe, ripe (almost overripe). They must be peeled, seeded and diced and then frothed with iced water and the best olive oil available. Quantities of iced water and olive oil create (along with the sweetness and the acidity of the ripe tomatoes) a flavoursome, light, frothy blend of pure chilled flavour, so right for the hot days and nights of southern Spain.

Now, at this point there are two optional additions you can make to your *gazpacho*. Some of the great restaurants in Spain whisk in a little double cream to add smoothness and sophistication to the blend. I rely on the emulsion of the liquids and the oil to do that. And others, classic country cooks, like to add a little wine or sherry vinegar at the last minute to 'spark' the flavour. Again, I prefer to let the ripeness of the tomatoes do that, though I have been known to add a little sherry at the last moment in a fit of over-generous madness. But if the cook can't be over generous and a little mad … who can?

Other possibilities are legion. Why not serve your *gazpacho* with a bouquet of fresh herbs in the centre of each chilled bowl? Or give it a lavish sprinkling of diced garlic croûtons, raw peppers, cucumber and tomato. Or add a little diced avocado kept colour-bright with lemon juice … or a few small ice cubes, small melon balls and seedless white grapes along with the tomatoes.

CHO

Gazpacho andaluz
Andalusian gazpacho

At its origins, *gazpacho* was a dish of the poor in Andalusia. Made with the remains of yesterday's bread, mixed with diced tomatoes and peppers from the garden, olive oil from their own trees and cold water from the well, this refreshing vegetable emulsion has since become one of the elegant mainstays of modern hot-weather cooking. Some say the recipe is Moorish, but as there were no tomatoes and peppers in the time of the Moors (Columbus, Cortés and the *conquistadores* didn't return from their voyages until much later) it is clearly a more modern dish, probably seventeenth- or eighteenth-century at the earliest. Old enough – and delicious enough – for me.

2 fat cloves garlic, sliced

sea salt

extra virgin olive oil

2 slices country bread (or 2 slices ciabatta), crusts removed, diced

1 red pepper, seeded and diced

1 small hot red chilli pepper, thinly sliced

1.4 kg / 3 lb very ripe summer tomatoes, peeled, seeded and diced (and 2 canned tomatoes for colour)

425 ml / ¾ pint cold water or light vegetable stock

2 tablespoons wine vinegar

2–3 teaspoons sugar

½ teaspoon *pimentón* (Spanish sweet paprika)

pinch of crushed dried chillies

2–4 tablespoons double cream (optional: cream is not used in a classic *gazpacho* but is sometimes added by modern restaurant chefs to soften the colour)

Garnish

finely chopped tomato, red and green pepper, onion, chives and fresh basil

I like to use a mortar and pestle to pound the sliced garlic with 1 teaspoon of sea salt until I get a smooth paste. I then add 4 tablespoons olive oil and pound the mixture again until the oil is well blended into the smooth paste. (You can also use the flat blade of a knife on the garlic and salt on a cutting board; the salt acts as an abrasive. Then transfer the paste to a bowl and add the oil.)

Spoon the contents of the mortar into the bowl of a food processor. Moisten the bread with a little water and then squeeze almost dry. Add the bread, red pepper, chilli pepper and tomatoes to the garlic. Process in short bursts, adding a little of the cold water (or stock) from time to time until a smooth, slightly thickened cold soup has formed. According to the ripeness of the tomatoes, you can use up to a litre of cold water. Season with the vinegar, sugar, *pimentón* and crushed dried chillies.

At the last minute, to improve the colour, add the double cream and process until the soup is uniformly coloured. Combine the garnish ingredients in a small bowl, mix well and spoon over the soup just before serving.

You can also serve the soup in deep bowls with a small cluster of fresh herbs – sprigs of basil, coriander, flat-leaf parsley and mint – in the centre of each bowl. Or serve the *gazpacho* in the traditional country manner with separate bowls of diced garlic croûtons, tomato, peeled and seeded cucumber, onion and hard-boiled egg. Each guest adds his or her own garnish to the soup.

Serves 4 to 6

Sopa de alubias rojas de Tolosa
Tolosa red bean soup

A Basque classic. This richly coloured, highly flavoured soup is made of the very special dried red beans from Tolosa but you can use red kidney beans. The beans, soaked overnight, are simmered with onion and garlic in olive oil before water, or a light vegetable stock, is added along with pieces of pork fat, blood sausage and *chorizo*.

450 g / 1 lb red kidney beans, soaked overnight and drained

1 large Spanish onion, finely chopped

2 cloves garlic, finely chopped

120 ml / 4 fl oz virgin olive oil

100 g / 4 oz pork fat, cut into small squares, about 6 mm / ¼ inch thick

2 *morcilla* (blood) sausages, about 100 g / 4 oz each

2 *chorizo* sausages, about ? g / ? oz each

sea salt and crushed dried chillies

Put the beans in a large pot and add enough cold water to cover. Bring to the boil, skimming off any impurities as they rise to the surface.

In a frying pan, sauté the onion and garlic in the olive oil until the vegetables begin to change colour. With a slotted spoon, transfer the vegetables to the pot with the squares of pork fat. Lower the heat and simmer the beans for 1 to 1½ hours, or until the beans are tender, adding more water from time to time as necessary.

In the fat remaining in the frying pan, sauté the *morcilla* and *chorizo* until they just begin to change colour. Remove from the heat and reserve.

Fifteen minutes before serving, add the *morcilla* and *chorizo* to the beans and heat through. Correct the seasoning, adding sea salt and crushed dried chillies to taste. Serve immediately.

Serves 4 to 6

Potaje de espinacas y garbanzos
Chickpea and spinach hot pot

In the eighteenth century, Spanish cooks used to soak their chickpeas in the broth of salt cod to give them extra flavour, much as our own cooks of that period used to soak dried legumes in water flavoured with a little ham or salt beef stock. I tried flavouring the broth for this soup with a very little shredded salt cod (just a tablespoon or two) and found it a delicious addition.

Presoaked chickpeas and baby spinach leaves are the basis for this classic soup, which resembles Provençal country dishes in feeling. Try it.

300 g / 10 oz chickpeas, soaked overnight
   and drained
boiling water
450 g / 1 lb potatoes, peeled and cut into pieces
150 ml / 5 fl oz olive oil
1 thick slice coarse-textured country bread, about
   25 g / 1 oz
2 cloves garlic, thinly sliced
1 Spanish onion, finely chopped
1 teaspoon *pimentón* (Spanish sweet paprika)

675 g / 1½ lb baby spinach leaves, washed and
   chopped
2 young leeks, trimmed and sliced into thin rounds
sea salt
2–4 small hot red chilli peppers, seeded and cut in half
   lengthways
2 tablespoons each chopped flat-leaf parsley, basil
   and chives
2 hard-boiled egg whites, chopped
2 hard-boiled egg yolks, sieved

In a large pot, cover the chickpeas with boiling water, bring to the boil and skim off impurities from the surface of the liquid. Then turn the heat down, cover the pot and gently simmer. After 45 minutes add the potatoes, another 900 ml / 1½ pints boiling water, and continue to cook for a further 30 minutes.

In the meantime, heat the oil in a frying pan. Add the bread and fry it until golden brown on both sides. Remove the bread from the pan and reserve. Add the garlic to the pan and sauté until golden. With a slotted spoon, remove the garlic and reserve. Add the onion to the pan and sauté, stirring constantly, until transparent and just starting to turn golden. Stir in the *pimentón* and then scrape the mixture into the pot of chickpeas. Add the spinach leaves, leeks, sea salt to taste, and hot red chillies, and cook for another 15 minutes, or until the chickpeas, spinach and leeks are tender.

Meanwhile, combine the fried bread and garlic in a mortar and pound to a smooth paste. Stir in the herbs and reserve for the garnish.

When ready to serve, pour the soup into a heated serving bowl or individual soup bowls. Sprinkle with the breadcrumb, garlic and herb mixture and top with a sprinkling each of egg white and egg yolk.

Serves 4 to 6

Sopa de ajo 1
Garlic soup 1

This is the real peasant soup of Spain. Richly flavoured, satisfying and soul-warming when served with an egg poached in it and garnished with tiny squares of *serrano* ham, it is almost a meal in itself. Serve it to friends on a cold winter's night. But I warn you, don't serve anything too substantial after it.

4 tablespoons olive oil

4 cloves garlic, blanched

225 g / 8 oz dense-textured day-old country bread,
   sliced

1 teaspoon *pimentón* (Spanish sweet paprika)

1 litre / 1¾ pints boiling water, or light vegetable
   stock

tiny squares of thinly sliced cured pork fat

tiny squares of thinly sliced *serrano* ham

sea salt and crushed dried chillies

4 eggs

1–2 tablespoons chopped flat-leaf parsley

In a medium-sized casserole, heat the olive oil. Add the blanched garlic cloves and sauté over a medium heat until the garlic begins to change colour. Rip each slice of bread into pieces and add to the garlic and oil, and continue to cook, stirring, until the bread begins to turn golden. Stir in the *pimentón* and pour in the boiling water or light vegetable stock. Add the squares of thinly sliced pork fat and *serrano* ham and cook over a medium heat for 20 minutes. Season with a little sea salt (note that the ham is already salty) and a pinch or two of crushed dried chillies.

During this time, preheat the oven to 180°C/350°F/gas 4.

Just before serving: place 4 warmed heatproof earthenware soup bowls on a baking tray. Ladle the soup into the bowls and carefully break an egg into each bowl. Place the tray with the soup bowls in the preheated oven and cook the eggs in the hot soup for a few minutes, or until the whites are just set. Sprinkle each serving with a pinch or two of flat-leaf parsley and serve immediately.

Sopa de ajo 2
Garlic soup 2

They say there are as many ways of making garlic soup as there are cooks in Spain. Most versions feature day-old bread, garlic, parsley leaves and poached eggs, as in the recipe on the left. This version, however, introduces tomato purée and foamy egg whites to the garlic-flavoured stock to ring the changes on a Spanish country classic.

1 litre / 1¾ pints cold water

2 tablespoons finely chopped garlic

2–4 tablespoons tomato purée

4 tablespoons olive oil

2 tablespoons finely slivered fresh mint leaves

sea salt and freshly ground pepper

pinch of crushed dried chillies

4 egg whites

4 slices day-old country bread, rubbed with a cut
   clove of garlic and dried out in a low oven

Garnish

slivered fresh mint leaves

In a large saucepan, combine the water, garlic, tomato purée and olive oil. Add the slivered mint leaves and season with salt, pepper and crushed dried chillies, to taste. Whisk well to amalgamate the flavours. Bring to the boil, skim off any froth or impurities, lower the heat and simmer for 10 minutes.

When ready to serve, whisk the egg whites until foamy and well blended and stir into the hot soup. Cook for 2 to 3 more minutes, or until 'threads' of egg white have formed. Place a slice of garlic-rubbed country bread in each of 4 soup bowls. Spoon over the hot garlic soup, sprinkle with additional slivered mint leaves and serve immediately.

Both serve 4

Sopa de almendras
Almond soup

One of the great soups that are thickened with cubes or crumbs of fresh bread is this interesting blend of ground blanched almonds, day-old bread cubes and water, flavoured with garlic, parsley, saffron and cumin. This soup has great flavour and contrast of texture – smooth (the blend of softened bread and water), crunchy (the crisp-fried garnish of croûtons and toasted almonds), and spicy (the finely chopped garlic, saffron threads and powdered cumin) all work their sophisticated taste magic in this blend of flavours and textures.

4 tablespoons olive oil

225 g / 8 oz blanched almonds, chopped

2 cloves garlic, finely chopped

4 sprigs flat-leaf parsley, finely chopped

2 slices country bread (or 4 slices ciabatta),
   crusts removed, diced

1 teaspoon powdered cumin

½ teaspoon saffron threads

¼ teaspoon *pimentón* (Spanish sweet paprika)

sea salt and freshly ground pepper

4–6 tablespoons extra virgin olive oil

900 ml / 1½ pints water

Garnish

garlic croûtons

slivered toasted almonds

threads of peel of ½ unwaxed lemon

flat-leaf parsley leaves

In a frying pan, heat the olive oil until it sizzles. Stir in the almonds, garlic and parsley and half the bread and sauté over a medium heat, stirring constantly, until the bread cubes are golden. Soak the remaining bread in a little water and reserve.

Transfer the contents of the frying pan to a mortar and pound with a pestle until the mixture is smooth. Then add the spices, salt and pepper to taste, and most of the extra virgin olive oil. Pound again until the mixture forms a highly flavoured paste, adding the remaining olive oil to taste.

When ready to cook the soup, add some of the water to the mortar, mix well with a wooden spoon and pour the contents of the mortar into a large saucepan. Fill the mortar with some more of the water, scraping any of the spicy mixture still in the mortar into the added water, and pour it into the saucepan. Add the remaining water to the saucepan and simmer the soup base for 8 to 10 minutes.

Remove the pan from the heat and stir in the presoaked bread cubes to swell up in the hot liquid.

When ready to serve, correct the seasoning and ladle the soup into 4 soup bowls. Sprinkle each bowl with a few garlic croûtons, a pinch of toasted almonds, threads of lemon peel and several parsley leaves.

Serves 4

Zarzuela
Fish stew

Colourful, dramatic *zarzuela* (the name itself means light operetta, or a play with music) is one of the world's great dishes: Spain's potent answer to France's bouillabaisse, Genoa's ciuppin and San Francisco's famous cioppino. *Zarzuela*, like *paella*, is made in a wide shallow pan, and seems to contain as many kinds of fish and shellfish as the spirit of the cook dictates.

4 baby squid

900g / 2lb firm white fish (choose from monkfish and halibut, or cod and hake), skin and bones removed

olive oil

2 Spanish onions, finely chopped

8 langoustines and/or ecrevisses (I sometimes substitute Dublin Bay prawns or large crevettes)

4 plum tomatoes, peeled, seeded and chopped

2–4 tablespoons tomato purée, dissolved in 300 ml / ½ pint dry white wine

300 ml / ½ pint well-flavoured fish stock

100 g / 4 oz *serrano* ham, in one piece

2 bay leaves

sea salt and freshly ground pepper

1–2 teaspoons *pimentón* (Spanish sweet paprika)

2–4 tablespoons Spanish brandy

Aromatic Thickener (Picada)

25 g / 1 oz toasted almonds, ground

2 tablespoons finely chopped flat-leaf parsley

1 packet saffron threads, warmed in 2 tablespoons wine vinegar

1 piece fried bread (such as ciabatta), crumbled

2 tablespoons olive oil

Just Before Serving

16–24 scrubbed mussels, beards removed

16–24 palourdes, scrubbed

4 tablespoons finely chopped flat-leaf parsley

Clean the squid, removing the blade and the dark external membrane (it is easy to rub off under cold running water) and then slice the flesh into strips or rings. Cut the white fish into pieces.

In a large frying pan, shallow casserole or *paella* pan, heat 6 tablespoons olive oil over a medium heat until it sizzles. Add the onions and sauté for 5 to 7 minutes, stirring occasionally, until the onions just begin to turn gold. Add the shellfish and squid and continue to cook for 2 to 3 minutes, stirring. Stir in the tomatoes and tomato purée (in white wine) and simmer gently for 5 minutes, stirring occasionally.

Add the fish stock, fish pieces, ham and bay leaves. Season with salt and pepper, to taste, and add the *pimentón*. Simmer over the lowest of heats for 10 minutes.

During this time, prepare the aromatic thickener (*picada*). Combine all the ingredients in a mortar and work to a paste with a pestle. Add a ladleful of the hot bouillon to the *picada*, mix well and then stir this into the cooking liquid. Add the mussels and palourdes and bring the *zarzuela* to the boil. As soon as the mussels and palourdes have opened, correct the seasoning, sprinkle with parsley and bring the *zarzuela* (right in the pan it was cooked in) to the table so that your guests can feast right from the steaming pot. Serve with lemon quarters and masses of crusty bread.

Serves 8

Chapter 7

SAUCES AND MARINADES

There are seven major preparations that give traditional Spanish cooking its unbeatable savour, including two of the most famous preparations in the world: *mayonesa*, and *allioli*, the Catalan version of Provence's famous *aïoli*. Only recently I first began to realize that if *pistou*, Provence's legendary vegetable soup, was almost certainly brought to Provence from what is now Italy by the early Ligurians, a culinary adaptation of their native *pesto* sauce, why couldn't we begin to admit that the equally famous Provençal sauce, *aïoli*, was probably first created in Spain (in Catalonia, in fact)? And, wonder of wonders – is there no end to this surmising once one gets going – could another famous Provençal dish, *brandade de morue* (a flavourful mix of pounded presoaked and poached salt cod, potato, olive oil and cream) have first been created in Spain (Catalonia again)? After all, there is no cod fished off the coasts of France and indeed, except for boutargue (the salted roe of grey mullet, a speciality of Martigues near Marseilles), there were no known fish salteries along the French coast. The salt cod was imported to southern France from the north.

Let us follow this peregrination: salt cod dishes have been famous for centuries in both Portugal and Spain, both much nearer by sea routes to Norway and Iceland than Provence is. The Spanish noble,

René de Beranger, was the count of Provence from the eleventh century. Catalonia ruled what we now call Roussillon/Languedoc in the 12th and 13th centuries. Nîmes (supposedly the birthplace of *brandade de morue*) is only a number of miles from the border of Roussillon.

Are you with me? Anyway, *aïoli*, *allioli* or *alioli* is used in far more imaginative ways in Catalan and Spanish cooking than it is in Provence. Until you have tasted a dollop of fragrant sauce stirred into a wood-fired *arroz a banda* or the black smokiness of a starchy *arroz negro con sepia*, you haven't met this fragrant golden mix at its best. They serve it, too, with *cordero al horno* (quarters of baby lamb cooked with half heads of green garlic, baked potatoes and herbs in wood-fired ovens). The fiery, pungent, mouth-tingling garlic and oil pomade provides the perfect punch for the meltingly tender lamb. It was high in the hills of the Sierra Nevada that I first tasted wild rabbit roasted in the same way and served with the garlic-flavoured exclamation mark, *alioli*. Whip it into mashed canned tuna and anchovies for a superlative *pincho* as they do in San Sebastián; blend it into a richly flavoured fish soup; or more simply, serve it with boiled or grilled artichokes, cooked snails or as a dip for grilled paprika-coated potatoes. The recipe for *alioli* is on page 93.

Sofrito and picada

These two much-used basic preparations serve more as basic aromatic flavouring blends and 'thickeners' than as sauces in their own right. They both go back to ancient times and – like Arab *chermoula* – give Spanish cooking its legendary layered flavours. Get to know both of these preparations as friends. Like *chermoula*, they will change the style, flavour, texture and aroma of your cooking.

Sofrito

Catalan cooks always start their recipes with the direction: First make a *sofregit*, just as in old French cookbooks, classic recipes began: Make a brunoise, a mirepoix, or a duxelles. *Sofregit*, or *sofrito*, as it is called in Spanish, is made from onion, garlic, parsley and tomatoes, and sometimes, for special recipes, or according to the whim of the cook, it has a few tablespoons of finely chopped *serrano* ham and/or red or green pepper for extra savour. This is the basic *sofrito*.

4–6 tablespoons olive oil
1 medium-sized Spanish onion, finely chopped
2 small cloves garlic, finely chopped
4 tablespoons water
2 tablespoons finely chopped flat-leaf parsley
4 plum tomatoes, peeled, seeded and diced
sea salt and freshly ground pepper
pinch of crushed dried chillies

In a large frying pan, over a low heat, heat 4 tablespoons of the olive oil. Add the onion and garlic and sauté, stirring constantly, until they begin to colour. Add the water and continue to simmer the vegetables, stirring, until the water evaporates and the vegetables are moist and pale gold in colour. Do not let them brown.

Then add the parsley and tomatoes, and continue to simmer gently, until the mixture has 'melted down' to a smooth sauce, adding a little more olive oil and/or water to moisten the sauce as it simmers. Season with salt, pepper and a pinch of crushed dried chillies to taste.

Use as the flavoursome base for Spanish rice dishes, soups, stews and sauces.

Picada

This is the prime seasoned thickening agent used to add special flavour to many Spanish soups, sauces, stews and casseroles. It is a must in Catalan cooking (sometimes called *picat* in the older cookbooks), a savant combination of garlic pounded with almonds and/or hazelnuts, smoothed down with a slice of country bread (try ciabatta) fried in olive oil. Where *sofrito* is a cooked preparation used to start off a dish, *picada* is an almost dry flavourer and thickener, added at the last minute. I must confess now that I like to use it, too, to 'season' meats, fish and poultry before grilling or roasting them, much as the Arabs use *chermoula*, the Jamaicans use *jerk* seasoning and the Thais use a blend of garlic, ginger, red chillies, lime juice and *nuoc mam*. But I am not sure that this is a truly 'classic' use for this classic preparation, which dates back to medieval times.

50 g / 2 oz shelled almonds or hazelnuts, chopped and
**   tossed in a dry nonstick pan until golden**
2 cloves garlic, peeled, chopped and tossed in a dry
**   nonstick pan until golden**
1 slice country bread (or 2 slices ciabatta) sautéed in
**   olive oil until golden and then crumbled**
½–¾ teaspoon each powdered cinnamon, *pimentón*
**   (Spanish sweet paprika) and saffron**
2–4 tablespoons olive oil
1–2 tablespoons wine vinegar
sea salt and freshly ground pepper, or cayenne

In a mortar, combine the nuts, garlic, crumbled fried bread and spices with the olive oil and wine vinegar and pound until smooth. Season with sea salt and pepper, or cayenne and use as directed by the recipe.

Salmorejo

Salmorejo – a simple Roman blend of pounded garlic, breadcrumbs and water (standard everyday fare for a Roman legionary stationed in the Hispanic province of Beatica) took on traits of nobility when Christopher Columbus first brought back the exciting peppers and tomatoes from the New World. This pink-tinted ambrosial sauce-cum-soup (first cousin, perhaps, of *gazpacho*) is used both as a frothy cold sauce (serve it chilled, as they do at Córdoba's famous El Churrasco restaurant, with paper-thin slices of hot crisp-fried aubergine – so thinly sliced and so quickly fried in hot oil that the thin golden vegetable shapes are card-crisp: see page 178) and as a delicious chilled summer soup.

For a chilled summer soup, whisk in more iced water or iced vegetable stock. Serve it in the traditional way with ham, chopped fresh herbs and chopped hard-boiled egg white. Or, in a more modern fashion, softened with crème fraîche and garnished with diced peeled and seeded ripe tomato, diced peeled and seeded cucumber, diced ham (*serrano*, of course), chopped herbs and sieved hard-boiled egg yolk. Delicious.

2 cloves garlic, sliced

1 teaspoon sea salt

700 g / 1½ lb large, very ripe tomatoes, peeled, seeded and diced

1 pinch each chopped fresh rosemary and thyme leaves

2 slices day-old country bread (or ciabatta), moistened with cold water and squeezed almost dry

6–8 tablespoons extra virgin olive oil

1–2 teaspoons wine vinegar

½–1 teaspoon *pimentón* (Spanish sweet paprika)

1 pinch crushed dried chillies

Garnish

2 hard-boiled egg whites, chopped

2 hard-boiled egg yolks, chopped

1–2 thin slices *serrano* ham, cut into tiny sticks

1 tablespoon chopped flat-leaf parsley

Pound the garlic to a smooth paste with the salt in a mortar. In a mixing bowl, combine the tomatoes with the garlic-and-salt, herbs and moistened bread. Then add the olive oil, little by little, beating with a balloon whisk until smooth. Add the wine vinegar, *pimentón* and crushed dried chillies, to taste. Chill in the refrigerator until ready to serve.

To serve, remove the *salmorejo* from the refrigerator and whisk it again. Taste and correct the texture and seasoning, adding a little more olive oil and vinegar, if desired. Transfer to a bowl and garnish with the egg white and yolk, ham strips and flat-leaf parsley. Serve cold with crisp, hot, pan-fried slices of aubergine as a starter or *tapa* as they do at El Churrasco, with hot mushrooms sizzled in olive oil with sliced garlic and hot red chillies, as a dip for a platter of raw vegetables, or extended with equal quantities of water and dry white wine to be a thick cold soup.

Serves 4 to 6

Marinadas
Marinades

Marinate the seafood of your choice for at least 4 hours (better, overnight in the refrigerator), turning the pieces over once or twice to ensure maximum flavour. When ready to cook, remove the seafood from the marinade, drain on a rack over a tray, pat dry with kitchen paper and then dredge in seasoned flour. Shallow-fry in sizzling oil for 2 to 3 minutes each side until crisp and hot. Serve at once with lemon wedges. Use small rouget (as shown here), for example, cleaned and scaled but with skins left on, and cut into sections. If fresh baby squid come your way, they are excellent given this treatment too.

Marinada de azafrán y pimiento
Cooked saffron and pepper marinade

1 packet saffron threads

6 tablespoons dry white wine

8–10 tablespoons extra virgin olive oil

2 medium onions, thinly sliced

½ each red and green pepper, stems, pith and seeds removed, cut into long thin sticks

4 tablespoons chopped flat-leaf parsley

2 tablespoons red wine vinegar

sea salt and freshly ground pepper

pinch of crushed dried chillies

Sprinkle the saffron threads into a small frying pan, place over a medium heat, add the wine and cook, stirring, until the wine has almost disappeared. Then add half the olive oil and the onions and cook, stirring constantly, until the onions are soft. With a slotted spoon, transfer the onions to a dish large enough to hold the seafood in one layer. Reserve.

Add the red and green pepper sticks to the pan and cook, stirring, for about 3 minutes or until soft. Transfer, along with the pan juices, to the onions. Pour the remaining olive oil into the hot pan, add the parsley and vinegar and season with salt, pepper and crushed dried chillies, to taste. Pour the oil and aromatics into the saffron-flavoured vegetables. Mix well. Allow to cool (it is important that the marinade is quite cold before it is poured over the raw seafood).

Put the marinade in a dish large enough to hold the seafood to be marinated in one layer, and use as above.

Marinada de jerez y aceite con ajo y berros
Sherry vinegar and oil marinade with garlic and watercress

8–10 tablespoons extra virgin olive oil

2–3 tablespoons Spanish sherry vinegar

2–3 fat cloves garlic, finely chopped

6 tablespoons chopped watercress leaves

sea salt and freshly ground pepper

pinch of crushed dried chillies

Combine the ingredients for the marinade, beat briefly with a whisk, season to taste, and use as above.

Marinada con lima y naranja
Citrus marinade with thin wedges of lime and orange

8–10 tablespoons extra virgin olive oil

2 tablespoons each orange and lime juice

1 tablespoon each freshly grated (unwaxed) lime and orange peel

8 thin wedges unwaxed lime with peel

4 thin wedges unwaxed orange with peel

pinch of saffron threads

sea salt and freshly ground pepper

pinch of crushed dried chillies

Combine the ingredients for the marinade, season to taste, and use as above.

Mayonesa
Mayonnaise

Mayonesa and alioli are two of the most famous Spanish sauces. Did they both originate in Spain, I wonder? *Larousse Gastronomique*, bible of French cooking, uncertain of the derivation of the word *mayonnaise* (one theory is that it comes from *magnonner*, 'to mix' in old Provençal), feels that it could have derived from the word *'mahonaise'* (named after Mahon, a port on the Balearic island of Minorca, where a famous French battle was fought). I certainly believe that Spain (or specifically Catalonia) was the originator of both of these brilliant sauces.

2 egg yolks

½ teaspoon fine salt

pinch of white pepper

150 ml / 5 fl oz olive oil, or peanut oil, or a half-way blend of both these oils

1–2 tablespoons of good Spanish wine vinegar

In a tall-sided mixing bowl, combine the egg yolks and the salt and white pepper. With a balloon whisk, or more simply with a fork, begin to beat in the oil, drop by drop, until a smooth emulsion forms. Beat in the vinegar, to taste. Use as desired.

Mayonesa catalana To a bowl of *mayonesa*, add 1–2 tablespoons tomato purée, ½–1 teaspoon *pimentón* and a pinch of cayenne

Mayonesa con pimiento In a mortar, pound 1 sliced garlic clove with ½ teaspoon salt until smooth. Add 1 canned red *pimiento* and pound again until the *pimiento* is amalgamated into the garlic. Then stir in 2 egg yolks, and whisk in olive oil, drop by drop (as if making a mayonnaise, which you are). Keep adding oil, little by little, and whisking continuously, until the sauce is smooth and thick. Add lemon juice, salt and freshly ground pepper, and a pinch of cayenne pepper, to taste.

Alioli
Oil and garlic sauce

Perhaps the origin of Provençal *aïoli* is Catalan *allioli*, a brilliant, highly flavoured cold sauce, thick, smooth and golden in colour, sometimes flecked with tiny white specks of pounded raw garlic. This pungent sauce, so loved by the Spanish (who call it *alioli*) that it is used in a variety of imaginative ways throughout Catalan and Spanish cuisine, pulls no punches where intense flavour is concerned. In Spain they use a whole head of fresh garlic to make their classic version of this famous sauce. If your taste for garlic is not quite so enthusiastic, use 2 to 3 cloves of garlic for each person. Or, if you make the classic version and find it too strong, beat in a mashed boiled potato and lemon juice, to taste, to 'soften' the potent garlic flavour.

1 whole small head of fresh garlic, skin removed

½ teaspoon fine salt

½ teaspoon freshly ground pepper

150 ml / 5 fl oz olive oil

2 egg yolks

1–2 tablespoons good Spanish wine vinegar

Combine the garlic cloves and the salt and pepper in a good-sized mortar and pound until smooth, adding a few drops of olive oil from time to time to moisten the mixture.

When the garlic has been well broken down to a smooth mass, add the egg yolks and pound again until they are completely amalgamated into the garlic mix. Then, as if you were making a highly flavoured mayonnaise, add the remaining olive oil, a few drops at a time at first, and then in more generous trickles as the sauce begins 'to take', continuing to pound until the emulsion is thick and smooth. Beat in the vinegar, to taste. Use as desired.

Alioli al azafrán To a bowl of *alioli*, add ½ packet saffron threads which you have soaked in 1–2 tablespoons boiling water. Or add the saffron threads to the egg yolks when you make the sauce from scratch.

Alioli a la naranja To a bowl of *alioli*, add the grated rind of 1 navel orange and 4 tablespoons orange juice which you have reduced over a high heat to half the quantity (2 tablespoons).

Romesco

Romesco in classic Catalan cooking terminology is not so much a sauce as the basic preparation in which other ingredients – especially fish and shellfish – are cooked. In modern times, however, this preparation, from the region of Tarragona, accompanies dishes of pan-seared or grilled seafood as a sauce, as well as providing the cooking medium for fish fricassees and dishes such as *zarzuela* and *suquet*.

 Romesco can be served cold (much as we serve *alioli* or *mayonesa*) or hot. In each case the basic preparation varies slightly.

450 g / 1 lb ripe tomatoes

1 large red pepper

4–5 garlic cloves, in their skins, smashed

extra virgin olive oil

1 slice country bread (or 2 slices ciabatta), fried in a little olive oil until golden brown, then drained and crumbled

25 g / 1 oz shelled almonds, grilled in a dry nonstick frying pan and then chopped (not ground)

2–4 tablespoons wine vinegar

salt and freshly ground pepper

pinch of crushed dried chillies

Preheat the grill. Brush the tomatoes, red pepper and garlic cloves generously with olive oil and grill them, turning occasionally, until their skins are charred and they are softened by the heat of the grill.

 Remove the vegetables from the grill and pack them into a plastic bag to steam until they are cool enough to handle. Then, under running water, rub off the skins of the tomatoes, the red pepper and the garlic.

 Once the skins, seeds and stems of the vegetables have been removed, combine the vegetables in a large mortar with the crumbled fried bread and the chopped grilled almonds.

 Pound the vegetables in the mortar, adding alternate spoonfuls of olive oil and wine vinegar, and a little water if desired, until the sauce is smooth and thick. Season with salt, pepper and crushed dried chillies, to taste.

Samfaina

Samfaina (*Chanfaina* in Spain, *Xanfaina* in Catalonia) is a sweet-tasting savoury sauce, rich in colour and savour, which combines onions, aubergines and, unusually, pumpkin to create its marmalade-like consistency. Red and green peppers and diced tomatoes add colour and Mediterranean flavour. I like to serve this comforting sauce with grilled meats and certain meat-like fish like tuna, turbot or salmon. It is excellent with grilled meats or roasted poultry.

1 medium-sized red pepper, stem, seeds and pith removed, cut into very thin long slices

1 medium-sized green pepper, stem, seeds and pith removed, cut into very thin long slices

2 medium-sized Spanish onions, peeled and cut into very thin slices

1 medium-sized aubergine, trimmed, peeled and cut into very thin long slices

225 g / 8 oz peeled and seeded pumpkin, cut into very thin slices

2 cloves garlic, peeled and very thinly sliced

extra-virgin olive oil

4–6 plum tomatoes, peeled, seeded and cut into small dice

sea salt and freshly ground pepper

In a medium-sized enamelled iron or stainless steel saucepan, combine all the vegetables except the tomatoes. Add 6 tablespoons of extra virgin olive oil and simmer the vegetables over a low heat, stirring constantly, until the onions start to melt. Then add the tomatoes and season with salt and pepper, to taste.

Lower the heat as low as you can. Cover the saucepan and simmer the vegetables very, very gently, stirring from time to time, until the sauce has completely melted down to become a thick, smooth coulis or fondue: about 20 minutes. If the sauce becomes a little too dry during cooking, add a tablespoon or two of olive oil or water from time to time, as you deem necessary.

Serves 4 to 6

Chapter 8
PAELLA
AND OTHER RICE DISHES

The most famous dish of all Spain, *paella,* was first created in Andalusia and made from the extra-quality short-grain rice grown in the Valencia region. *Paella* is not a single dish, but a diversity of rice dishes united by the pan in which they are cooked – the wide flat *paella* pan sometimes – and, I am told, mistakenly – called a *paellera.*

My first authentic *paella* experience took place on the banks of the Guadalifcar. It was an inland *paella, paella del país,* cooked over the embers of an outdoor fire overlooking the Albufera lagoon, a monster *paella* in the biggest *paella* pan I had ever seen. The wonderful rice, picked in the rice paddies that surrounded us on all sides, the flavour of the wood smoke from the open fire, the excitement and pleasure of the *al fresco* feast – all made this the best *paella* I had ever tasted. Monica Lewinsky and El Niño are beginning to fade from my mind

but I can still taste that meal: a poem of saffron-flavoured rice, sautéed rabbit and chicken, baby broad beans and wild greens, and the occasional land snail and slice of freshwater eel baked in the fragrant rice. A superb *paella,* equalled only, perhaps, by the *paella valenciana* created for me more recently by Don Rafael Vidal at his country restaurant Levante, at Benissanó on the outskirts of Valencia. Don Rafael's country *paella* is famous in Spain; so famous indeed, that King Juan Carlos invited the Don and his chefs to come to the palace in Madrid to prepare it.

Paella was first eaten from the pan in which it was cooked, set down in the centre of the table and enjoyed, Arab fashion, with each guest dipping with a tablespoon or fork into the nearest part of the pan to him. I still love to serve this great communal dish in this way; each guest is given a

spoon and crusty bread, and a bowl of *alioli* is passed from hand to hand throughout the meal.

In Spain, many households have different-sized *paella* pans – from small individual pans to several larger sizes for groups and parties. For the secret of a good *paella* is that the rice, to be evenly cooked, must never be more than 4 cm / 1½ inches high at any point in the pan. Most households here are not so lucky. At most they are the proud owners of one *paella* pan. So if your pan seems too small for the rice indicated in the recipes below, use a shallow heatproof casserole instead.

In Britain, and in the Basque country of France, we know *paella* as a colourful mix of golden saffron rice, chicken, mussels, prawns and *chorizo*, topped with an artichoke heart for gala occasions and garnished with a cascade of emerald green peas or asparagus tips. And you will find these composite dishes masquerading as *paella* in the tourist resorts of Spain as well. But for the original great *paella del país*, you will have to go inland as far as Benissanó to discover Don Rafael's original recipe.

Paella valenciana de Don Rafael
Don Rafael's Valencian paella

This wonderful country recipe (further described on pages 96-7) calls for a traditional garnish of a dozen snails and/or slices of eel, added to the pan at the same time as the rice, to give the dish an unctuosity and a special taste. If you want to be thoroughly traditional, add some snails and/or eel slices (seized for a few minutes in a little olive oil) at the same time as the rice.

1 small free-range corn-fed chicken

1 small wild rabbit, skinned

125 ml / 4 fl oz virgin olive oil

2 large tomatoes (or 4 plum tomatoes), peeled, seeded and chopped, or a 400 g / 14 oz can chopped peeled tomatoes

225 g / 8 oz green beans, trimmed and halved

100 g / 4 oz young chard (or red chard) leaves (optional)

900 ml /1½ pints water or stock

2 sprigs fresh rosemary

350 g / 12 oz *paella* rice

½ teaspoon *pimentón* (Spanish sweet paprika)

½ teaspoon saffron threads

225 g / 8 oz baby broad beans

sea salt and freshly ground pepper

1–2 pinches crushed dried chillies

Optional Extras

12–18 snails or 4–6 slices conger eel

alioli sauce (page 93)

To prepare the chicken and rabbit garnish, first cut the chicken and rabbit into serving pieces. Place a large *paella* pan (or shallow heatproof casserole) over a high heat, add the olive oil and heat the pan until the oil is sizzling hot. Then add the rabbit and chicken pieces, a few at a time, and sauté until golden brown in colour. With a slotted spoon, transfer the pieces to a serving dish and continue to sauté the remaining chicken and rabbit pieces in the same way.

When ready to cook the *paella*, return the chicken and rabbit pieces to the pan, add the tomatoes, green beans and chard leaves (if using), and simmer the meats and vegetables, stirring from time to time, for 20 minutes, or until the chicken and rabbit pieces are tender but not quite cooked through. Add the water or stock and the rosemary to the pan, and, if you have managed to get them, the snails and/or eel. Turn the heat to high. Once the water begins to boil; stir in the rice, *pimentón*, saffron and broad beans; season with salt, pepper and crushed dried chillies, to taste. After 10 minutes, reduce the heat and let the *paella* simmer gently for another 10 to 15 minutes, or until the grains of rice are soft but still quite firm inside. This is the mark of a good *paella*. Remove the pan from the heat and allow the *paella* to rest for 5 minutes before serving. It will continue to cook in its own heat. Serve with a bowl of *alioli*.

Serves 4 to 6

Paella 'catalana'
'Catalan' seafood paella

Spanish friends of mine who have the good fortune to manage their own vineyard not far from Barcelona like to serve what they call *paella catalana*: a savant mixture of *paella* rice cooked over an open fire of vine stumps and trimmings, with tiny monkfish tails, langoustines, mussels and palourdes (clams) in a well-flavoured fish stock, with, in addition, quarters of red pepper, green beans and a whole head of fresh garlic. This dish might just as well be called *paella de mariscos*, as it is in Valencia, or *arroz al caldero*, as it is in Murcia. But *paella catalana* it is at the *hacienda* of my friends, and that is the name I give it here.

2 small monkfish tails

8 langoustines, or scampi

16 mussels, cleaned and bearded

16 palourdes (clams), if available

1 Spanish onion, finely chopped

6 tablespoons dry white wine

6 tablespoons water

8 tablespoons olive oil

½–1 packet saffron threads

½ teaspoon *pimentón* (Spanish sweet paprika)

2 large or 3–4 medium-sized tomatoes

100 g / 4 oz fine green beans

1 head of fresh garlic

1–2 red peppers, quartered

450 g / 1 lb *paella* rice

1.2 litres / 2 pints hot well-flavoured fish stock

8–12 tablespoons garden peas

sea salt and freshly ground pepper

crushed dried chillies

Using a serrated knife, cut each monkfish tail into 4 to 6 slices across the bone. Remove the shells from the langoustines (or scampi) and, with a sharp knife, remove each black thread.

In a large frying pan, combine the mussels, palourdes and langoustines (or scampi) with the onion, white wine and water. Cover the pan and cook over a high heat, shaking the pan once or twice, for 3 to 5 minutes, or until the mussels have opened. Remove the pan from the heat. Remove the langoustine (or scampi) shells and discard them along with any mussels and palourdes that have not opened, and allow the shellfish and their aromatic pan juices to cool until ready to use.

Meanwhile, in a large *paella* pan, or large shallow heatproof casserole, sauté the monkfish tails in 4 tablespoons of the olive oil until golden. Add the shelled langoustine (or scampi) tails and cook for 3 more minutes. Allow to cool.

Pour off the liquor from the mussels and palourdes into a small bowl. Stir in the saffron threads and *pimentón* and reserve.

Roughly chop the tomatoes. Top and tail the green beans. Cut the garlic head in half across the cloves. Save the bottom half for another dish.

Add the remaining 4 tablespoons of olive oil to the *paella* pan (or shallow casserole). Add the half head of garlic cut-side down, and heat the hot oil and cook until the cut side is a pale gold colour. (Too much and it will be bitter). Remove the garlic and reserve. Add the tomatoes and red pepper to the pan and cook for 5 minutes, or until the vegetables soften. Add the rice and allow it to cook over a low heat, stirring, for 5 more minutes, or until the rice is well coated with the oils and flavourings.

Then add the green beans, the reserved saffron and *pimentón*-flavoured pan juices and the hot stock and bring to the boil, stirring. Place the sautéed half head of garlic (cut-side up) in the centre of the pan, tucking it well down into the rice. Lower the heat and simmer the rice and vegetables very gently, uncovered, for 20 minutes, or until the rice has absorbed almost all the liquids and is cooked through.

Five minutes before serving, add the peas to the shellfish and heat through. Arrange the shellfish and peas, with their pan juices, over the rice and serve immediately from the pan. Or, as in *la nueva cocina*, mix the rice and seafood gently together and serve on individual plates.

This is party food, and serves 8 with enough left over for a *tapa* the next day

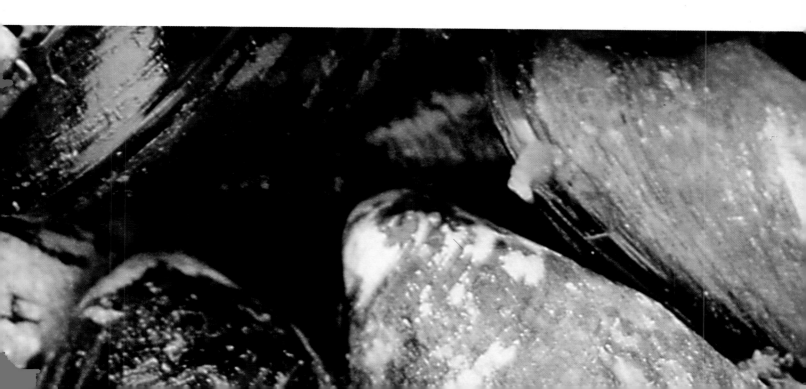

Arroz al horno con chorizo
Oven-baked saffron rice with chorizo

A dish to savour as a heart-warming country meal on its own, or as a sublime accompaniment for fish (John Dory or sea bass) baked in a salt crust, or even to serve alongside a platterful of grilled lamb chops with a chopped onion, garlic, parsley and basil marinade. The rice is simmered lovingly in the oven in an earthenware dish that comes happily to the table, cooked with a choice of meat garnishes: sliced *chorizo* and/or blood pudding, left-over chunks of cooked meats from a *cocido* ... or a combination of all three. Here I give you the (easily adaptable) *chorizo* and *morcilla* version.

2 medium-sized Spanish onions, finely chopped

2 cloves garlic, finely chopped

6 tablespoons olive oil

2 red peppers, seeds and pith removed, diced

225 g / 8 oz *paella* rice

16–20 slices *chorizo* sausage

4–8 slices *morcilla* (Spanish black pudding)

900 ml / 1½ pints well-flavoured vegetable stock

1 packet saffron threads

sea salt and crushed dried chillies

In a large frying pan sauté the onion and garlic in the olive oil over a medium heat until the vegetables begin to change colour. Remove the vegetables with a slotted spoon and reserve. Add the red peppers to the pan and continue to cook, stirring constantly, for 5 minutes. Remove the pepper with a slotted spoon and reserve. Then add the *paella* rice to the pan and continue to cook, stirring constantly, until the rice begins to change colour. With a slotted spoon, transfer the rice to the heatproof earthenware casserole (or your usual casserole) in which you are going to bake it. Set it aside.

Add a little water to the frying pan. Add the *chorizo* and *morcilla* slices and simmer them in the pan juices for a few minutes, then transfer to a plate and keep warm. Add the vegetable stock along with the saffron threads to the frying pan and heat to simmering point. When piping hot, pour the contents of the pan over the rice. Stir the aromatics (sautéed onion, garlic and red pepper) into the rice; season with sea salt and a pinch or two of crushed dried chillies, and arrange the *chorizo* and *morcilla* slices over the top. Bake in a preheated oven – 190°C/375°F/gas 5 for about 20 minutes or until the liquids have evaporated and the rice, *chorizo* and *morcilla* are crisp and well coloured.

Serves 4

Arroz a banda
Rice and fish served apart

In this traditional recipe of seafood and rice, the fish and squid are cooked in a well-flavoured stock which is then used to cook the saffron rice, resulting in an incredibly rich dish, which, when well made, is to me one of the most exciting dishes in all Spanish cooking. In the classic version of this famous dish, the fish used to make the stock is served separately, sometimes with the rice, or as a separate course with a well-flavoured *alioli* sauce made with extra virgin olive oil. This version is the more modern one, as served at the Picata restaurant, at the port in Valencia. Either way, this is a heavenly dish.

4 tablespoons olive oil

2 small squid, cleaned and thickly sliced

450 g / 1 lb Spanish onions, coarsely chopped

2 cloves garlic, thinly sliced

450 g / 1 lb potatoes, thickly sliced

sea salt

powdered cinnamon, *pimentón* (Spanish sweet paprika) and crushed dried chillies

4 sprigs flat-leaf parsley, leaves only, chopped

300 ml / ½ pint fish stock or water

½ packet saffron threads

450 g / 1 lb fresh fish (1 or 2 fillets, or steaks, such as rouget, tilapia, monkfish or sea bass)

The Rice

6 tablespoons olive oil

4 cloves garlic, sliced

½ packet saffron threads

350 g / 12 oz *paella* rice

900 ml / 1½ pints fish stock

In a heatproof casserole, heat the olive oil until it starts to sizzle. Add the squid rings and sizzle for 2–3 minutes. Remove the squid rings and reserve for later use. Add the onions, garlic and potatoes. Season with sea salt and a pinch or two each of cinnamon, *pimentón* and crushed dried chillies. Add the parsley and stir well to make sure the vegetables do not stick to the bottom of the casserole. Then add half the cold water and the saffron threads and simmer over a low heat until the potatoes and onions are almost tender: 10 to 15 minutes. Lay the fish pieces over the vegetables, add the remaining water, cover the casserole and continue cooking for 10 more minutes, or until the fish flakes easily with a fork. Remove the casserole from the heat and set it aside.

To prepare the rice, heat the oil in a medium-sized saucepan, stir in the garlic and when the garlic begins to sizzle stir in the rice. With a wooden spoon, over a medium heat, stir the rice and garlic for 2 to 3 minutes, or until the rice begins to change colour.

Add the saffron, the fish stock and the fish and vegetable juices from the first casserole and cook for about 20 minutes, or until the rice has absorbed almost all of the liquid.

Serve the saffron rice in the pan with an accompaniment of hot cooked vegetables, fish and squid. Or, as served in the Pepico restaurant in the port of Valencia, spoon the seafood (fish and squid rings), potatoes and aromatics into the hot saffron rice and serve immediately.

Serves 6 as a first course, 4 as a main course

Arroz negro
Rice with squid and squid ink

Spanish paella rice cooked with squid and black squid ink is a famous recipe all along the coasts of Spain. This version comes from Cadaqués. For extra colour, add tiny palourdes (clams), scallops or slices of lobster, as shown.

1.2 litres / 2 pints well-flavoured fish stock (made as
   below)

6 tablespoons olive oil

350 g /12 oz baby squid, cleaned

125 g / 5 oz ripe tomatoes, peeled, seeded and
   chopped

½ Spanish onion, finely chopped

2 fat cloves garlic, finely chopped

350 g / 12 oz *paella* rice

3 small packets squid ink

pimentón (Spanish sweet paprika)

sea salt

Prepare a well-flavoured fish stock by simmering 500 g / 1 lb fish heads, bones and trimmings (whatever your fishmonger will give you) in 2 litres / 3½ pints of water with a 15-cm / 6-inch piece of conger eel (for added flavour and sapidity) with 1 Spanish onion, 2 bay leaves and 2 stalks of celery. Cook over a medium heat until the broth has reduced to half its original quantity. Season with *pimentón*, sea salt and a tiny pinch of crushed dried chillies to taste, and reserve.

In a *paella* pan, or shallow heatproof casserole, heat the olive oil until sizzling then sauté the baby squid for about 3 minutes, or until they stiffen. (If the squid are a little on the large side, cut them into pieces before cooking them in the hot oil.) Add the tomatoes, onion and garlic and sauté, stirring constantly, until the onions are transparent. Then add the rice and stir until the rice is well mixed with the tomatoes, onion and garlic in the pan.

Bring the fish stock to the boil. Pour half the stock over the rice, squid and vegetable mixture and simmer gently over a low heat for 10 minutes. Mix the squid ink into the remaining stock. Pour this over the rice, squid and vegetables and cook for 10 minutes more, or until the rice is cooked through, adding a little more liquid, if necessary, in the form of hot water (hot stock if you still have some). True *arroz negro* should not be too moist. The rice should be puffed up and tender, but with a slight bite to it, and intensely flavoured. Cover the pan and let the dish rest for 5 minutes before serving.

Serves 6

Fideuá con gambas y calamares
Fideuá with tiger prawns and ribbons of baby squid

Spanish noodles called *fideos* provide the base for this delicious variation on *paella*. I first enjoyed it at a charming sea-front restaurant in the little town of Sitges, near Barcelona. The intense flavour of the dish is achieved by the use of tomato and *pimentón*-flavoured fish stock. Home-made, of course.

6 tablespoons olive oil, plus extra to sprinkle over the fideuá

1 medium onion, finely chopped

2 cloves garlic, finely chopped and pounded to a smooth paste with 2 tablespoons each finely chopped flat-leaf parsley and lemon juice

100 g / 4 oz tomatoes, peeled, seeded and chopped

1 red pepper, stem and pith removed, seeded and finely chopped

24 raw tiger prawns

6 baby squid, cleaned and cut into wide ribbons

1 litre / 1¾ pints well-flavoured fish stock

1 teaspoon *pimentón* (Spanish sweet paprika)

sea salt and freshly ground pepper

crushed dried chillies

350 g / 12 oz *fideo* noodles (available in Spanish food stores, or substitute spaghetti or thin egg noodles cut or broken into short even lengths)

Accompaniments

alioli sauce (page 93)

lemon wedges

Heat the olive oil in a large *paella* pan and gently sauté the onion until it just begins to change colour. Stir in the pounded garlic and parsley mixture together with the tomatoes and red pepper and cook, stirring, for 3 minutes. Then add the tiger prawns and squid ribbons and sauté for a few more minutes, until the prawns turn pink.

With a perforated spoon, remove the prawns and squid and reserve. Tip the aromatics and pan juices into a flameproof casserole, add the fish stock, season with the *pimentón* and salt, pepper and crushed dried chillies, to taste. Cover the casserole and simmer the stock and aromatics over a low heat for 20 to 30 minutes.

When ready to cook the *fideuá*, pour the broth into the *paella* pan and bring to the boil. Add the noodles, spreading them out evenly in the pan. Garnish with the prawns and squid ribbons. Sprinkle with a little olive oil and cook over a medium heat for 15 to 20 minutes, or until the noodles are cooked through. Serve immediately, accompanied by *alioli* and lemon wedges.

Serves 4 to 6

Fideuá con chorizo y mejillones
Fideuá with chorizo and mussels

Fideuá **is known by my rice-loving Spanish friends** as the poor man's *paella*. This is poor-mouthing this great fisherman's dish of noodles, fish or shellfish and intricate fish stock. The basis of the stock is similar to that of *arroz negro*. The short curved noodles absorb all the intense fish flavours of the stock, *pimentón* and saffron with wonderful results.

6 tablespoons olive oil, plus extra to sprinkle over

1 medium-sized onion, finely chopped

2 cloves garlic, finely chopped

100 g /4 oz tomatoes, peeled, seeded and chopped

1 red or green pepper, stem and pith removed, seeded and finely chopped

100 g / 4 oz *chorizo* sausage, thinly sliced

12 langoustines, or 24 raw tiger prawns

1 litre / 1¾ pints well-flavoured fish stock

1 teaspoon *pimentón* (Spanish sweet paprika)

sea salt and freshly ground pepper

pinch of crushed dried chillies

1 kg / 2 lb fresh mussels

100 ml / 3 fl oz dry white wine

225 g / 8 oz *fideo* noodles (available in Spanish food stores, or substitute spaghetti or thin egg noodles cut or broken into short even lengths)

Accompaniments

alioli sauce (page 93)

lemon wedges

Heat the olive oil in a 40-cm / 16-inch *paella* pan and gently sauté the onion and garlic until they just begin to change colour. Stir in the tomato and red or green pepper and cook, stirring, for 3 minutes more. Then add the *chorizo* and langoustines (or raw tiger prawns) and sauté for a few more minutes, until the langoustines (or prawns) turn pink.

Remove the *chorizo* and langoustines (or prawns) and reserve. Then tip the aromatics and pan juices left in the pan into a flameproof casserole. Add the fish stock, season with the *pimentón*, and salt, freshly ground pepper and crushed dried chillies, to taste. Cover the casserole and simmer the stock and aromatics over a low heat for 20 to 30 minutes.

In the meantime, clean and beard the mussels, discarding any that are cracked or open. Place the mussels in a clean saucepan with the white wine. Cover the pan and cook the mussels over a medium to high heat for 3 to 5 minutes, until they open. Remove the shells from half the mussels and reserve.

When ready to cook the *fideuá*, pour the stock into the *paella* pan and bring to the boil. Add the noodles, spreading them out evenly in the pan. Garnish with the mussels, *chorizo* and langoustines (or prawns). Strain the mussel liquor over the pan. Sprinkle with a little olive oil and cook over a medium heat for 15 to 20 minutes, or until the noodles are cooked through. Serve immediately, accompanied by *alioli* and lemon wedges.

Serves 6

Arroz con pasas y piñones
Rice with raisins and pine nuts

The Moors and the Jews left many culinary traces behind in Spanish cooking. Any dish with raisins, pine nuts, saffron, cinnamon or honey hints at this exotic heritage. Try this intriguing mix of oven-simmered rice, saffron, cinnamon, raisins and pine nuts as a vegetarian main course, or as an accompaniment to roast quail, pigeon, chicken, guinea fowl, duck … or pork. It will work wonders.

4–6 tablespoons olive oil

1 medium-sized onion, finely chopped

1 clove garlic, finely chopped

225 g / 8 oz long-grain rice

1–2 pinches each cinnamon, *pimentón* (Spanish sweet paprika) and saffron threads

1 vegetable stock cube

425 ml / 15 fl oz boiling water

sea salt and freshly ground pepper

pinch of crushed dried chillies (optional)

squeeze or two of lemon juice (optional)

Garnish

50 g / 2 oz seedless raisins, soaked in boiling water, and drained

25 g / 1 oz pine nuts, sautéed in olive oil until golden

Preheat the oven to 190°C/375°F/gas 5.

Heat the olive oil in a flameproof shallow casserole until it sizzles. Add the onion and garlic, and simmer, stirring from time to time, until the vegetables are soft: about 10 minutes.

Add the rice and spices and stir over a moderate heat for 2 to 3 minutes, or until the grains are thoroughly coated with the oil.

In the meantime, dissolve the stock cube in the boiling water in a saucepan and bring back to the boil. Pour the boiling stock into the casserole (take care, as the stock will sizzle up when it comes into contact with the hot oil). Season with salt and pepper, to taste, and quickly cover the casserole to prevent too much stock evaporating. Transfer the casserole to the preheated oven and bake for 15 to 20 minutes, or until the rice grains are tender but still quite firm in the centre and the liquid has been absorbed.

Note: It is always wise when cooking rice in the oven to check whether it needs just a little more moisture during the cooking time.

To serve, transfer the rice to a serving dish. Add the soaked raisins and sautéed pine nuts and toss with a fork to mix them in lightly. Taste, and add more salt and pepper, if necessary. I sometimes add a pinch of crushed dried chillies and a squeeze of lemon juice.

Serves 4 to 6

Arroz al azafrán
Virgin paella

Saffron rice made in the Spanish way – I like to call it virgin *paella* – makes a wonderful accompaniment for grilled, roasted or poached fish, or grilled lamb or veal. Serve it, too, as a flavourful go-with for an oven-roast leg of lamb (especially when served with a bowlful of pungent *alioli*), and use this fragrant golden rice to stuff roasted red peppers – the colour contrast is striking – or as a basis for a fabulous *paella* salad.

2–3 shallots, finely chopped

2–3 garlic cloves, thinly sliced

6–8 tablespoons olive oil

225–300 g / 8–11 oz *paella* rice

1 packet saffron threads

200 ml / 7 fl oz dry white wine

400–600 ml / 14–20 fl oz well-flavoured hot stock
   (vegetable or chicken)

sea salt and freshly ground pepper

pinch of crushed dried chillies

In a large frying pan or *paella* pan, sauté the shallots and garlic in the olive oil, stirring constantly, until the vegetables soften and begin to turn gold. Remove from the pan with a slotted spoon and reserve.

Add the *paella* rice to the pan and cook, stirring, for 1 to 3 minutes. Then stir in the saffron threads and dry white wine, return the onion and garlic to the pan, and cook, stirring from time to time, until the wine has reduced to a syrupy consistency. Now it is time to add 300 ml / 10 fl oz of stock, and to lower the heat to simmer the rice for 12 to 14 minutes.

Season the rice generously with salt and pepper, and with just a hint of crushed dried chillies, while it is simmering. Moisten with more stock from time to time. Don't stir the rice from this moment on. One of the nicest results of this low-heat, top-of-the-stove cooking technique is the lightly browned, nutty flavoured, slightly crunchy texture of the bottom of a true *paella*. Your virgin rice should be tender, with a slight bite. Taste from time to time, so that you know when it is ready.

Serves 4 to 6

Chapter 9

FISH
AND SHELLFISH

The Spanish do many things extremely well. But their almost reverential treatment of seafood is among their most impressive (for me) attributes. This is one reason I always want to return to Spain. Food from the sea abounds on all the coasts and fills the markets in most cities, even inland Madrid. Málaga boasts fresh fish fried with a delicacy and lightness that is hard to find anywhere else in Europe. Japan is the only country that can rival it – and I find it interesting to note that the fishing fleet of Spain is second in size only to that of the Japanese.

Andalusian fried fish, although apparently such a simple dish, can be exceptional, provided the freshness of the fish is not in question and the quality of the oil and the temperature at which it is cooked is just right. The secret here is to use a big pot and lots of top-quality oil so that the fish are cooked quickly, crisp on the outside and wonderfully moist within.

Spanish cooks love fish and shellfish. And thanks to an incredible organization of chilled express lorries that travel to the major cities fresh from the coastal ports, the fish of that night's catch are on the vast market slabs of the inland cities in the morning. It was my first early-morning visit to the fish counters of La Boqueria, Barcelona's great central market, that made me realize how exciting the fresh fish markets in the major Spanish cities could be. In the centre of the great round hall reserved for fish and shellfish, I saw many kinds of fish I never knew existed. In great quantities and in every size and shape and colour and form imaginable. It was a revelation.

Cooking methods on the southern coasts of Spain seem to divide at Málaga. From Málaga eastwards fish is usually cooked in water or stock flavoured with saffron, bay leaves and olive oil. On the other side is where cooking *a la plancha* (on a sheet of iron, or even an oiled, garlic-rubbed slate, over an open fire) comes into its own, as does the custom of frying fish in the lightest of batters. Perhaps the greatest of simple fish dishes in Spain is *merluza*, fresh-as-fresh hake, pan-simmered with baby clams and chopped fresh parsley, creating its own sauce that emulsifies by the simple expedient of the cook shaking the pan. See page 118, and you will be able to make it yourself.

Percebes
Goose barnacles

A rare seafood speciality from the rocky Galician coasts in northern Spain is a prehistoric shellfish, called *percebes* in Spain, *pousse pied* in France and goose barnacle in Britain and Ireland, where they were once gathered along the Cornish and Irish coasts. These rare sea barnacles look like miniature elephant legs with wrinkled grey outer skins and a sort of hard shell hoof at their extremities. They once grew in clusters on the rocky cliffs, but are now so rare that they have to be gathered by deep-sea divers.

Available now only in their local habitat, and in the best of the great markets of San Sebastián and Madrid, you will be lucky to find them. If you do, simply cook them for 4 to 5 minutes only in boiling salted water. Teach your guests to pull off the delicate grey skin-like casing (it easily slips away) to reveal a slim coral 'finger' of incredible sea savour. Fingerfood at its best. Serve with lemon wedges and fingerbowls.

Pescado frito
Deep-fried seafood

Spanish cooks are famous for their deep-fried seafood. Take a leaf from their culinary repertoire when deep-frying seafood: you will find that baby squid, squid rings, prawns, small rougets and squares of pre-soaked *bacalao* (dried salt cod) are at their best when marinated in an aromatic marinade (see facing page, and page 91) before they are coated with plain flour, seasoned flour or a light batter ahead of frying.

Plain Flour
100 g / 4 oz plain flour

Seasoned Flour

100 g / 4 oz plain flour

¼ teaspoon each salt, *pimentón* (Spanish sweet paprika) and powdered saffron
a pinch of cayenne

For seasoned flour, mix all the ingredients together well. Spread the plain or seasoned flour in a large flat soup plate or shallow bowl. Before frying, dip the seafood of your choice in the flour to cover all sides.

Rebozado a la romana
Light frying batter

100 g / 4 oz plain flour
1 teaspoon baking powder
¼ teaspoon fine salt

1 egg
200 ml / 7 fl oz milk (or milk and water)

Sieve the flour, baking powder and salt into a bowl. Break the egg into the centre and blend with a fork. Add the milk (or milk and water) and whisk until smooth. Allow the batter to stand for 20 to 30 minutes before using.

This recipe makes enough batter for 500–600 g / 1–1½ lb baby squid, prawns, baby rougets, presoaked *bacalao* (cut into squares or rectangles), or 6 baby squid (cut into rings: see the recipe on page 116).

Aromatic marinades for seafood

Before I coat the seafood, I often marinate it.

Marinade 1 (Arabo-Andaluz)

2 cloves garlic, finely chopped

1 bay leaf, crumbled

¼ teaspoon each powdered cumin and dried oregano

2 tablespoons red wine vinegar (or lemon juice)

4–6 tablespoons olive oil

sea salt and freshly ground pepper

pinch of crushed dried chillies

Marinade 2 (Sherry vinegar)

2 cloves garlic, finely chopped

2 tablespoons finely chopped flat-leaf parsley

2 tablespoons Spanish sherry vinegar (or lemon juice)

4–6 tablespoons olive oil

sea salt and freshly ground pepper

pinch of crushed dried chillies

Combine the ingredients in a bowl. Marinate the seafood of your choice for 1 to 2 hours, turning the pieces in the marinade once or twice during this period. Pat dry with kitchen paper before flouring.

Calamares fritos
Deep-fried squid rings

Deep-fried tender squid rings, whether plain-flour-coated, seasoned-flour-coated or batter-coated, are generally served in Spain as a piping hot *tapa* with a glass of chilled *manzanilla* or white wine, or a cold beer.

8 small squid (100–125 g / 4–5 oz each, to ensure tenderness), cut into even-sized rings about 6 mm / ¼ inch thick

marinade of your choice (if using), page 115

plain flour or seasoned flour (page 114)

batter (page 114)

oil for deep-frying

Garnish

lemon wedges

Most small squid come today already cleaned by your fishmonger or supermarket, ready to cut into rings. If this has not been done, stretch each squid out and remove the head section (discarding the eyes, ink sac and intestines) and pull out the transparent central bone from the interior. Then, under cold running water, wash off the purple-coloured outer covering, rubbing well, inside and out, then pat dry with kitchen paper. With a sharp knife, cut each squid into rings.

If you are going to marinate the squid rings, proceed as on page 115. Make sure you pat the squid dry with kitchen paper before coating with batter.

When ready to cook, dip the prepared squid into plain or seasoned flour and then into the batter, allowing any surplus to drip back into the bowl. Deep-fry a few rings at a time in hot oil until they are crisp and golden. Drain thoroughly on kitchen paper (or a folded clean tea towel) and serve 2 or 3 rings on small individual plates for *tapas*. Accompany each *tapa* with a lemon wedge.

Note: Large squid need to be bashed with a wooden rolling pin (or a meat tenderizer) to tenderize them before marinating.

Serves 8 as a *tapa*; 4 as a first course

Angulas
Baby eels

***Angulas* – the delicate baby eels of northern Spain**, fried for what seems like seconds only in garlic-flavoured olive oil with thin slices of golden-fried garlic and bits of thinly sliced hot red chilli pepper – are now found throughout Spain thanks to commercially chilled packs on sale in the major markets. This is a special dish. I love it.

8 tablespoons extra virgin olive oil

2–3 cloves garlic, thinly sliced lengthwise

450 g / 1 lb *angulas* (baby eels)

1 little hot red chilli pepper, seeded and thinly sliced

2 teaspoons finely chopped flat-leaf parsley (optional)

Place 4 individual flat flameproof earthenware dishes on the heat. Add 2 tablespoons olive oil to each dish and divide the garlic between the dishes. Sauté the garlic slices in the piping hot oil, stirring until the slices are golden on both sides. Add the *angulas*, sprinkle with the chilli, turn the *angulas* with the prongs of a dinner fork, and remove from the heat immediately. The delicate baby eels continue cooking in their little dishes as you bring them to the table. I sometimes sprinkle flat-leaf parsley on each dish before serving.

Serves 4

Merluza con almejas en salsa verde
Hake with clams in green sauce

This is one of the most famous fish dishes of Spain. Hake – top-favourite Spanish fish – is pan-seared, skin-side down, in olive oil in a large nonstick frying pan wide enough to contain six pieces of hake comfortably in one layer. If necessary, use 2 nonstick pans.

The recipe itself is so straightforward that it hardly seems possible to make it so quickly, so easily and with such simple ingredients. The secret is, of course, that it can only be made successfully with fish fresh from the sea (hake traditionally, but truly fresh cod or turbot would also be delicious). The constant shaking of the pan is important too: it allows the generous quantity of olive oil to emulsify with the juices and stock during cooking. So next time you are by the sea in Spain, or in Cornwall, Devon, or on the Norfolk coast, try your hand. You will love it.

2 cloves garlic, peeled but kept whole
100 ml / 3 fl oz olive oil
300 g / 10 oz palourdes (clams)
2–3 tablespoons finely chopped flat-leaf parsley

6 fillets, steaks or top ends of fillet of hake,
200 g / 7 oz each, dusted with seasoned flour
½ glass water, dry white wine or well-flavoured fish
stock

In a large nonstick frying pan (or 2 pans, see above), sauté the whole garlic cloves in the olive oil until they just begin to turn colour. Add the clams and 1 tablespoon of the parsley, cover the pan and shake it over a high heat for 3 minutes, or until the clams have opened (discard any that don't open). Then add the lightly floured pieces of hake, skin-side down. Cover the pan and continue to cook, shaking the pan from time to time, for 3 more minutes to steam the fish.

With a fish slice, or wide spatula, turn the fish over. Moisten the pan juices with the water, wine or fish stock, and continue to cook, constantly shaking the pan gently to amalgamate the sauce, for 3 more minutes.

Just before serving, make certain that the sauce is quite liquid (adding a little more water or stock if necessary). Then, with a fish slice or spatula, transfer the fish and clams to heated plates (gently turning the fish skin-side down as you do so). Add the remaining parsley to the sauce in the pan, bring it to the bubble and then spoon over the clams and fish.

Serves 6

Vieiras a la plancha con pimentón y jerez
Grilled scallops with paprika and sherry

Scallops in the half shell – anointed with olive oil and butter – become a thing apart when seasoned with *pimentón* and dry sherry. Try this idea, too, with live lobsters, halved and grilled.

8–12 scallops in the shell

4–6 tablespoons extra virgin olive oil

4 tablespoons butter

6 tablespoons finely chopped onion

6 tablespoons dry sherry

pimentón (Spanish sweet paprika)

salt and cayenne pepper

Preheat the grill to hot.

Scrub the closed scallop shells thoroughly. Then, with a sharp knife, prise them open. Wash any sand or impurities away and cut the muscle free from each shell. Wash the scallops again under cold running water and return to their bottom shells.

Combine the olive oil, butter, onion and dry sherry in a small saucepan and cook over a low heat until the liquids begin to bubble. Season with *pimentón*, salt and cayenne, to taste. Divide the mixture between the scallops and grill until golden.

Serves 4 to 6

Vieiras con cava
Scallops with a sauce of Spanish champagne

Pan-seared scallops in champagne seems more French somehow than Spanish. But I first encountered this elegant dish that combines *cava* and saffron with a hint of tomato in one of Madrid's top restaurants. This is my version.

2 tablespoons butter

16–20 small scallops

2 teaspoons tomato purée

300 ml / ½ pint dry *cava* (Spanish champagne)

pinch of saffron threads

150 ml / 5 fl oz single cream or crème fraîche

sea salt and freshly ground pepper

pinch of crushed dried chillies

2 tablespoons finely chopped flat-leaf parsley

Melt the butter in a large thick-bottomed frying pan until it just starts to sizzle. Add the scallops in one layer and quickly sauté them over a medium to high heat until they are lightly coloured on each side: about 2 minutes altogether. Then, with a spatula, transfer them to a heated serving plate.

Dissolve the tomato purée in the *cava* and add it to the pan with the saffron threads. Cook over a high heat, stirring constantly, until it is reduced to half the original quantity. Add the cream and cook again until it is reduced to a sauce consistency: about 5 minutes.

Taste the sauce and season with salt, pepper and crushed dried chillies to taste. Return the scallops to the sauce and heat through. Divide the scallops and sauce between 4 heated plates, sprinkle each with a little parsley and serve immediately.

Serves 4

Sardinas al horno
Oven-baked sardines

There are many ways of preparing fresh sardines in Spain; grilling over vine roots in the open air, over charcoal, or, more rustically (and to my mind more glamorously), *a la plancha* (seared on a sheet of iron over an open fire). I like them, too, pan-fried and served with wedges of lemon and a cascade of finely chopped fresh herbs, or *en escabeche* (pan-fried and then marinated in a zesty *escabeche* sauce of olive oil, vinegar and aromatics). But perhaps my favourite way is to serve them oven-baked with finely chopped garlic, breadcrumbs and parsley and a splash of extra virgin Spanish olive oil.

12–16 medium-sized fresh sardines, gutted and scaled
extra virgin olive oil
3–4 cloves garlic, finely chopped
1 large bunch flat-leaf parsley, finely chopped
50 g / 2 oz fresh breadcrumbs
salt and freshly ground pepper
crushed dried chillies

Garnish
sprigs of fresh watercress
lemon wedges

Preheat the oven to 180°C/350°F/gas 4.

Wash the sardines under running water and pat dry with kitchen paper. Remove the backbones and brush with olive oil. Brush a large baking dish, roasting tin or 2 smaller baking dishes with olive oil to keep the sardines from sticking.

In a large flat dish, combine the garlic, parsley and breadcrumbs. Season generously with salt, pepper and a pinch or two of crushed dried chillies. Mix well so that the breadcrumbs and aromatics are evenly distributed.

Dip each fish in the savoury breadcrumb mixture and arrange them (in a single layer) in the oiled dish, dishes or roasting tin. Bake in the preheated oven for about 15 minutes. Serve immediately with a splash of extra virgin olive oil, sprigs of fresh watercress and wedges of lemon.

Serves 4

Lubina hervida con salsa de alcaparras y azafrán
Poached sea bass with saffron caper sauce

Fillets of sea bass, poached for minutes only in a simple *court-bouillon*, come into their own when dressed with a bright saffron sauce sparked with tiny capers.

4 x 225 g / 8 oz sea bass fillets

2 bay leaves

sea salt and black peppercorns

fish stock, to cover

boiled new potatoes or rice, to serve

Saffron Caper Sauce

2 tablespoons small capers

flat-leaf parsley leaves (2–3 sprigs)

125 ml / 4 fl oz virgin olive oil

150 ml / 5 fl oz double cream

1 generous pinch saffron threads

sea salt and freshly ground pepper

crushed dried chillies

Put the bass fillets in a shallow saucepan with the bay leaves, a pinch of sea salt and 12 peppercorns and add enough cold fish stock to cover the fish by 2.5 cm / 1 inch. Bring to a simmer and cook for 5 minutes. Set aside and keep warm.

To prepare the saffron caper sauce, drain the capers and rinse under running water. Drain and reserve in a small bowl. Pour a little boiling water over the parsley leaves. Drain and combine with the capers.

Combine the olive oil and double cream in a saucepan and whisk until well blended. Add the saffron threads and season with sea salt, pepper and crushed dried chillies, to taste. Cook over a high heat until reduced to a sauce consistency. Then add the drained capers and parsley leaves, and keep the sauce warm over a low heat.

Drain the bass fillets and place one on each of 4 heated plates. Spoon the fillets with the sauce, and serve with boiled new potatoes or rice.

Serves 4

Salmonete con naranja y lima
Red mullet with orange and lime

In the country behind the sea coasts of southern Spain, many houses boast their own little orchards of orange, lemon, lime and avocado trees. Even the smallest patios in the southern cities of Córdoba, Sevilla and Granada feature a citrus tree or two so it is only natural that many recipes of the region use these fruits imaginatively.

4 medium-sized (or 8 small) red mullet, scaled and cleaned
1 orange
1 lime
6 sprigs fresh rosemary
6 tablespoons fish or vegetable stock
6 tablespoons dry white wine
2 tablespoons chopped flat-leaf parsley

Citrus Marinade
juice and grated zest of 1 lime
juice of 1 small orange
6 tablespoons extra virgin olive oil
sea salt and freshly ground pepper
pinch each of saffron threads and crushed dried chillies

To make the marinade, strain the juice of 1 lime and 1 orange into a small bowl. Add the lime zest and olive oil and season generously with salt, pepper, saffron and crushed dried chillies.

Arrange the red mullet in a rectangular flameproof baking dish. Pour over the marinade juices and allow the fish to marinate in this mixture for at least 2 hours.

When ready to cook, preheat the oven to 180°C/350°F/gas 4.

In the meantime, scrub the unpeeled orange and lime with a vegetable brush. Cut each fruit into quarters and garnish the fish with them. Arrange the rosemary sprigs around the dish. Add the stock and dry white wine. Heat the baking dish over a medium heat until the liquids begin to bubble. Transfer the dish to the preheated oven to cook for 20 to 25 minutes, or until the fish flakes at the touch of a fork.

Scatter chopped parsley over the dish and serve immediately.

Serves 4

Ragu de mariscos y pescados
Spanish fish casserole

A seafood extravaganza, the succulent fish and shellfish – red snapper, John Dory, mussels and langoustines – or the fish and shellfish of your choice – are gently simmered with leeks, garlic, tomatoes and white wine, the broth lightly tinted with saffron.

6 tablespoons olive oil

6 leeks, white parts only, sliced

sea salt and freshly ground pepper

4–6 cloves garlic, finely chopped

8 large ripe tomatoes, peeled, seeded and diced

½ packet saffron threads

1 bouquet garni (2 sprigs fennel, 2 sprigs parsley,
   1 bay leaf)

1 teaspoon cornflour

1 glass white wine

1 red snapper (or talapia), cut into thick slices

1 small John Dory (or sea bass), cut into thick slices

450 g / 1 lb mussels, cleaned and bearded

6 langoustines

freshly squeezed lemon juice

crushed dried chillies

garlic croûtons, sprinkled with finely chopped flat-leaf
   parsley to serve

In a medium-sized *paella* pan or a large shallow casserole, heat the olive oil. Add the leeks, season with sea salt and pepper, and sprinkle with the chopped garlic and tomato. Add the saffron and the bouquet garni and simmer for 20 minutes.

Add the fish slices in one layer and moisten with water to cover. Dissolve the cornflour in the white wine and stir into the pan juices. Cover the pan and cook over a high heat for 5 minutes.

Add the mussels and the langoustines and allow to cook for 10 minutes more. Correct the seasoning, adding a little salt, pepper and lemon juice, to taste. Add a pinch of crushed dried chillies and serve immediately, with garlic croûtons sprinkled with flat-leaf parsley.

Serves 4

Rape andaluz con miel y azafrán
Andalusian monkfish with honey and saffron

Monkfish, sea bass, or small monkfish tails – cooked in the ancient Arabian manner of Córdoba, Granada and Sevilla – combine with finely chopped onion and coriander, raisins, honey and Arabian spices to create a wonderful dish evocative of Moorish Spain. This same combination of Arab flavours combined with fish can be found in the Maghreb today.

olive oil

¼ teaspoon each crushed dried chillies and cracked black pepper

½ teaspoon powdered cinnamon

¼–½ teaspoon saffron threads

4 small monkfish tails or 2 sea bass (about 175 g / 6 oz each)

350 g / 12 oz Spanish onion, diced

2 tablespoons chopped flat-leaf coriander

4 tablespoons each liquid honey and vinegar

175 g / 6 oz seedless raisins, plumped up in hot water to cover

sea salt

To prepare the marinade, combine 4 tablespoons each olive oil and water in a bowl. Add the crushed dried chillies, cracked pepper, cinnamon and saffron.

Place the fish in a rectangular baking dish or roasting pan, pour over the marinade juices and let the fish rest in this bath for 30 minutes, turning the fish once during this time.

When ready to cook, add 4 tablespoons of olive oil to a large frying pan or flameproof shallow casserole. When the oil is hot, add the fish and sauté on each side until golden. Remove the fish from the pan and reserve.

Add the onion to the pan, with a little more olive oil if necessary, and sauté, stirring constantly, until it just begins to turn gold. On no account allow the onion to burn, or it will taste bitter. Add the coriander and the juices from the marinade, and stir in the honey, vinegar and drained raisins. Turn the heat down to low and simmer the sauce for 15 minutes. Season with salt, to taste.

Return the fish to the pan, arranging the pieces in one layer, and making sure the sauce covers them, at least partly. Cover the pan and continue cooking over a very low heat for 5 to 8 minutes, or until the fish is warmed through. Serve immediately.

Serves 6

Lubina con brandada de bacalao
Sea bass with brandada

One lazy summer afternoon, while lunching on the shaded terrace of the Maricel seafront restaurant in Sitges, I took time out (while eating my main course) to photograph the pan-seared sea bass, set on a scrumptious bed of dynamite *brandada*, softened, I think, with a touch of whipped potato. At least that's the way I have been serving it ever since, with the pan juices spooned over the crisp-skinned bass. It's an incredible concept. Try it.

4 tablespoons olive oil or butter

4 x 200-g / 7-oz sea bass fillets

sea salt and freshly ground pepper

flour

4–6 tablespoons white wine

2 tablespoons chopped chives or spring onion tops

Brandada

2–4 cloves green garlic, chopped

olive oil

225 g / 8 oz presoaked salt cod (see page 54), poached in simmering water until tender (about 5 minutes)

1 small boiled potato, whipped to a soft purée with 2 to 3 tablespoons each olive oil and double cream, or the water in which the potato was cooked

First prepare the *brandada*. Pound the chopped garlic with 2 tablespoons of olive oil in a mortar until you have a smooth paste. Add the freshly poached cod and pound again, adding more olive oil, little by little, as you pound (as you would for a *mayonesa*). When the *brandada* is smooth, whisk in the whipped potato to soften the flavour. Keep hot in the top of a double saucepan (over simmering water) until you are ready to serve.

To prepare the sea bass, heat the oil (or butter) in a large frying pan over a medium heat until it just begins to sizzle. Season the fillets with salt and pepper and dredge with flour. Shake off excess flour and then add the fillets, skin-side down, to the frying pan. Cook for 5 to 6 minutes or until the skin is crisp and brown. With a palette knife, carefully turn the fillets over and continue to cook for another 4 to 5 minutes, until tender.

To serve, spoon a little hot *brandada* on each of 4 heated dinner plates. Place a fillet of sea bass on the *brandada*, strain over the pan juices, to which you have added the white wine, and top with a sprinkling of snipped chives or spring onion tops. Serve at once.

Serves 4

Besugo a la sal
Sea bream baked in sea salt

From Cádiz, on its promontory, along the glittering sandy coast past Playa de la Barrosa, to far-off Tarifa, the beaches all along the sun-washed coast of the Costa de la Luz are brilliant … an unbroken sandy bay of bright yellow sands. I based myself in the stunning hill town of Vejer de la Frontera, a white-washed town that still guards its Muslim heritage with steeply tortuous streets winding up the rock to the Saracen castle. It was here that I first tasted a glorious sea bream baked in a thick salt crust, accompanied by steamed new potatoes, lemon quarters and a great bowl of *alioli*. A feast.

1 sea bream, about 1.4 kg / 3 lb, gutted, cleaned
   and scaled
1.4 kg / 3 lb coarse sea (or kosher) salt
crushed peppercorns
extra virgin olive oil

To Serve
a bowl of freshly made *alioli*
lemon quarters
steamed new potatoes

It couldn't be simpler. All you need is a super-fresh fish large enough to serve 4 (magnificently) to 6 people, a mountain of coarse salt and a baking dish large enough to hold the fish comfortably.

Preheat the oven to 200°C/400°F/gas 6. Cover the bottom of a large roasting tin or flameproof ceramic dish with a 2.5-cm / 1-inch layer of coarse salt. Lay the whole fish on this aromatic bed and cover completely with the rest of the salt. Place the dish (on a diffuser if necessary, if the dish is ceramic) over a medium heat for 5 minutes before transferring it to the preheated oven, where it will bake until the salt is hard-crusted and golden brown (about 40 minutes).

When ready to serve, bring the still salt-encrusted fish to the table (on a large chopping board to protect the tabletop) and with a wooden steak tenderizer, or a hammer, crack open the crust, scraping the top away completely to leave the moist white fish accessible to your guests. All it needs is a splash of olive oil and a grind of black pepper for each serving. Accompany with *alioli*, lemon quarters and new potatoes.

Serves 4 to 6

Chapter 10

COCIDO
AND OTHER MEATS

Cocido, the most glamorous of Spanish pot dinners, and its even more remarkable ancestor *olla podrida*, go back in time to the sixteenth- and seventeenth-century cookery books *Arte de Cocina* by Martínez Montino, master of Philip II's kitchens, and *Libro de Arte de Cocina* by Diego Granado, published in 1599. *Olla podrida* was a feast made of up to seven separate courses and is said to have included salted breast of pork, salted leg of lamb, unsalted beef and wild boar, as well as chickens, game birds and pigeons, and, if that were not enough, every sort of fresh and dried vegetable you can imagine cooked in the delicious bouillons of the meats and game.

No wonder this great Spanish dish caught the attention of cooks throughout Europe – along with that other great Spanish culinary invention, the deep-coloured, deep-flavoured, classic brown sauce still known today as 'espagnole' in professional kitchen terminology. This greatly reduced sauce made from browned bones and vegetables and rich beef stock, coloured by seared onions and enriched by roasted tomatoes, and its resulting sophisticated meat 'glazes', which originated in classic Spanish court kitchens, forms the culinary backbone of most great cooking throughout the world even to this day. And *cocido* – or at least the many courses of this

great dish, some old cookery books mention as many as seven – is one of the treasures of Spanish gastronomy. Even the simpler versions of *cocido* that we find today in Spain's top restaurants, usually a combination of beef, fresh and salt pork, ham, preserved pork fat, *chorizo*, *morcilla*, chickpeas, cabbages, spinach and green beans, can be the worthy centrepiece – like Provençal bouillabaisse, Moroccan couscous, New England boiled dinner, Austrian tafelspitz and Mexican chile con carne – of a weekend feast (a bumper Sunday lunch would be great) that you can make for your favourite friends.

This is a dish that cries out for 6 to 8 hungry eaters. And if you feel that it is a lot of trouble, relax. You will need nothing else. No first courses, no complicated desserts, no accompanying vegetables – this meal is complete in itself. Another plus: except for the fresh vegetables, your fabulous three-course *cocido* can be prepared on the day before the party, leaving you calm, cool and collected as your guests arrive. You will need nothing more than a few bottles of excellent Rioja, some good country bread to mop up the sensational juices, perhaps a mixed leaf salad to follow, and a glittering fruit sorbet to finish. Then sit back and listen to the groans of pleasure and fulfilment from your happy guests.

Top-quality meats – beef, veal and lamb – grilled over the embers is a speciality of Juan Mari Arzak's restaurant in San Sebastián. One of the top restaurants of Spain, Arzak is well worth a visit.

Cocido madrileño
Classic cocido Madrid-style

Enjoying a *cocido* in one of the venerable restaurants in Madrid is quite an event. The meal starts out with a steaming bowl of fragrant broth poured out for you from large ceramic jugs. Then come the steaming platters of meats and poultry, spicy *chorizo* and heady black puddings, the salty tips of pigs' ears and melting pork belly (yes, you heard me: utterly delicious), and then platters of fresh vegetables, quarters of cabbage, carrots, potatoes, green beans and chickpeas. More than you ever thought you could eat. And then some. You'll need a speciality Spanish food store or a Caribbean market for some of the ingredients, but you could also try your local friendly butcher, giving him a few days' notice.

Cocido is served at lunchtime only in Spain. Far too rustic and far too filling for an evening meal. Now I know why the long afternoon siesta is still such a regular pastime with the Spanish. Taste *cocido* and die seems to be the motto. Of pleasure, of course!

225 g / 8 oz dried chickpeas

½ salted pig's ear

700 g / 1½ lb lean brisket of beef, in 1 piece

1 roasting chicken

225 g / 8 oz *serrano* ham in 1 piece (or
 175 g / 6 oz gammon)

175 g / 6 oz unsalted pork fat (optional)

10 black peppercorns

2 small *chorizo* sausages

175 g / 6 oz *morcilla* (Spanish blood sausage)

1 green cabbage, outer leaves removed, cut into
 8 wedges

6–8 medium-sized potatoes, peeled

6–8 medium-sized carrots, peeled

2 bay leaves

1 head of garlic, cut in half horizontally

450 g / 1 lb green beans, topped and tailed

100 g / 4 oz macaroni

extra virgin olive oil

6–8 small 'bouquets' of fresh herbs, to garnish

On the day before you are going to serve the *cocido*, soak the chickpeas and the salted pig's ear in cold water for 12 hours, changing the water 2 or 3 times during the soaking period. Then leave overnight in fresh cold water. The following day, drain in a colander, rinse under cold running water, drain again and reserve.

To prepare the *cocido*, combine, in a large casserole or stockpot, the pig's ear, beef, chicken, *serrano* ham, pork fat (if using) and peppercorns. Add water to cover by at least 7.5 cm / 3 inches and bring gently to the boil. Skim the froth and impurities from the surface, reduce the heat, loosely cover the casserole (to let a little of the steam escape) and simmer the meats gently for 1 hour. Then add the drained chickpeas to the bouillon and continue to simmer for another hour.

At the same time (during the second hour of cooking), combine the *chorizo* and *morcilla* in a medium-sized saucepan, add the cabbage wedges and enough bouillon from the *cocido* to just cover the cabbage, and bring to the boil. Lower the heat to a simmer, cover the pan and gently cook the sausages and cabbage for 30 minutes.

After a total of 2 hours' cooking time for the *cocido*, remove the meats from the bouillon and reserve them on a platter while you separate the chickpeas from the bouillon in the following manner: place a colander over a bowl large enough to contain the bouillon, and then pour the bouillon and chickpeas into the colander, allowing the bouillon to drain into the bowl, leaving you with the chickpeas in the colander.

Skim the fats from the *cocido* bouillon and return to the cleaned casserole (or stockpot). Add the potatoes and carrots to the pan along with the bay leaves and garlic and cook for another 10 minutes. Then add the green beans, place the colander containing the chickpeas over the bouillon, cover and continue to cook the vegetables for another 20 minutes.

At the same time, cook the macaroni for 15 minutes in boiling salted water. Drain and reserve.

Drain the vegetables, reserving the bouillon. Transfer the vegetables, including the chickpeas, to a heated serving platter and sprinkle with a few tablespoons each of the hot bouillon and olive oil. Keep warm.

Cut the meats, chicken and pork products into 6 to 8 serving pieces each. Pour one third of the bouillon into a clean casserole. Add the prepared meats and warm through, then arrange on another heated serving platter.

Heat the remaining bouillon in a saucepan, add the cooked macaroni and bring to the boil.

Serve the cocido in three services: first the bouillon, in which you warmed the macaroni; second the chickpeas and other vegetables; and finally the meats, garnished with bouquets of herbs. Or you can serve all three courses at the same time.

Serves 8

Cocido sencillo
A simpler cocido

Here is a simpler version of the classic *cocido* – but still quite delicious – if you find it difficult to procure the speciality pork products. This recipe substitutes raw gammon and salt pork for the pig's ear and salted pork fat. It uses *serrano* ham and *chorizo* sausages from the supermarket (for the superior imported *serrano* ham and Spanish *chorizo*) and British black pudding for the imported *morcilla* sausage of the classic recipe. To give added flavour to this simplified recipe, I like to add half a boiling fowl, or a small boiled free-range chicken.

450 g / 1 lb lean brisket of beef, in 1 piece

½ boiling fowl, cut into 4 pieces (or 1 small free-range chicken)

4 slices supermarket *serrano* ham

225 g / 8 oz raw gammon, soaked overnight

100 g / 4 oz salt pork, soaked overnight

225 g / 8 oz chickpeas, soaked overnight

2 medium supermarket *chorizo* sausages, halved

100 g / 4 oz black pudding

½ medium-sized green cabbage, cut into 4 pieces

4 medium-sized potatoes

4 medium-sized carrots

1 bay leaf

4 cloves garlic, unpeeled, flattened

extra virgin olive oil

little bouquets of herbs, as in the preceding recipe

In a large flameproof casserole, or stockpot, combine the beef, fowl, ham, gammon and salt pork; add water to cover the meats by at least 7.5 cm / 3 inches and bring gently to the boil. Skim the froth and impurities from the top of the liquids in the casserole; reduce the heat and simmer gently for 1 hour.

Cook the chickpeas in the *cocido*, as in the preceding recipe.

Cook the *chorizo* sausages, black pudding and cabbage, as in the preceding recipe, for 30 minutes.

Remove the chickpeas from the casserole as in the preceding recipe and reserve. Add the potatoes and carrots, the bay leaf and garlic cloves to the bouillon and cook for 30 minutes.

Serve the *cocido* as in the classic recipe.

Serves 4

Cordero a la plancha con habas
Pan-grilled lamb with baby broad beans

Tender lamb cutlets, brushed with extra virgin olive oil and sprinkled with chopped fresh thyme and rosemary, make for quick and easy cooking when served with baby broad beans.

The young cutlets are quickly grilled in an oiled ridged pan or over the open fire. The baby broad beans need hardly any cooking at all; more mature beans need more simmering. Rub the skin off with your fingers to reveal the bright green beans in all their tender glory.

The Lamb

12 trimmed lamb cutlets (or 6 trimmed lamb chops)

4 tablespoons extra virgin olive oil

3 sprigs each fresh thyme and rosemary, leaves only
   (reserve the stems to flavour the broad beans)

sea salt and freshly ground pepper

crushed dried chillies

The Broad Beans

1 teaspoon sea salt

2 tablespoons olive oil

reserved fresh thyme and rosemary stems

1 kg / 2 lb fresh baby broad beans

1 roasted red pepper, seeded and diced
   (or 1 canned *pimiento*, seeded and diced)

2 tablespoons chopped chives or flat-leaf parsley

2 tablespoons butter

1 squeeze fresh lemon juice

To prepare the lamb, brush the cutlets (or chops) with the olive oil and sprinkle with the thyme and rosemary leaves. Season with sea salt, pepper and crushed dried chillies, to taste. Leave the lamb to marinate in this seasoned oil for at least 2 hours to absorb its flavours.

To prepare the broad beans, bring a large saucepan of water to the boil, add the salt, olive oil, and thyme and rosemary stems, and simmer for 3 minutes. Add the beans and blanch in the boiling bouillon for 3 minutes, depending on their age. With a slotted spoon, remove the beans and drain. Then remove the skins from the beans by rubbing them with your thumb and forefinger as soon as they are cool enough to touch. Reserve.

Heat a ridged grill pan (or large non-stick frying pan) over a medium heat until a drop of water sizzles on contact with it. Arrange the lamb cutlets (or chops) in the pan, lower the heat and grill for 3 to 4 minutes each side for rare; a little longer for well cooked. Transfer the lamb to a heated serving dish, or to individual heated serving plates, and serve with the warm broad beans. Spoon over chopped chives, which you have warmed in butter with lemon juice.

Serves 4 to 6

Salchichas de cordero con comino y pimentón

Grilled lamb sausages with cumin and paprika

These great-tasting home-made sausages, cumin and *pimentón* flavoured, combine with a Spanish potato salad and watercress and rocket leaves to make a superb light main course packed with flavour.

Use a sausage-stuffing machine and sausage casings to make these, or you can quite easily fill the casings by hand as long as you have a rod to stuff them with. Or, more simply, wet your hands and form the mix into sausage-like kefta shapes, or into flat round patties. It's the flavour that counts.

And let's admit it: your favourite supermarket lamb sausages (craftily dusted with a little powdered cumin and *pimentón* before grilling) wouldn't come amiss with this combination of salads.

Sausages (or Patties)

500 g / 1 lb boneless leg or shoulder of lamb

500 g / 1 lb boneless pork shoulder

100g / 4 oz unsmoked fatty bacon

2 cloves garlic, finely chopped

6 tablespoons fresh breadcrumbs

3 teaspoons salt

1 teaspoon each *pimentón* (Spanish sweet paprika) and cumin

freshly ground pepper

2 pinches crushed dried chillies

4 tablespoons chopped fresh coriander leaves or flat-leaf parsley leaves

sausage casings, unless you're making patties

Dressing

150 ml / 4 fl oz extra-virgin olive oil

2 tablespoons fresh lime juice

1–2 tablespoons dry sherry

salt and freshly ground pepper

pinch of crushed dried chillies

1 small red onion, finely diced

½ green pepper, seeded and finely diced

½ red pepper, seeded and finely diced

1 clove garlic, finely chopped

Salads

1 kg / 2 lb new potatoes, unpeeled

1 bunch fresh watercress, stems removed

1 bunch (or 1 packet) rocket leaves, stems removed

To prepare the sausage mix, cut the lamb, pork shoulder and bacon into 2.5 cm / 1 inch cubes. Combine in an electric food processor and process, in short bursts, until the meats are coarsely and evenly ground. Add the garlic, breadcrumbs, seasonings and spices and grind again until well mixed. Transfer the mixture to a mixing bowl. Add the chopped coriander or parsley and a tablespoon or two of cold water, and mix well.

To taste the sausage mix, roll a tablespoon of the mixture into a ball and sauté it for a minute or two in a little olive oil until cooked through. Taste and correct the flavours, adding a little more seasoning, or spices, if desired. If the mix is too dry, add a little more water, or a little olive oil. Mix again. Stuff into casings to make 8 sausages, or, failing this, form by hand into 8 sausage-shaped kefta or little round patties. Make any leftover mixture into sausages or patties to reserve for another meal. Reserve.

To make the dressing, combine the olive oil, lime juice and dry sherry in a medium-sized bowl. Season with salt, pepper and crushed dried chillies, to taste, and stir in the red onion, peppers and garlic.

For the potato salad, cook the potatoes in boiling salted water until tender but not mushy. Peel while they are still quite warm (the potatoes will absorb the flavours of the dressing better). Slice and toss with one third of the dressing.

To serve, grill the sausages (or sausage patties) over a medium charcoal fire (or pan-grill them, using an oiled ridged grill pan over a medium heat) for 10 to 15 minutes, turning the sausages 2 or 3 times during grilling to ensure they are evenly marked by the grill.

Place 2 sausages on each of 4 heated plates. Combine the watercress sprigs and rocket leaves in a bowl, pour over the remaining dressing and toss well. Then garnish each plate with the greens and the potato salad. Serve immediately.

Serves 4

Caldereta de cordero a la malagueña
Málaga lamb stew

One of the great lamb stews of southern Spain is *caldereta*. Serve this country stew with a garnish of boiled potatoes and artichoke hearts as they do at the Castillo de Monda. This recipe serves 4. Better double the quantities … they'll ask for seconds.

1 kg / 2 lb boned leg or shoulder of lamb (weighed
    after the lamb is boned), cut into cubes
1 large leek, or 2 trimmed leeks, cut into 5-cm / 2-inch
    segments
6 tablespoons olive oil
4 carrots, cut into segments
1 large Spanish onion, cut into quarters
3 cloves garlic, smashed
4 plum tomatoes, cut in half

1 bay leaf
125 ml / 4 fl oz dry white wine
4 tablespoons Spanish brandy

Garnish
4 artichoke hearts, with stems intact, boiled with 4
    large new potatoes in salted water to which you
    have added 4 tablespoons of olive oil and the juice
    and peel of ½ unwaxed lemon

Combine the lamb and leek in a large flameproof casserole. Place over a high heat, add the olive oil and sauté, stirring constantly, until the meat and leeks have browned on all sides. Then add the carrots, onion, garlic, tomatoes and bay leaf. Lower the heat to medium and continue to cook, stirring, for 5 minutes more.

    Then add the dry white wine and enough water to cover the meat. Cover the casserole and simmer the stew over a very low heat for 45 minutes. Just before serving, flame with the brandy. As a last touch, arrange the garnish of cooked artichoke hearts and potatoes over the meat and vegetables, cover the casserole and warm through.

Serves 4

Cordero asado con miel, romero, migas y foie gras, 'Albacar'
Roast lamb with honey, rosemary, migas and foie gras, 'Albacar'

Tender roast lamb, brushed with rosemary-infused honey, accompanied by a round of crisp bacon-enclosed *migas* (topped with pan-flashed fresh foie gras) is about as elegant a dish as you could wish for. A creation of the Albacar brothers (whose top-rated restaurant in Valencia is given 7.5 out of 10 by Spain's most prestigious restaurant guide), this brilliant dish is modern Spanish cooking at its surprising best. To serve 6 generously, you will need 3 to 4 slices of lamb per person (18 to 24 slices), so count on 3 racks of lamb. Ask your butcher to cut the meat from the bones, making 3 long 'fillets', and be sure to ask him for the bones and trimmings. You will need them to make the sauce for the lamb. And rehearse the *migas* in bacon rings before a big dinner. It's worth the extra trouble.

3 racks of lamb (see note above)

6 teaspoons honey flavoured with ¼–½ teaspoon
   powdered rosemary

sea salt and freshly ground pepper

1–2 tablespoons chopped fresh rosemary

6 slices fresh foie gras, 12mm / ½ inch thick

Migas Parcels

6 thin slices bacon, rinds removed

6 tablespoons finely chopped onion

3 tablespoons finely chopped green pepper

1 clove garlic, finely chopped

1 tablespoon olive oil

175 g / 6 oz crustless day-old bread, finely diced

sea salt and freshly ground pepper

The Sauce

bones and trimmings from the lamb

½ chicken stock cube

1 tablespoon tomato purée

½ Spanish onion, finely chopped

1 bay leaf

4 tablespoons dry white wine

2–4 tablespoons Spanish brandy

1 tablespoon each butter and flour mashed together
   to a smooth paste

salt and freshly ground pepper

To make the sauce, chop the lamb bones coarsely and combine in a thick-bottomed saucepan with the meat trimmings and scraps, stock cube, tomato purée, onion, bay leaf and wine. Add water to cover and simmer gently until the meat on the bones is cooked through. Strain the stock into a clean pan and cook over a high heat until reduced by half. Then flavour with the brandy and whisk in the butter and flour mixture. Season with salt and pepper, to taste, strain and keep warm.

To prepare the parcels of *migas*, preheat the oven to 200°C/400°F/gas 6. Roll each piece of bacon around a 5-cm / 2-inch ring mould and fasten with a cocktail stick. Cook in the hot oven for 3 to 5 minutes, until the bacon is crisp but not too browned. Slip the bacon from the moulds and reserve. Meanwhile, put the onion, green pepper and garlic in a small frying pan with a little water. Add the olive oil and cook over a medium heat, stirring, until the vegetables are tender and the water has evaporated. Then stir in the bread with a wooden spoon, allowing it to brown lightly in the hot pan. If the bread does not brown, put

the pan under a preheated grill until the top crisps and begins to turn a light golden brown. Reserve.

Now it's time to pan-sear the lamb. First preheat the oven to 200°C/400°F/gas 6. Brush the racks of lamb with the rosemary honey, season generously with salt and pepper and sprinkle with fresh rosemary. Pan-sear in a hot nonstick frying pan on all sides until well browned on the outside: about 10 minutes. Then put the fillets in the preheated oven and roast for 15 to 20 minutes, until moist and pink on the inside.

Transfer to a carving board and reserve while you sauté the fresh foie gras for a minute on each side in the pan juices. Reserve and keep warm.

To serve, cut a thin slice off both ends of each fillet and then carve the lamb into 18 to 24 slices (3 to 4 slices per person). Keep warm. Place a crisp bacon ring near the top edge of each heated dinner plate. Spoon the lightly browned *migas* into each bacon ring and top with a slice of pan-seared foie gras. Arrange 3 to 4 slices of lamb, overlapping, on each plate. Spoon strained sauce around the meat and serve immediately.

Serves 6

Rabo de toro
Bullfighter's oxtail stew

It is said that *rabo de toro* simmered with vegetables and aromatics in red wine is a bullfighter's favourite dish. When the cross-cut sections of tail cut from a bull slaughtered in the ring are marinated in a bottle of the best regional red wine for 36 hours, as I first had the dish in Córdoba, it is certainly mine. You might have to make do with a package of oxtail from a supermarket, but the Spanish wine marinade will still make it a memorable dish.

12–16 pieces of oxtail

2 Spanish onions, finely chopped

2 leeks, white parts only, cut into thin rounds

2 stalks celery, cut into thin rounds

4 large carrots, peeled and finely chopped

1 strip orange peel, dried in a low oven

2 sprigs fresh thyme

2 bay leaves

8 peppercorns

1½ bottles Rioja

4 tablespoons plain flour, seasoned with a little salt and freshly ground pepper

6 tablespoons olive oil

2 tablespoons tomato purée

crushed dried chillies

In a large mixing bowl, combine the pieces of oxtail and the vegetables (onion, leeks, celery and carrots). Add the oven-dried orange peel, thyme, bay leaves and peppercorns, cover with the red wine and leave to marinate at room temperature overnight, or in the refrigerator for 36 to 48 hours.

When ready to cook, place a large colander or sieve over a clean mixing bowl, and pour the meat, vegetables, aromatics and red wine into it, allowing the liquids to settle in the bowl.

Carefully remove the pieces of meat. Pat them dry with kitchen paper and then toss in the seasoned flour. Heat the olive oil in a large shallow flameproof casserole and sauté the oxtail pieces quickly on all sides. Remove the meat from the pan and reserve. Add the marinated vegetables to the pan and sauté in the remaining fats for 5 minutes. Return the meat to the pan, add the marinade juices and herbs and simmer on the lowest of heats for 1½ to 2 hours, or until meltingly tender.

Serves 4 to 6

Conejo relleno de setas
Leg of rabbit stuffed with wild mushrooms

Spain loves rabbit. Delicious rabbit dishes are served in restaurants and farm kitchens throughout the Spanish countryside. I particularly enjoy this recipe of stuffed rabbit – easy to prepare if you can coax your butcher into boning the thighs, and not too difficult to do even if you bone the rabbit yourself. The secret is a highly flavoured stuffing of wild mushrooms and aromatics, simmered in olive oil before being inserted into the upper leg of the rabbit. Try this recipe, too, with free-range, corn-fed chicken. A treat.

4 rabbit hind legs (with thigh)

100 g/4 oz dried wild mushrooms (less 4 tablespoons reserved for the stock: see right)

4 tablespoons dry white wine

boiling water

olive oil

1 Spanish onion, finely chopped

2 cloves garlic, finely chopped

2 sprigs fresh thyme, leaves only

2 sprigs fresh marjoram, leaves only

sea salt and freshly ground pepper

pinch of crushed dried chillies

4 slices unsmoked bacon, coarsely chopped

50 g/2 oz fresh breadcrumbs

425 ml/¾ pint light mushroom stock, made ahead of time with the rabbit bones and trimmings, a vegetable stock cube and 4 tablespoons of the reserved dried mushrooms

2–3 tablespoons diced butter

Ask your butcher to bone the rabbit thighs, leaving the bones in the lower leg intact (or, if you are using chicken, have the thighs boned, leaving the drumsticks intact).

Combine the mushrooms with the dry white wine in a small bowl and add enough boiling water to cover. Set aside.

In a large frying pan, heat 6 tablespoons olive oil until it sizzles. Add the onion, garlic and herbs and season with salt, pepper and crushed dried chillies, to taste. Cook over a medium heat, stirring constantly, until the vegetables are transparent and just beginning to turn gold. Remove from the heat.

Press the soaked mushrooms almost dry, chop them coarsely and add to the vegetable mixture with the chopped bacon. Return to the heat and continue to cook for 3 to 5 minutes more, or until the bacon begins to crisp. Stir in the fresh breadcrumbs. Taste the mixture, add more seasoning if desired, then allow to cool.

Stuff the rabbit (or chicken) thighs loosely with the mixture and fasten the edges of the thigh openings together with a little sewing thread or with cocktail sticks which you have soaked in cold water. (You can prepare the recipe in advance to this point. Keep the stuffed legs in the refrigerator until half an hour before you want to cook them.) Add any remaining stuffing ingredients to the stock.

To cook the rabbit (or chicken), preheat the oven to 180°C/350°F/gas 4. Place the stuffed legs on a rack in a roasting tin. Pour the stock into the roasting tin. Brush the rabbit (or chicken) with additional olive oil, season with sea salt and pepper and cook for 40 to 45 minutes until golden brown and cooked through. Remove from the oven and place the rabbit (or chicken) on individual heated plates. Make a sauce by pouring the cooking juices into a small frying pan, bringing to the boil then thickening by swirling in the butter. Strain the sauce over the rabbit (or chicken) pieces, garnish with mushrooms from the sauce, and serve.

Serves 4

Conejo con ajo y limones en conserva
Rabbit with garlic and preserved lemons

Even without a wild mountain rabbit, and the very special *andaluz* flavours of preserved lemons and half-heads of green garlic, this is a great dish. But complete, in the original Moorish version, as served at the Castillo de Monda, a hotel built on the remains of an old fortified Moorish castle, it is beyond compare.

2 tender rabbits

50 g / 2 oz flour, seasoned with salt and freshly ground pepper

olive oil

1 head of green garlic, cut in half crossways

2 Spanish onions, finely chopped

2 cloves garlic, finely chopped

2 leeks, trimmed and thinly sliced

8–10 tablespoons dry white wine

2–4 sprigs fresh thyme

2 preserved lemons, in halves or quarters (see opposite)

sea salt and freshly ground pepper

water, or light stock

Preheat the oven to 190°C/375°F/gas 5.

Cut the rabbits into serving pieces. Dredge the rabbit pieces lightly in seasoned flour and set aside. In a large frying pan, heat 2 tablespoons olive oil until it begins to sizzle. Sear the 2 half-heads of garlic, cut-side down, in the oil until golden brown. With a slotted spoon, transfer the garlic halves to a large flameproof casserole and reserve. Add a little more olive oil to the pan and, when it sizzles, stir in the onion and chopped garlic cloves and sauté, stirring from time to time, until they just begin to turn golden. Transfer to the casserole with the garlic half-heads and reserve.

Add a little more olive oil to the pan, and sauté the pieces of rabbit, a few at a time, turning them to brown on all sides. Transfer the browned rabbit pieces to the casserole, place the casserole over a moderate heat, and continue to sauté the rabbit pieces with the garlic and onions, adding a little more olive oil if necessary. Meanwhile, to the fats remaining in the frying pan, add the leeks and wine and cook, stirring, for 2 minutes. Pour the leeks and pan juices over the rabbit. Add the thyme, the preserved lemons (rind only) and their juice, and season with salt and pepper, to taste. Pour over enough water or light stock to cover the rabbit and cook in the preheated oven for 1 to 1½ hours, or until the rabbit is tender.

Serves 6 to 8

Limones en conserva
Preserved lemons

A nostalgic leftover from the reign of the Moors in Andalusia, preserved lemons are sometimes encountered even today in kitchens in southern Spain, a wonderful encounter indeed when combined with a succulent wood-fired roast of rabbit, or even lamb. When you come to use the lemons, it is only the skins, and the juice from the pulp, that go into a recipe. The flavour is unique. The peel has lost its bitter taste, and adds a surprisingly different, pungent flavour to ancient Andalusian recipes.

16 small, thin-skinned ripe lemons
coarse salt and lemon juice

Scrub the lemons with a stiff brush, then place in a large glass, plastic, stainless steel or glazed earthenware container, cover with cold water, and allow to soak for 3 to 5 days, changing the water each day.

Drain the lemons. Insert the point of a sharp knife 6 mm / ¼ inch away from the bud end of each lemon and make 4 lengthways incisions to within 6 mm / ¼ inch of the other end. Then cut through the incisions so that the lemons are cut completely through but still held together at the ends.

Squeezing each lemon open, insert ¼ teaspoon coarse salt into the centre. Arrange the lemons in sterilized Kilner jars. Sprinkle each jar with 1 tablespoon coarse salt and the strained juice of 1 lemon. Pour in enough boiling water to cover the lemons, and seal the jars. Leave the lemons to steep in this mixture for at least 3 weeks before use. You'll find that the salty, oily pickling juice is honey-thick and highly flavoured. The lemons will keep in this mixture indefinitely if stored in a dry place.

To use the lemons, remove each one you need from the jar and rinse well under cold running water. Cut into quarters and cut away the pulp (squeezing the juice from it before you discard it). Never touch preserved lemons in the jar with an oily spoon, as fat will spoil the pickling mixture. Don't worry if a white film forms on the preserved lemons in the jar. Just rinse it off before using the lemons.

Pollo vasco
Basque chicken

***Cocina vasca* (Basque country cooking) always means red and green peppers to me,** and this attractive casserole of chicken, tomatoes and coloured peppers is no exception. Serve it hot straight from the casserole … or prepare it the day ahead and make it the centrepiece of a cold buffet.

1 free-range corn-fed chicken, about 1.4 kg / 3 lb

2 green peppers, halved

2 red peppers, halved

4 tablespoons olive oil

4 tablespoons flour seasoned with sea salt, *pimentón* and freshly ground pepper

75 g / 3 oz *serrano* ham, in 1 piece, diced

1 Spanish onion, finely chopped

800 g / 1 lb 12 oz tomatoes, peeled, seeded and chopped

bouquet garni (parsley, bay leaf and thyme)

2 cloves garlic, finely chopped

300 ml / ½ pint dry white wine

Garnish

1 lemon cut into 8 wedges (optional)

pimentón (Spanish sweet paprika)

2 tablespoons finely chopped flat-leaf parsley

Divide the chicken into serving pieces using a serrated knife, cleaver, or poultry shears. Heat the grill to hot. Place the peppers, cut-side down, under the grill for 10 minutes or until their skins blacken and blister all over. Rub off the skins under cold running water, remove the seeds and cut each half into fat strips. Reserve.

Heat the olive oil in a large, thick-bottomed frying pan or flameproof shallow casserole. Dredge the chicken pieces with seasoned flour and sauté in the hot oil, turning them from time to time, until they start to turn golden on all sides. Then add the ham and 2 tablespoons of the onion and continue to sauté until the onions and chicken pieces are golden in colour. Remove the chicken, ham and onion from the pan.

In the oil remaining in the pan, sauté the pepper strips for 5 minutes. Remove using a slotted spoon and reserve. Add the remaining onion to the pan and sauté for 8 to 10 minutes, until soft and a light golden colour. Stir in the tomatoes, bouquet garni, garlic and wine. Simmer for 10 minutes, uncovered, then return the chicken, ham, onion and pepper to the pan, and combine well with the tomato mixture. Cover and simmer for 30 to 40 minutes, or until the chicken pieces are tender.

When ready to serve, remove the bouquet garni and correct the seasoning, adding more salt and pepper if necessary. Arrange the chicken pieces on a heated serving dish. Spoon over the vegetables and sauce, and garnish with lemon wedges. Sprinkle with *pimentón* and parsley and serve immediately.

Serves 4

Pollo asado con pimientos rojos
Roast chicken with red peppers

Peppers in Spanish hands become vivacious and versatile food, especially in this pepper-stuffed, pepper-garnished roast chicken. The wild mix of Andalusian flavours keeps the mood sunny, with its golden glazed chicken and brilliant red garnish.

1 free-range corn-fed chicken, about 1.4 kg / 2 lb

olive oil

sea salt and freshly ground pepper

pimentón (Spanish sweet paprika)

2½ red peppers, stems, seeds and membranes
  removed, quartered and tossed in olive oil

Basting Sauce

4 tablespoons each olive oil and water

6 tablespoons dry white wine

Stuffing

4 slices country bread (or 6 slices ciabatta), diced

4 tablespoons olive oil

2 cloves garlic, finely chopped

1 tablespoon chopped fresh thyme or rosemary leaves

2 tablespoons each chopped flat-leaf parsley and
  onion

1½ red peppers, stems, seeds and membranes
  removed, diced

sea salt and freshly ground pepper

Preheat the oven to 170°C/325°F/gas 3.

In a mixing bowl, combine the first 6 stuffing ingredients. Season generously with salt and pepper. Mix well, adding a little more olive oil if the mixture seems too dry.

Stuff the bird loosely with this mixture and truss it. Rub the outside of the chicken with a little olive oil and sprinkle generously with salt, pepper and *pimentón*.

Roast the chicken in the preheated oven for about 1 to 1¼ hours, basting with the olive oil, water and wine mixture from time to time. After 45 minutes, surround the chicken with the quartered red peppers which you have tossed in olive oil, and serve.

Serves 4

Pollo al chilindrón
Chicken with tomato and red peppers

If *zarzuela* is a musical concert and *chilindrón* is a game of cards, one wonders where Spanish recipe names come from. Perhaps elegant silver dishes of red-painted chicken and bright green peas were first handed around by white-gloved *mayordomos* in seventeenth-century gaming circles. Anyway, down to the nitty gritty: finely chopped *serrano* ham is the secret here, joined with finely chopped Spanish onions and green garlic simmered in white wine to give the chicken and the sauce its intense flavour and silky texture, and ripe red tomatoes and red peppers do the rest. This is a gutsy dish, easy to cook and easy to serve. Let it be the culinary trick up your sleeve the next time you're hosting a game of bridge *en casa*.

1 small free-range corn-fed chicken, about 1.2 kg / 2½ lb

4 tablespoons olive oil

1 medium onion, finely chopped

4 cloves garlic, peeled but kept whole

100 g / 4 oz *serrano* ham in 1 piece, cut into finger-sized strips

225 g / 8 oz carrots, sliced

4 plum tomatoes, peeled, seeded and chopped

1 red pepper, seeded and chopped

2 sprigs flat-leaf parsley, leaves only, finely chopped

1 clove garlic, finely chopped

1–2 tablespoons tomato purée

6 tablespoons dry white wine

150 ml / 5 fl oz chicken stock

sea salt and crushed dried chillies

175 g / 6 oz fresh peas

Divide the chicken into serving pieces using a serrated knife, cleaver, or poultry shears. Heat the olive oil in a large frying pan, add the onion, garlic cloves and ham and sauté for 1 minute. With a slotted spoon transfer the ham and garlic to a flameproof casserole and reserve. Add the chicken pieces to the flavoured oil and sauté, stirring, until well coloured on all sides. Transfer them to the casserole with the ham and garlic. Add the carrots, tomatoes and pepper to the pan and sauté, stirring, for 3 to 5 minutes. Transfer the vegetables to the casserole.

Add the parsley and chopped garlic to the frying pan with the tomato purée dissolved in the white wine and the chicken stock, and cook until the pan juices begin to bubble. Scrape the pan juices into the casserole. Season with salt and crushed dried chillies, to taste, cover the casserole and cook, over a medium heat, shaking the pan frequently to ensure the vegetables and meats do not stick to the bottom, for 30 to 40 minutes. Add the peas, lower the heat and simmer in the sauce until tender: 15 to 20 minutes more.

Serves 4

Pollo en salsa de almendras
Chicken in almond sauce

Almonds, saffron and fried breadcrumbs join forces to create this Arab-inspired chicken dish from Castille. The chicken pieces are dusted with flour and sautéed in olive oil with chopped onions, before being simmered in the aromatic sauce thickened with pounded fried bread, garlic, almonds and spices in the manner of the Arabian courts. I like to garnish this dish with chopped hard-boiled egg white and flat-leaf parsley and slivered toasted almonds.

8–12 chicken pieces (thighs, breasts and legs)

4 tablespoons flour, seasoned with powdered cumin, salt and freshly ground pepper

6 tablespoons olive oil, plus extra if needed

1 large onion, chopped

1 thick slice country bread (crusts trimmed), diced

2 cloves garlic, chopped

12 almonds, chopped

600 ml / 1 pint chicken stock

¼ teaspoon each salt, saffron threads, *pimentón*

(Spanish sweet paprika) and powdered cumin

2 hard-boiled eggs, shelled and cut in half lengthways

juice of ½ lemon

boiled rice, to serve

Garnish

chopped egg whites (from hard-boiled eggs above)

2 tablespoons chopped flat-leaf parsley

2 tablespoons slivered almonds, toasted

To prepare the chicken, dredge the pieces in the seasoned flour. Reserve. Heat 4 tablespoons olive oil in a flameproof casserole, add the onion and sauté until it begins to take on colour. With a slotted spoon, transfer the sautéed onion to a bowl and reserve.

Add the diced bread to the pan with the garlic and almonds and sauté, stirring, until the garlic is golden. With a slotted spoon, transfer the mixture to a mortar. Reserve.

Add the remaining 2 tablespoons olive oil to the casserole and sauté the floured chicken pieces, 3 or 4 at a time, turning the chicken pieces over in the hot oil from time to time, adding a little more oil if necessary until golden brown on all sides. Return the sautéed onion to the casserole, pour in the chicken stock, cover and simmer over a very low heat for 40 minutes.

In the meantime, prepare a *picada.* Pound the fried bread, garlic and almonds in the mortar until smooth. Add the salt, saffron, *pimentón*, cumin and the mashed yolks from the hard-boiled eggs. Moisten with 4 tablespoons of the pan juices and pound again until the mixture is well blended. Stir the *picada* into the casserole of cooked chicken and onions and cook for 5 to 10 minutes more, or until the chicken is cooked through. Chop the hard-boiled egg whites for the garnish. Add the lemon juice to the casserole and correct the seasoning.

To serve, transfer the chicken pieces to a heated serving dish. Pour over the sauce, garnish with the chopped egg whites and parsley, and scatter with the toasted almonds. Serve immediately with boiled rice.

Serves 4 to 6

Braseado de ternera con ajillo
Braised veal steak with garlic

Fat cloves of fresh garlic – blanched to remove their strong garlic taste – and a thickened tomato confit (or concentrate) simmered in dry white wine give this Catalan recipe for pan-cooked veal its wonderful flavour. The sauce is thickened in the age-old manner with fresh breadcrumbs. Use this recipe, too, with shoulder or a slice of the top leg of pork or lamb. Serve with boiled rice or green vegetables.

1 kg / 2 lb veal steak (cut across the leg of veal)

4 tablespoons olive oil

4 tablespoons fresh breadcrumbs

10 fat cloves garlic, peeled but kept whole, and
   blanched

4 tablespoons tomato purée

salt and freshly ground pepper

150 ml / 4 fl oz dry white wine

60 ml / 2 fl oz water

Cut the veal steak into 2.5 cm / 1 inch pieces and sauté in the olive oil until golden. Add the breadcrumbs, blanched garlic cloves and tomato purée to the pan. Cook over a gentle heat, stirring continuously, for 5 to 7 minutes. Season with salt and pepper to taste. Moisten with white wine and water and simmer gently for 45 minutes to 1 hour, or until tender.

Serves 4 to 6

Pimientos rellenos de codorniz y arroz de azafrán

Red peppers stuffed with quail and saffron rice

Fat red peppers stuffed with saffron rice and a hidden bounty of pan-seared quail were the hit of a recent luncheon in the hills behind Málaga. They were served cold as an intriguing first course with finger bowls so guests could use their fingers to enjoy the last shreds of the roasted quail.

4 red peppers, roasted whole

4 quail, trussed and ready for roasting

6 tablespoons olive oil

salt and freshly ground pepper

pinch of crushed dried chillies

Tomato Sauce

6 tablespoons olive oil

½ Spanish onion, chopped

2 cloves garlic, finely chopped

450 g / 1 lb tomatoes, peeled and chopped (or a
    400 g / 14 oz can peeled, chopped plum tomatoes)

2 tablespoons chopped flat-leaf parsley

1–2 tablespoons Spanish sherry vinegar

sea salt and freshly ground pepper

pinch of crushed dried chillies

Saffron Rice

½ Spanish onion, finely chopped

4 tablespoons olive oil

8 tablespoons *paella* rice

¼–½ teaspoon saffron threads

425 ml / ¾ pint hot chicken stock

sea salt and freshly ground pepper

pinch of crushed dried chillies

To make the tomato sauce, heat the olive oil until it sizzles. Add the onion and garlic and sauté, stirring, until they just begin to change colour. Then add the tomatoes, parsley and sherry vinegar and season with sea salt, pepper and crushed dried chillies, to taste. Simmer the sauce over a low heat for 20 minutes. Remove from the heat and reserve.

Preheat the oven to 180°C/350°F/Gas 4. To prepare the peppers for stuffing, slice the cap off each one and scrape out the seeds and pith. Trim off just enough from the bottom of each pepper (without cutting through into the cavity) to allow them to stand up in a baking dish. Brush with 2 tablespoons olive oil and soften in the oven for 10 minutes while you prepare the saffron rice and quail.

To prepare the saffron rice, sauté the onion in the olive oil in a large frying pan until the onion is transparent. Add the rice and continue to cook, stirring, until the rice is translucent. Add the saffron and a ladleful of the hot chicken stock and continue to cook, stirring, until the stock is absorbed by the rice and onions. Add another ladle of the hot stock and continue to cook, adding a little more stock from time to

time, until the rice is tender but not mushy. Season with salt, pepper and crushed dried chillies, to taste. Remove from the heat and reserve.

In the meantime, cook the quail. Brush the quail with 2 tablespoons olive oil, season with salt, pepper and crushed dried chillies, to taste, and sauté in a nonstick pan until the little birds are well browned on all sides. Remove from the heat, cut away the strings and reserve the birds and their pan juices.

When ready to cook the softened peppers, stuff them loosely with the saffron rice, tuck a quail into the centre of each rice-filled pepper and replace the stuffed peppers in the baking dish. Drizzle with the remaining olive oil and roast in the preheated oven for 20 minutes. Pour the tomato sauce around the peppers; sprinkle the remaining olive oil over the top of the peppers and cook for another 20 minutes.

Serves 4

Oca con peras
Goose with pears

Two poultry dishes in classic Spanish cuisine have always intrigued me. So on my last visit I determined to search them out and cook them while staying in a friend's house just outside Barcelona. The two recipes are goose with pears (a very old recipe dating back, as far as I could discover, to the seventeenth century, and probably earlier) and partridge cooked in chocolate (a seventeenth-century import from the fabled court of Montezuma, brought back to Spain by the *conquistadores*).

The classic way of cooking goose with pears was to cook the bird whole and then cut it up into serving portions. But if you are going to cook a goose whole in stock, you will need a huge oval casserole to hold the great bird and its vegetables. A large deep roasting pan, such as is found in professional kitchens, might do the job, but even then only with heavy-duty aluminium foil to cover the bird and the pan to keep in the fragrances and moisture of the goose while it is cooking. My solution (and you'll have to ask your butcher to help you with this when you order the goose, unless, of course, you are handy with a cleaver) cuts both thighs across the bone into 2 pieces each, and across both breasts into 3 pieces each, which, plus the drumsticks, allows 2 portions of goose for each guest. And ask him to chop the neck and backbone into segments to help improve the flavour of this magnificent dish. Now you can cook the bird and its vegetables comfortably in a large oval casserole.

The Goose

1 goose (2.7–3.5 kg / 6–8 lb), cut into 12 serving
   pieces, plus segments of backbone and neck to
   improve the flavour of the sauce (see above)
sea salt and freshly ground pepper
100 g / 4 oz lard
2 Spanish onions, cut into eighths
6 plum tomatoes, chopped
1 bay leaf
900 ml / 1½ pints water or light chicken stock
2 cloves garlic, peeled but kept whole
50 g / 2 oz almonds, toasted
2 digestive biscuits (or 2 slices ciabatta, fried in 1
   tablespoon of the lard until crisp and golden on
   both sides)
2 tablespoons white wine
2 tablespoons wine vinegar

The Pears

300 ml / ½ pint white wine
2 tablespoons sugar
1 bay leaf
1 cinnamon stick
pinch of saffron threads
4 peppercorns
6 small hard pears, peeled, but with stems intact

Garnish

sprigs of fresh mint and watercress, tied into 6 tiny
   bouquets

To prepare the pears, first combine the wine, sugar, bay leaf, cinnamon, saffron and peppercorns in a medium-sized saucepan. Bring the mixture to the boil and skim any froth from the surface. Add the pears, bring to the boil again, lower the heat, cover the pan loosely and simmer gently until the pears are tender but not mushy: about 30 minutes. Remove the pan from the heat and let the pears cool in the cooking liquid.

To prepare the goose, season the pieces of goose with a little sea salt and pepper. Melt the lard in a flameproof casserole large enough to hold the goose pieces and vegetables comfortably. Sauté the goose pieces in the sizzling fat until golden. Transfer the pieces to a large plate and sauté the onions and garlic cloves in the goose fat and lard until they just begin to turn colour.

Remove the garlic cloves and set aside. Add the tomatoes and bay leaf to the casserole and cook, stirring, for 2 to 3 minutes more before returning the goose pieces to the casserole. Add the hot water (or chicken stock), cover the casserole and cook for 1¼ to 1½ hours. The exact cooking time will depend on how tender the goose is.

In the meantime, make a *picada* by crushing the semi-cooked garlic cloves in a mortar with the almonds and the digestive biscuits (or fried ciabatta) to form a smooth paste.

When you are ready to finish the dish, remove the 12 best goose pieces from the casserole with a cooking fork or slotted spoon, leaving the segments of neck and backbone to continue to give flavour to the broth. Skim all of the fat from the surface of the pan juices. Add the white wine and wine vinegar and stir over the heat, allowing the alcohol to evaporate.

Take a small ladle of the broth and add it to the mortar to dilute the *picada* mixture. Then add this mix to the casserole and continue to cook the broth over a high heat, stirring from time to time, until the sauce is reduced to one third of its original quantity. Strain the reduced sauce into a clean casserole, pressing down on the vegetables and meats with the back of a ladle or a wooden spoon to extract all the flavour.

Return the saucepan containing the pears to the heat to reheat the pears and put the goose pieces in the casserole to heat through in the reduced sauce.

When ready to serve, use a slotted spoon to remove the pieces of the goose and arrange them in the centre of a heated serving dish. Remove the hot pears from the wine and arrange them around the edges of the serving dish. The pears can be served whole, or sliced and fanned out for a more elegant presentation.

Add enough of the wine juices from the pears to flavour the pan juices in the casserole while it is still on the heat. Taste the sauce and adjust the seasoning. Then strain it into a clean saucepan or jug so that you can spoon a little of the hot sauce over the goose and pears. Garnish each pear with a tiny bouquet made up of sprigs of mint and watercress and serve immediately. Serve the remaining sauce separately.

Serves 6

Perdiz con chocolate
Partridge cooked in chocolate

Brought back from the fabled courts of the Aztecs by the Conquistadores in the early sixteenth century (Cortés and his troops rode through the Mexican jungles to Tenochtitlán, Mexico City, in 1519) were two flavoursome beans that were to change the world's culinary history: cacao and vanilla. Chocolate, in particular, was to prove of major importance, both as a drink in the Aztec manner (deliciously flavoured, sweetened with honey and vanilla, and served ice cold, chilled with snows brought down from the mountains) and in a surprising recipe for venison and wild birds such as partridge and turkey. This ancient recipe is still served today in Mexico, and, even more surprisingly, in Spain. The recipe combines the flavours of finely chopped onion, garlic and herbs with cinnamon, cloves, vinegar and bitter chocolate.

2–4 young partridges (if small, serve 1 each, if a good size, cut in half after cooking and serve half each), ready for cooking

2 tablespoons flour, sifted and seasoned with salt and freshly ground pepper

4 tablespoons olive oil

½ medium-sized onion, finely chopped

2 cloves garlic, finely chopped

2–3 teaspoons ground cinnamon

2 whole cloves

1 dried bay leaf, crumbled

450 g / 1 lb baby white onions, blanched

2 tablespoons tomato purée

300 ml / ½ pint well-flavoured chicken stock

50 g / 2 oz deluxe dark chocolate (such as Valrhona), grated

2 tablespoons red wine vinegar

Dust the partridges with the seasoned flour. Heat the olive oil in a flameproof casserole and brown the partridges on all sides in the hot oil. Then transfer the birds to a large dish and reserve. Add the onion and garlic to the casserole and sauté, stirring constantly, until the vegetables just begin to change colour. Return the partridges to the casserole and add all the remaining ingredients, except the chocolate and the vinegar. Reduce the heat to very low, cover the casserole and simmer the birds and onions for about 45 minutes or until tender. Then transfer the partridges and onions to a heated serving dish and keep warm while you finish the sauce.

Skim excess fat from the juices remaining in the casserole. Stir in half the chocolate and half the vinegar and cook over a medium heat for 5 minutes, whisking constantly, until the sauce is smooth and thick. Taste and correct the seasoning, adding more grated chocolate, vinegar, salt, pepper and cinnamon, if desired. The sauce should be rich and highly flavoured.

Serve at once, with the hot sauce strained over the birds and onions.

Serves 4

Pichón en escabeche con ensalada de higos
Pigeon escabeche with ripe fig salad

Fat little birds, squab pigeon or quail, pink roasted and then cooked in an *escabeche* sauce, make delicious eating when combined in an appetizer or luncheon main course salad with warmed figs.

3 squab pigeons, or 6 quail, ready for roasting	*Escabeche*
extra virgin olive oil	150 ml / 5 fl oz olive oil
salt and freshly ground pepper	2–3 cloves garlic, thinly sliced
pinch of crushed dried chillies	4 tablespoons wine vinegar
½ head of young curly endive, cleaned and	4 tablespoons dry white wine
separated	150 ml / 5 fl oz fish stock
1 packet rocket leaves, tough stems removed	2 bay leaves
18 sprigs fresh watercress	2 sprigs fresh thyme
lime juice	6 peppercorns
3 ripe purple figs, halved	6 thin slices lemon (with peel), cut into quarters

Preheat the oven to 240°C/475°/gas 9.

Place the pigeons (or quail) in a baking dish. Brush with olive oil and season each bird with salt, pepper and a pinch of crushed dried chillies, to taste. Roast the pigeons in the preheated oven for 10–12 minutes, keeping the pigeons quite pink. (Roast quail for about 8 minutes.)

In the meantime, prepare the *escabeche* by combining the ingredients in a frying pan and bringing gently to the boil. Simmer for 5–10 minutes to reduce the liquid to a quarter of its original amount. Take off the heat and set aside.

When the birds are cooked to your liking (slightly undercooked really), remove them from the oven and let them rest for 10 minutes. Then cut the breasts off the bone and remove the legs. Heat the *escabeche* sauce in the pan, add the breasts and legs and heat through in the sauce. Correct the seasoning, adding a little more lime juice, salt or pepper, if desired.

To make the salad, combine the endive leaves with the rocket and watercress. Add olive oil, lime juice, and salt and pepper, to taste. Toss well to blend the flavours, and arrange a little salad on each salad plate. Garnish each plate with breasts and legs. Warm the halved figs in the *escabeche* pan juices over a medium heat and then arrange 2 halves on each plate. Pour a little of the hot pan juices over each salad and serve immediately.

Serves 6

Chapter 11

VEGET

Christopher Columbus and the *conquistadores* brought more than Incan gold and silver back from the New World to enrich the coffers of Ferdinand and Isabella. They brought even more valuable treasures, which changed the eating habits and lifestyles of the European courts, and revolutionized world cuisine. Imagine the cookery of Spain, Italy, France and North Africa without tomatoes, dried beans and sweet and hot peppers. Where would Ireland be without the potato? Italy without polenta? Add New World pumpkins and squashes, sweet potatoes, avocados and exotic fruits such as pineapples, bananas, melons, lemons and oranges …

Spain was ready for these excitements. After 600 years of Moorish rule, while the rest of Europe was ravaged by feudal wars, the Spanish court was recognized as the most elegant and sophisticated in Europe. The Arabs had brought intricate architecture, lavishly watered pleasure gardens, wondrous silks and ceramics. The scene was ripe for a culinary revolution. But in the first years, the New World foods were looked upon with suspicion, wonder and fear. Yet tomatoes gradually began to be used to add flavour, sharpness and colour to native dishes when the pale mixtures of pounded breads, olive oil and aromatics left by the early Romans, enriched by Eastern spices under Moorish rule, found their soul with Mayan tomatoes, making possible the *gazpachos*, raw and cooked salads, tomato-based stews and sauces that we know today. The hot red pepper plants produced a sweet, mild fruit on Spanish soil. It was found that when dried and pounded they produced a pungent but mild spice: *pimentón*. Made in Spain in three seasonings – mild, sweet and pungent – this led to a whole new range of creations, in particular the distinctive curing of pork products like *chorizo*. Spain never looked back.

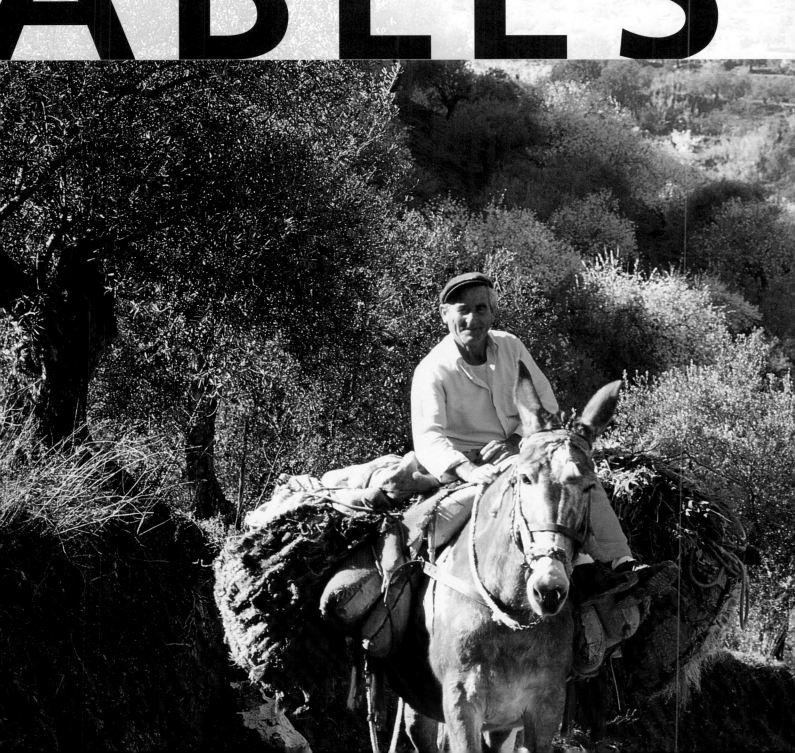

Verduras asadas
Roasted vegetables

Pimientos rojos asados
Roasted red peppers

In Spain, red peppers, roasted (for a meltingly soft flesh) or char-grilled (for a slightly firmer flesh) until their blackened skins can be rubbed off easily, are regular accompaniments for grilled fish and meats (especially veal and lamb); are used extensively in sauces and stews; and, cut into thin strips, feature in *tapas* and salads.

4 whole red peppers
extra virgin olive oil

To 'roast', place the peppers whole under a hot grill, about 5 to 7.5 cm / 2 to 3 inches away from the heat, turning frequently until charred and blistered on all sides.

To 'char-grill', grill the pepper whole over a gas flame or on a very hot ridged grill pan, turning frequently until charred and blistered on all sides.

Whichever method you use, put the peppers in a plastic bag and leave them to 'steam' for 15 minutes. Then remove the peppers from the bag and, under cold running water, gently rub the blackened skin off. Pat dry with kitchen paper. Pull out the stem (it comes away easily, complete with seeds), slice each pepper in half, quarters or strips, and brush with olive oil. Use as desired.

Tomates asados
Roasted tomatoes

Roasted tomatoes make a vibrantly flavoured vegetable accompaniment for grilled seafood, veal or lamb. Or chopped and dressed with a little extra virgin olive oil, flat-leaf parsley and red onion, they make a fabulous garnish for dishes of crushed boiled potatoes, rice, or even green salad.

12 ripe vine tomatoes
extra virgin olive oil
1 small bunch basil or flat-leaf parsley, leaves chopped
sea salt (or celery salt) and crushed dried chillies

Preheat the oven to 140°C/275°F/gas 1. Cut the tomatoes in half lengthways and press lightly to remove excess liquids. Place the tomatoes, cut-side down, on a platter to drain while you prepare the baking tray.

Brush a baking tray lightly with a thin coating of olive oil, sprinkle with the chopped basil or parsley leaves (or a combination of the two), to flavour the tomatoes, then drizzle over a little more oil. Sprinkle the herbs with sea salt and just a hint of crushed dried chillies.

Place the tomatoes, cut-side down, on this bed of aromatics, and brush each half with a little more oil. Cover with greaseproof paper and wrap the whole in aluminium foil. Bake for about 30 minutes, or until the tomatoes are soft and the skin comes away easily from the flesh. Remove from the oven, carefully remove the skins from the tomatoes and allow to cool until ready to use.

Maíz asado
Roasted corn on the cob

Along with tomatoes and peppers, one of Montezuma's gifts. This is best cooked over the hot coals of a barbecue.

8 sweetcorn
8 thin slices *serrano* ham
extra virgin olive oil
sea salt and crushed dried chillies

Discard the outer husks of the sweetcorn. Carefully pull back the inner husks and remove the silky threads that turn from pale green to golden brown as the corn matures. Wrap a slice of *serrano* ham around the bared corn. Brush each corn with olive oil, sprinkle with sea salt and a pinch of crushed dried chillies, and pull the husks back around the ear, twisting them to seal in the flavours of corn, ham and chillies.

Before cooking over coals, soak the wrapped ears in water to prevent the corn husks from overcharring. Then cook for 15 minutes, turning the corn over from time to time during cooking. Serve at once.

Potaje andaluz 'Castillo de Monda'
Andalusian vegetable hotpot 'Castillo de Monda'

A comforting medley of country vegetables is given added flavour with *chorizo, morcilla* (Spanish black pudding) and a thin half pork chop (with the bone). Half vegetable stew, half farmhouse soup, this mix of beans, pumpkin, chard and potatoes is comforting food at its best. Substitute a pounded *picada* (see page 88) for the meat products and you have a vegetarian dish to crow about.

100 g / 4 oz presoaked chickpeas

50 g / 2 oz presoaked kidney beans

100 g / 4 oz green beans, cut into short lengths

100 g / 4 oz pumpkin (weighed after peel and seeds removed), cubed

50 g / 2 oz courgettes, thickly sliced

2 ripe tomatoes, peeled, seeded and chopped

1 onion, cut into 6–8 wedges

100 g / 4 oz young chard (or red chard) leaves

100 g / 4 oz potatoes, peeled and thickly sliced

2 *chorizo* sausages, sliced

100 g / 4 oz *morcilla* (Spanish black pudding), sliced

1 thin pork chop, with bone

4–6 tablespoons olive oil

2 cloves

sea salt and freshly ground pepper

pinch of crushed dried chillies

600 ml / 1 pint well-flavoured vegetable stock

In a large saucepan, or flameproof casserole, combine the chickpeas, kidney beans, other vegetables and pork products. Moisten with olive oil and cook over a medium heat, stirring, for 5 minutes. Season with cloves and salt, pepper and crushed dried chillies, to taste. Then add the vegetable stock and simmer, uncovered, for 30 minutes, or until the vegetables are tender, but not mushy. Add a little water from time to time if necessary. Remove the half pork chop, correct the seasoning and serve immediately.

Serves 4

Pisto manchego
Stewed vegetables from La Mancha

Pisto manchego is the Castilian version of mixed stewed vegetables. Not unlike Provençal ratatouille – it uses the same mix of vegetables: onions, peppers, aubergines, courgettes and tomatoes – in Spain the vegetables are diced rather than cut into chunks, strips or slices. Try pisto in a variety of ways: as a vegetarian lunch or supper dish on its own, as a hot or cold first course or vegetable accompaniment, or, more importantly, with scrambled eggs or sausages as a main course.

6 tablespoons olive oil

2 Spanish onions, diced

2 large cloves garlic, finely chopped

2 green peppers, diced

2 medium aubergines, diced

2 courgettes, diced

6 large ripe tomatoes, peeled, seeded and diced (or a 400 g / 14 oz can peeled, chopped plum tomatoes)

salt and freshly ground pepper

pinch of crushed dried chillies

2 tablespoons chopped flat-leaf parsley

Heat 2 tablespoons of olive oil in a thick-bottomed saucepan. Add the onion and garlic and sauté until transparent. Add another 2 tablespoons olive oil and the peppers; lower the heat and cook, stirring from time to time, for 5 minutes more. Transfer the vegetables to a bowl.

Add the remaining olive oil to the pan. Add the aubergines and courgettes and cook for 5 minutes. Return all the vegetables to the pan. Add the tomatoes and season with salt, pepper and crushed dried chillies (just a hint), to taste, and cook for 2 to 3 minutes more. With a slotted spoon, transfer the vegetables to a serving dish or bowl. Sprinkle with freshly chopped parsley and serve immediately. If the *pisto* is to be served cold, do not add the freshly chopped parsley until just before serving.

Serves 4 to 6

Hervido de verduras
Valencian boiled vegetables

The simplest of boiled vegetable dishes can become vegetarian party fare if the vegetables are prepared in a home-made vegetable stock and served with lemon wedges, extra virgin olive oil, sea salt and crushed dried chillies.

3 medium-sized parsnips, quartered	*Vegetable Stock*
3 medium-sized turnips, quartered and blanched	1.5 litres / 4 pints water
4 medium-sized carrots, quartered	2 onions, peeled
4 potatoes	2 leeks, quartered
4 leeks, trimmed and cut in half crossways	2 stalks celery, quartered
2 medium-sized Spanish onions, halved	2 carrots, halved
4 cloves garlic, peeled but kept whole	1 turnip, quartered
450 g / 1 lb fine green beans, trimmed	1 vegetable stock cube, crumbled
2 bay leaves	
sea salt and crushed dried chillies	
extra virgin olive oil	
lemon wedges	

Make the vegetable stock by combining all the ingredients in a large saucepan and bringing to the boil. Simmer for 20 to 30 minutes, then strain and cool. Use 1.2 litres / 2 pints of strained stock for this recipe and keep the remaining stock in the refrigerator for use during the week. It will keep refrigerated for 5 days.

To prepare the vegetables, combine them with the bay leaves and stock in a large saucepan or medium-sized casserole. Bring gently to the boil, skim off froth and impurities, lower the heat and simmer for 20 to 30 minutes, or until the vegetables are cooked through. Parsnips may take a little less time to cook, so test after 20 minutes of cooking time. The turnips usually take a little longer, they are blanched (brought to the boil in water, to cover) before cooking.

With a slotted spoon, transfer the vegetables to a heated serving platter or individual flat soup bowls. Season the hot broth with a little sea salt and crushed dried chillies and spoon a little over the vegetables. Season the vegetables with a splash of extra virgin olive oil. Accompany with lemon wedges, twin jugs of hot stock and extra virgin Spanish olive oil, and little ramekins of sea salt and crushed dried chillies.

Serves 4

Verduras de verano con arroz al azafrán

Summer vegetables with saffron rice

Grilled summer vegetables – red onions, yellow peppers, courgettes and ripe tomatoes – make a wonderfully light luncheon or supper dish when served as a savoury vegetable topping over saffron rice or steamed couscous.

Mini versions of this recipe – served hot with a final fillip of chilled *alioli* or cold with a *vinagreta* or *salsa* dressing – vie for top place on my *tapas* table. Try it.

2 large courgettes, sliced

2 small to medium-sized onions, cut into wedges

4–6 plum tomatoes

2 yellow peppers, stems, seeds and pith removed, cut into quarters

1 recipe virgin *paella* (page 111)

alioli (page 93)

vinagreta (page 38)

Aromatics

6 tablespoons extra virgin olive oil

2 garlic cloves, finely chopped

2 tablespoons finely chopped parsley

sea salt and freshly ground black pepper

pinch of crushed dried chillies

Preheat the oven to 220°C/425°F/gas 7. Combine the aromatics in a small bowl.

Arrange the prepared vegetables in one layer on a large baking tray, or 2 smaller ones. Drizzle the vegetables with the aromatic mixture and roast in the preheated oven for 15 to 20 minutes, or until the vegetables are softened.

In the meantime, prepare the saffron rice (or the steamed couscous).

When ready to serve hot, spoon the hot saffron rice (or couscous) onto 4 to 6 heated plates. Divide the hot roasted vegetables among them. Top each with a dollop of chilled *alioli*.

If you are serving the dish cold, prepare the saffron rice (or couscous) and the roasted vegetables the day before. Toss the cold saffron rice with the well-flavoured *vinagreta* dressing. Divide the rice among 4 to 6 plates and top with the cold roasted vegetables and a dollop of chilled *alioli*.

Serves 4 to 6

Verduras con jamón serrano
Vegetables with serrano ham

This is the Spanish version of *primavera* vegetables – wonderful baby artichokes, carrots, new potatoes, green beans, spring onions and baby broad beans simmered in vegetable stock and white wine. Here the delicate bouillon is intriguingly flavoured with a slice or two of *serrano* ham. It makes a great difference.

12 small artichokes, cut in quarters, choke removed

12 baby carrots, trimmed

½ packet small green beans, trimmed

450 g / 1 lb small new potatoes

2 fat cloves garlic, peeled but kept whole

1½–2 small green peppers, cut in eighths

2 slices *serrano* ham

4 tablespoons olive oil

300 ml / ½ pint vegetable stock

12 salad onions, cut into segments

½ small packet frozen baby broad beans

1 glass dry white wine

sea salt and crushed dried chillies

lemon juice

In a flameproof casserole, combine the artichokes, carrots, green beans, new potatoes, garlic, peppers and ham. Add the olive oil and just enough vegetable stock (or water) to cover. Bring gently to the boil, then skim any impurities and lower the heat. Cover the casserole and simmer for 15 minutes.

Add the salad onions, broad beans and white wine and continue to cook over a low heat for 10 to 15 more minutes, or until the vegetables are tender.

Remove the ham. Taste the pan juices and season with sea salt, crushed dried chillies and a squeeze of lemon juice.

Serves 6

Alcachofas
Artichokes

The best artichokes for this recipe (you won't have to cut out the chokes) and for the dish opposite are the baby ones picked just before the choke forms. They are sometimes available in speciality greengrocers' and Italian food stores. Otherwise, a little extra effort is needed for more mature artichokes. But it's worth it.

6 artichokes
600 ml / 1 pint cold water
juice and rind of 1 lemon

4 tablespoons olive oil
sea salt

To prepare the artichokes, use a strong, sharp knife to slice all the leaves off level with the tips of the shortest ones. Strip away any tough outer leaves. Trim the base and stem. With a sharp-edged teaspoon, scoop and scrape out the fuzzy chokes (if necessary; see the introduction), taking care not to leave a single fibre. Remember that an artichoke is the flower bud of a thistle and these fibres are not called 'chokes' for nothing. While you are working on the artichoke, keep dipping it into a bowl of water to which you have added the juice and rind of 1/2 lemon. Do this each time you cut a fresh surface to prevent it turning brown. (The artichoke contains oxidizing enzymes which cause it to discolour very quickly when exposed to the air. This is not dangerous, but it makes the artichoke look unattractive and spoils its flavour.)

To cook the artichokes, add the olive oil, remaining lemon juice and rind, and a pinch or two of salt to a large saucepan of water. Bring to the boil. Immerse the artichokes and simmer for 30–40 minutes, or until you can pull a leaf out easily.

Lift out the artichokes and leave them to drain, standing on their heads in a colander. When cool, squeeze them gently to get rid of excess moisture.

Serve the cooked artichokes cold with the *vinagreta* of your choice (pages 38, 40 and 45), *mayonesa* (page 92) or *alioli* (page 93).

Serves 6

Alcachofas a la granadina
Artichokes Granada-style

Young artichokes, placed on a bed of aromatics, are simmered until tender in olive oil and chicken stock in this recipe. In Granada, this dish is served with an unthickened sauce. I sometimes add a teaspoon or two of cornflour to the pan juices to give a sheen to the vegetables.

6 artichokes	**sea salt and freshly ground pepper**
6 tablespoons olive oil	**pinch of crushed dried chillies**
1 medium onion, finely chopped	**300 g / ½ pint well-flavoured chicken stock**
4 cloves garlic, peeled but kept whole	**1 tablespoon cornflour**
2 small carrots, finely chopped	**4 tablespoons cold water**
1 bay leaf	**juice of ½ lemon**
1 sprig each fresh thyme and rosemary	

Prepare the artichokes as described opposite.

In a large saucepan or casserole, heat the olive oil until it sizzles. Add the onion, garlic cloves and carrot and simmer until tender.

Place the artichokes on this bed of aromatics. Add the bay leaf and the sprigs of fresh herbs and sprinkle with salt, pepper and crushed dried chillies, to taste. Add the chicken stock, cover the pan and simmer until the artichokes are tender.

With a slotted spoon, transfer the artichokes to a heated serving dish and reserve. Mix the cornflour and water. Add a little of the chicken stock and then pour the stock and cornflour into the sauce. Stir over a medium heat until the sauce is slightly thickened. Add the lemon juice, correct the seasoning and then spoon the hot sauce and vegetables over the artichokes. Serve immediately.

Serves 3 to 6

Espárragos salteados
Sautéed asparagus

Spanish asparagus are fine and fat, as white as pearls, and full of juicy flavour. For me the finest come from the region around Córdoba. Often served as a garnish, or as a delicious vegetable accompaniment for grilled or poached fish, asparagus can also be served, as in this recipe, as a vegetable on its own. Our green asparagus can be substituted in this country for Spanish white asparagus, or served alongside it, as here.

extra virgin olive oil

1 bunch green asparagus, poached until just tender

1 bunch white asparagus, poached until just tender

sea salt and freshly ground pepper

pinch of crushed dried chillies

juice of 1 lemon

Garnish

2 hard-boiled egg yolks and whites, chopped

2–3 tablespoons chopped flat-leaf parsley

2 thin slices *serrano* ham, cut crossways into
   thin strips

1 canned *pimiento*, or 1 small roasted red pepper,
   cut into short thin strips

In each of 2 frying pans, heat 3 tablespoons olive oil until it sizzles. Add the poached green asparagus to one pan, and the white asparagus to the other, and sauté, turning the asparagus with a palette knife, until they just begin to change colour. Season with salt, pepper and a hint of crushed dried chillies, and transfer both kinds of asparagus to a heated serving dish.

Squeeze the lemon juice into one of the pans, mix well, then spoon those pan juices into the other pan. Add the garnish to this pan, with a little more olive oil to make a sauce, and heat through. Spoon the sauce over the asparagus and serve immediately.

Serves 6

Espárragos asados con pimiento
Baked asparagus with pimiento

Of special note when you are travelling in Spain is a special sort of wild asparagus hand-gathered from the fields and vineyards. This very expensive springtime treat is much prized served grilled or poached with a herb-flavoured vinaigrette or, as in Provence, in a 'soft scramble' of farm-fresh eggs. Don't miss it. This recipe, however, is perfect for whatever kind of asparagus you are lucky enough to have.

1 kg / 2 lb fresh white or green asparagus

4 tablespoons olive oil

3 tablespoons finely chopped onion

1 stalk celery, finely chopped

4 tablespoons diced canned *pimiento* (or roasted red
    pepper)

1–2 teaspoons rubbed fresh marjoram

1–2 teaspoons rubbed fresh thyme

1 x 400 g / 14 oz can chopped tomatoes

salt and freshly ground pepper

pinch of crushed dried chillies

Garnish

2 slices of *serrano* ham, diced

5 tablespoons freshly grated *manchego* cheese

Trim the woody ends from the asparagus and scrape off any scaly parts. Wash under running water. Drain. Place the asparagus in a shallow casserole or frying pan, add cold water to cover and bring to the boil. Remove the blanched asparagus from the heat and drain.

Preheat the oven to 180°C/350°F/gas 4.

Heat the olive oil in a small frying pan and sauté the onion and celery for 2 to 3 minutes, stirring, until the onion is transparent.

Place the poached asparagus in a rectangular baking dish. Scatter the sautéed onion and celery over the asparagus, then sprinkle with the *pimiento* and herbs. Spoon over the chopped tomatoes and their juices and season with salt, pepper and crushed dried chillies, to taste. Cover the dish loosely with foil and bake in the preheated oven for 40 to 50 minutes, or until tender.

Just before serving, garnish with ham and *manchego* cheese.

Serves 4 to 6

Espinacas con piñones y pasas
Spinach with pine nuts and raisins

This dish, which I always thought of as Italian – I had eaten it many times in Tuscany and Sicily – turns out to be Catalan in origin, which makes perfect sense, I suppose, as Sicily and parts of Italy and France were once ruled by Catalonia. Which might also explain *brandada* and *alioli* in Spain (they are both Catalan in origin), well known to us as *brandade* and *aïoli* (two of the best-known dishes of Provence and neighbouring Languedoc, one-time fiefdoms of Catalonia as well).

3 tablespoons olive oil

4 tablespoons finely chopped onion

2 cloves garlic, finely chopped

4 tablespoons diced *serrano* ham

900 g / 2 lb baby spinach leaves, washed and drained

4 tablespoons seedless raisins, plumped up in a little
   hot water

4 tablespoons pine nuts

sea salt and crushed dried chillies

Heat 2 tablespoons of olive oil in a large heavy-bottomed frying pan and sauté the onion and garlic for 1 minute. Add the *serrano* ham and 1 more tablespoon of oil and continue to cook, stirring, for 1 minute more. Then add the spinach leaves and stir over a medium heat until the spinach wilts.

Add the plumped-up raisins and the pine nuts (which you have browned for a minute in a small dry pan). Stir and cook for 2 minutes. Season with sea salt and a pinch of crushed dried chillies.

Serves 4

Boniatos a la plancha
Grilled sweet potatoes

Orange-fleshed sweet potatoes are left unpeeled for a grilled vegetable accompaniment that goes well with poultry, game and pork. The cooked potatoes are sliced, brushed with olive oil, seasoned with salt, freshly ground pepper and a hint of crushed dried chillies and then pan-grilled until golden. Good, too, in combination with grilled red peppers, onions and aubergines.

2 sweet potatoes (orange-fleshed)
salt

olive oil
freshly ground pepper and crushed dried chillies

Leave the sweet potatoes whole. Scrub them well under running water, but do not peel. Put them in a saucepan, cover with cold water and add 1 tablespoon of salt. Bring to the boil and cook for 20 minutes, or until you can pierce the flesh with the point of a sharp knife or a skewer.

Drain the potatoes and leave to cool. Cut crossways into 25-cm / 1-inch slices, brush with olive oil, season with salt, pepper and crushed dried chillies and pan-grill (or pan-sear) for 2 to 3 minutes on each side.

Serves 4

Berenjena frita
Pan-fried aubergine slices

Top and tail 2 or 3 unpeeled aubergines and cut lengthways with a serrated knife into 6-mm / ¼-inch slices. Dredge with seasoned flour. Heat 4 tablespoons of olive oil in a large frying pan (large enough to hold several slices in one layer without touching) until the oil begins to sizzle. Divide the aubergine slices into batches and fry one batch at a time, for 2–3 minutes on one side. Then, with a palette knife, turn the aubergine slices over and fry for a minute or two on the other side. They should be crisp and pale gold in colour. If they are too dark, they will be bitter. Keep warm while you proceed in the same way for the other batches, heating more olive oil in the pan if necessary. Arrange in a fan shape on heated plates with individual bowls of *salmorejo* (page 89).

Serves 4 to 6

Patatas bravas
Potatoes with paprika sauce

The Spanish love sautéed potatoes – or sautéed potatoes and *chorizo* – with a spicy paprika sauce. This is a dish that is often served as a *tapa* or a first course. I like it, too, without the *chorizo* as a potato accompaniment to simple grills of fish or poultry. I give you my favourite version of this spicy dish.

900 g / 2 lb walnut-sized new potatoes
150 ml / 5 fl oz olive oil
sea salt

The Sauce
4 tablespoons olive oil
1 Spanish onion, finely chopped
2 cloves garlic, finely chopped

1 large tomato, peeled, seeded and chopped (or
 2 canned plum tomatoes, seeded and chopped)
¼ teaspoon dried sage
1–2 tablespoons *pimentón* (Spanish sweet paprika)
pinch of crushed dried chillies
sea salt and freshly ground pepper
1 tablespoon plain flour
300 ml / ½ pint chicken or vegetable stock

To prepare the sauce, heat the olive oil in a large frying pan until it sizzles. Stir in the onion and garlic and cook, stirring, until the vegetables just begin to change colour. Add the tomato, sage, *pimentón*, crushed diced chillies and salt and freshly ground pepper to taste. Simmer the sauce for about 5 minutes. Then stir in the flour and continue to cook, stirring, for 5 minutes more.

In a small saucepan, bring the stock to the boil. Gradually add the hot stock to the sauce. Bring it to the boil, reduce the heat and simmer over a low heat for 10 minutes. Remove from the heat, process until smooth in a food processor, pour into a small saucepan and reserve.

Wash the potatoes thoroughly but leave the skins on. Put them on to boil with just enough water to cover, leaving the lid off so that the water evaporates during cooking. When it has all evaporated, leave the pan on the heat for about 30 seconds more, shaking the pan to thoroughly dry out the potatoes. Then add 1 tablespoon of olive oil and a little sea salt.

While the potatoes are cooking, reheat the sauce, reducing it over a medium heat to the desired consistency.

To serve, shake the pan once and then divide the potatoes among 5 or 6 individual shallow earthenware bowls. Everyone spears his own potatoes with a fork and dips them into the hot sauce.

Serves 5 to 6

Pimientos rellenos
Stuffed red peppers

Peppers were brought to Spain by the *conquistadores* and have played a large part in Spanish cooking ever since. Here, we stuff the peppers with a highly flavoured savoury rice mixture, softened with toasted breadcrumbs for a delicious hot main dish or cold appetizer. I sometimes cut the cold stuffed peppers into quarters for a cold *tapa*.

4 large red peppers

6 tablespoons olive oil, plus extra to top the peppers

1 medium-sized onion, finely chopped

225 g / 8 oz minced pork

6 anchovy fillets, chopped

50 g / 2 oz fresh breadcrumbs, toasted

75 g / 3 oz seedless raisins

12 black olives, pitted and chopped

100 g / 4 oz rice, parboiled in saffron-flavoured water for 10 minutes and drained

2 tablespoons finely chopped flat-leaf parsley

1 teaspoon chopped fresh thyme or rosemary leaves

salt and freshly ground pepper

Tomato Sauce

1 x 400 g / 14 oz can chopped peeled tomatoes

½ medium-sized Spanish onion, finely chopped

2 tablespoons finely chopped flat-leaf parsley

2 cloves garlic, finely chopped

olive oil

300 ml / ½ pint water

½ teaspoon *pimentón* (Spanish sweet paprika)

¼ teaspoon cayenne pepper

sea salt

To make the tomato sauce, combine all the ingredients in a large saucepan except the sea salt. Simmer gently for ½ hour. Season with the sea salt to taste. Reserve.

To prepare the peppers, preheat the oven to 180°C/350°F/gas 4. Wash the peppers, cut off the caps (reserve for lids) and remove the seeds. Level the peppers to even height.

In a large frying pan, heat the oil until it sizzles. Sauté the onion in the oil until it begins to turn pale gold. Add the pork and continue to cook, stirring, until the meat begins to brown.

Meanwhile, in a bowl, combine the anchovy fillets, toasted breadcrumbs, raisins, olives, saffron-flavoured rice and herbs. Season with salt and pepper, to taste. Mix well, then stir into the frying pan with the meat and continue to cook, stirring from time to time, for 10 to 15 minutes more (adding a little more olive oil, or a little water, if the mixture is too dry).

Stuff the peppers with this savoury mixture and stand them in an oiled baking dish just large enough to hold them upright. Top each pepper with a little olive oil, then fix the caps to the peppers with wooden cocktail sticks. Spoon 2 tablespoons of the tomato sauce over each pepper cap and bake the peppers in the preheated oven for 45 to 50 minutes, or until tender.

When ready to serve hot, heat the remaining tomato sauce and spoon around the peppers. Also delicious cold.

Serves 4

Calabacines con pimientos rojos
Courgettes with red peppers

Diced roasted red peppers (or, if you are in a hurry, canned or bottled Spanish *pimientos*) add a touch of colour to this flavoursome southern dish. Serve it hot as a vegetable, or cold as a first course.

8 courgettes
150 ml / ¼ pint simmering salted water
6 tablespoons olive oil
1 medium-sized onion, chopped
1 clove garlic, finely chopped
1 roasted red pepper (or 1 *pimiento*), diced
4 ripe tomatoes, peeled, seeded and diced
sea salt and freshly ground pepper

Score the courgettes lengthways with a cannulator (or the triangular tip of a bottle opener, or the end of a pointed teaspoon). Poach them lightly in the salted water with 2 tablespoons of olive oil for 6 to 8 minutes, depending on the size of the courgettes. Keep them warm in the cooking liquid.

Sauté the onion and garlic in the remaining olive oil until transparent. Add the red pepper and tomatoes and cook until soft but not mushy. Season generously with sea salt and pepper.

Remove the courgettes from the cooking liquid and arrange in a heated oblong gratin dish. Spoon over the red pepper and tomato mixture and serve immediately.

Serves 2 to 4

Judías verdes con pimiento
Green beans with pimiento

Thin ribbons of canned or bottled Spanish *pimiento* (or use strips of roasted red and yellow peppers) make a welcome addition to crisp-tender green beans, especially when sprinkled with chopped flat-leaf parsley and walnuts.

450 g / 1 lb green beans, topped and tailed and cut into 5-cm / 2-inch lengths

4 tablespoons finely chopped onion

6 tablespoons olive oil

2 canned *pimientos*, drained and thinly sliced

lemon juice

salt and freshly ground pepper

crushed dried chillies

2 tablespoons finely chopped flat-leaf parsley

2 tablespoons chopped walnuts

Cook the green beans in plenty of boiling water for 3 to 8 minutes, according to size, until tender but still crisp. Drain and refresh in cold water.

Sauté the onion in the olive oil for about 5 minutes until transparent. Add the cooked green beans and toss for a few minutes more, or until the beans are warmed through.

Add the *pimiento* to the beans, and sprinkle with lemon juice and salt, pepper and crushed dried chillies to taste. Cook for a few minutes until the *pimiento* is heated through.

To serve, transfer the green beans and *pimiento* to a heated serving dish. Sprinkle with parsley and walnuts and serve immediately.

Serves 4

Coliflor frita
Deep-fried cauliflower

Crisp-poached cauli florets, dipped in a light batter and then deep-fried in olive oil, take on a new authority when served with a zesty Spanish tomato sauce. A good dish for vegetarians if you use a crumbled vegetable stock cube in the sauce. Or serve 2 to 3 pieces of batter-fried cauliflower with the sauce as a dip for a hot *tapa* with drinks.

Easy to do: the batter is made, the cauliflower is poached. All that you have to do now is dip and fry.

1 large cauliflower

Batter
1 egg
150 ml / ¼ pint milk
2 tablespoons dry white wine
100 g / 4 oz flour, sifted
salt
oil for deep-frying

Fresh Tomato Sauce
450 g / 1 lb tomatoes
¼ large Spanish onion, finely chopped
1 whole unpeeled clove garlic
4 tablespoons olive oil
¼ chicken stock cube, crumbled
2 tablespoons tomato purée
150 ml / ¼ pint water
salt and freshly ground pepper
pinch of cayenne pepper
lemon juice
2 tablespoons finely chopped flat-leaf parsley

To prepare the tomato sauce, peel the tomatoes: first make a tiny cut in the top of each one. Place in a bowl, cover with boiling water and leave for 10 seconds, then remove from the water and slip off their skins. Cut the tomatoes in half, squeeze out the seeds and juice, and dice the flesh finely.

Sauté the onion and garlic clove in half the olive oil until the onion is soft. Discard the garlic. Add the stock cube, tomatoes, tomato purée and water, then simmer for 5 minutes. Season with salt, pepper, cayenne pepper and lemon juice, to taste. Blend until smooth, then stir in the parsley and remaining oil.

To make the batter, beat the egg briefly with a wooden spoon in a mixing bowl, then beat in the milk and white wine. Add the flour, with salt to taste, and beat until smoothly blended. Reserve.

To prepare the cauliflower, trim away the green outer leaves and then rinse under cold running water. Place in a bowl of cold salted water and leave for 30 minutes, then drain and separate into florets. Poach in boiling water for 5 minutes, drain, and pat dry on kitchen paper.

Pour enough oil into a deep-fat fryer to come one-third of the way up the sides. Set the pan over a low heat and heat the oil to 190°C/375°F. (At this temperature a small cube of bread will brown in 50 seconds.) Dip the poached florets in the batter, then deep-fry them until golden brown, using skewers to lower them into the oil and cooking in batches, if necessary. Remove from the pan with a slotted spoon and drain on kitchen paper. Serve the deep-fried florets hot, accompanied by tomato sauce.

Serves 4

Calabaza 'El Molino'
Puréed pumpkin

There is a charming old mill just below the little town of Dúrcal in the Alpujarra mountain region just below Granada. Part museum, part cooking school, part restaurant, the old mill is the dream child of Manolo and Javier Carrillo-Diaz, who have set up an association for research into Moorish influences on Andalusian food. Going there is an adventure. On my last visit I enjoyed an intriguing puréed pumpkin starter, served with *longaniza* sausages and a light tomato coulis. I give you my version.

900 g / 2 lb pumpkin, peeled, seeded and coarsely grated
4 tablespoons olive oil or butter
1 Spanish onion, finely chopped
2 cloves garlic, finely chopped
½ teaspoon ground cumin
½ teaspoon ground ginger

½ teaspoon ground *pimentón* (Spanish sweet pepper)
1 teaspoon ground cinnamon
salt and freshly ground pepper
pinch of crushed dried chillies
8–12 x 6.5-cm/2½-inch *longaniza* sausages, simmered in tomato coulis (see below)

First, prepare the pumpkin purée. In a casserole, heat the olive oil or butter until it just begins to sizzle. Add the onion and garlic and sauté, stirring from time to time, until the vegetables are soft without taking on colour. Then stir in the grated pumpkin and spices, cover and cook over a gentle heat for 10 to 15 minutes, or until the pumpkin is very soft.

Leave the pumpkin to cool, then purée in a blender or food processor.

Return the purée to the saucepan and reheat gently. Season with salt, pepper and a hint of crushed dried chillies, and serve immediately with *longaniza* sausages, which you have pan-seared in 3 tablespoons each olive oil and water with 1 clove finely chopped garlic. When the water and oil has reduced to a glaze and the sausages are golden brown, add a 400-g / 14-oz can of chopped tomatoes and a little more olive oil, and simmer gently for 20 minutes, or until the sausages are cooked through.

Serves 4 to 6

Garbanzos a la sevillana
Quick chickpeas Sevilla-style

This Andalusian recipe uses canned chickpeas and chopped tomatoes for a quick answer to a vegetable dinner high in flavour. It uses 1½ cans of chickpeas, so save the remaining half a can to use as a garnish for a Spanish soup or salad at another meal, or mash them with a little lemon juice, olive oil and crushed black peppercorns to serve on crusty rounds of country bread as a *tapa*.

1½ x 400-g / 14-oz cans chickpeas, drained

2 small sweet potatoes (orange-fleshed)

4 tablespoons olive oil

½ large Spanish onion, finely chopped

2–3 cloves garlic, finely sliced

1 x 400-g / 14-oz can chopped peeled tomatoes

4 tablespoons rice

300 ml / ½ pint vegetable stock

salt and freshly ground pepper

pinch of crushed dried chillies

lemon juice

4 tablespoons chopped flat-leaf parsley

Pour the chickpeas into a colander and rinse well in cold water. Drain again and reserve. Peel the sweet potatoes and cut into 2.5-cm / 1-inch cubes. Reserve.

When ready to cook, heat the olive oil in a medium-sized saucepan or flameproof casserole. When the oil sizzles, add the onion and garlic and sauté, stirring constantly, until the vegetables are pale gold. Watch carefully: do not let them brown.

Add the chickpeas, sweet potato cubes, tomatoes, rice and vegetable stock. Season with salt, pepper and crushed dried chillies, to taste. Lower the heat and simmer, covered, for about 20 minutes, or until the rice and sweet potatoes are tender.

Just before serving, correct the seasoning. Add a squeeze or two of lemon juice and garnish with the parsley.

Serves 4 to 6

Chapter 12

CREMA AND OTHER

I have rounded up a dessert trolley for you of the exceptional sweets and puddings that I have enjoyed on my visits to Spain over the past five years. If you are going to Spain this year, make sure you try their tarts and cakes, not to mention their wonderful fruit, still grown for flavour and perfume rather than commercial viability. Try, if you can, the granddaddy of melted chocolate puddings, *pastel al chocolate*, as served by its creator Juan Mari Arzak at his restaurant, Arzak, deservedly one of San Sebastián's, and thus Spain's, best. Or *leche frita*, fried cream, served at Valencia's noted Albacar, or *torrijas*, an old-fashioned bread and honey pudding from Castillo de Monda, a charming castle/hotel in Andalusia.

And above all, wonder of wonders, a remarkable orange-flavoured *crema catalana* that I first enjoyed in a private home in Sevilla. If you have only previously tasted *crema catalana* in restaurants, you may not know what I am talking about, for often in Spain restaurant sweets are bought in. Only the better restaurants produce their own desserts and puddings *en casa*. And a bought-in *crema catalana* is, after all, even at its best, only a custard cream, and we've all had plenty of those. But this five-egg recipe, with its subtle citrus flavouring, is in a class of its own.

CATALANA
POSTRES

Crema catalana
Catalan custard cream

This is the beginning and end of all custard creams, although you might not know it from those on offer in non-caring restaurants who mistakenly fall back on commercial mixes. You just have to make this wonderful recipe: it is the comfort food that dreams are made of.

500 ml / 16 fl oz milk

250 ml / 8 fl oz whipping cream

finely grated zest of 1 orange

5 egg yolks

100 g / 4 oz sugar, plus extra to caramelize

1 tablespoon cornflour

6 tablespoons orange juice

2 teaspoons vanilla essence

In a medium-sized saucepan, combine the milk, cream and orange zest. Place the pan over a low heat and simmer for 5 minutes. Then remove the pan from the heat.

While the milk and cream are heating, combine the egg yolks and sugar in a medium-sized bowl and whisk with an electric hand-held beater until the mixture is thick and lemon-coloured.

Stir the infused milk, cream and orange zest into the egg and sugar mixture, a little at a time, beating with the electric beater after each addition. Dissolve the cornflour in the orange juice and then beat into the milk and cream. Transfer the mixture to a large saucepan and cook over a very low heat, whisking continuously, for about 5 minutes or until the mixture thickens, being careful not to let it come to the boil or it will curdle. When the mixture is thick enough to coat the back of a spoon, stir in the vanilla essence and divide the custard cream between 6 large ramekins or little bowls. Allow to cool.

When cold, sprinkle each *crema catalana* with a little sugar and caramelize the sugar under a preheated grill or with a cook's blowtorch.

Serves 6

Arroz con leche y pétalos de rosa
Rose-petal rice pudding

The simplest sweets are often the best. This creamy rice pudding – flavoured with orange zest, vanilla and cinnamon – is given a Moorish touch with its infusion of rose water and its last-minute scattering of pink rose petals and grated nutmeg.

100 g / 4 oz pudding rice
1 litre / ¾ pint milk
1 teaspoon grated orange zest
1 cinnamon stick
1 teaspoon vanilla essence
150 ml / ¼ pint single cream
75 g / 3 oz caster sugar
2–4 teaspoons rose water

Decoration
10–20 small pale pink rose petals
freshly grated nutmeg

In a medium saucepan, cover the rice with water and bring to the boil. Boil for 5 minutes. Drain. Add the milk, orange zest and cinnamon stick to the rice. Reduce the heat and simmer gently, stirring occasionally, for 20 minutes, or until the rice has absorbed most of the milk. Remove the cinnamon stick. Add the vanilla essence and the cream and continue to simmer the pudding for 10 to 20 minutes, or until the rice is thick and creamy.

Add the caster sugar, and rose water to taste, and stir until the sugar has completely dissolved. Remove the pan from the heat and allow to cool to room temperature.

To serve, spoon the rice puddings into individual small bowls. Decorate each serving with 2 or 3 small rose petals and a dusting of nutmeg.

Serves 4 to 6

Naranjas al Rioja
Oranges in Rioja

4 navel oranges, peeled and sliced crossways
2 tablespoons sugar
2 teaspoons ground cinnamon
Rioja wine

Decoration
fresh mint leaves

Place the orange slices in a fruit bowl, sprinkle with the sugar and cinnamon and pour over enough Rioja wine to cover. Chill until ready to serve. Decorate with mint leaves just before serving.

Serves 4 to 6

Naranjas al coñac
Oranges with Spanish brandy

2 tablespoons liquid honey
4 tablespoons Spanish brandy (or golden rum)
6 tablespoons white dessert wine
1 teaspoon ground cinnamon
4 navel oranges, peeled and sliced crossways

Decoration
ground cinnamon
pomegranate seeds, or slivered mint leaves

In a small bowl, whisk the honey and brandy until smooth. Whisk in the dessert wine and cinnamon.

Place the orange slices in a shallow bowl and drizzle the spicy brandy mixture over them. Just before serving, sprinkle with a little more cinnamon and the pomegranate seeds (or mint leaves), and serve.

Serves 4 to 6

Macedonia de frutas
Fruit salad

4 fresh yellow-fleshed peaches, peeled and sliced
2 oranges, peeled and diced
1 small punnet strawberries, hulled and cut in half
2–4 tablespoons sugar
4 tablespoons Spanish brandy (or golden rum)

Decoration
sprigs of fresh mint

In a shallow bowl, combine the peaches, oranges and strawberries. Sprinkle with sugar, to taste, and spoon over the brandy. Turn the fruits carefully in the sugar and brandy and chill until ready to serve.

Just before serving, stir the fruits gently in their juices and decorate with a few sprigs of fresh mint.

Serves 4

Higos en almíbar con helado de cardamomo
Fresh figs in syrup with cardamom ice cream

100 g / 4 oz sugar

300 ml / ½ pint water

1 cinnamon stick

2 strips orange peel

12 ripe purple figs

juice of 1 orange, strained

Decoration
fresh berries (raspberries, blueberries, small strawberries)

4 sprigs fresh mint

1 recipe cardamom ice cream (page 197), or serve the figs with store-bought vanilla ice cream or orange sorbet, or crème fraîche

In a saucepan, combine the sugar, water, cinnamon stick and orange peel and bring gently to the boil. Cook over a medium heat for 10 minutes, or until a syrup has formed.

Add the ripe figs to the syrup and simmer gently for 10 to 15 minutes, or until tender. With a slotted spoon, transfer the poached figs to small individual bowls. Stir the orange juice into the syrup and cook for 2 to 3 minutes, then transfer to a small bowl and allow to cool to room temperature. Spoon the orange syrup over the figs and decorate with fresh berries. Serve with ice cream or sorbet, or, more simply, crème fraîche.

Serves 4

Higos con helado y vino malagueño
Purple figs with Málaga wine and ice cream

1 tub good-quality vanilla ice cream, slightly softened

4 tablespoons Málaga wine

12 ripe purple figs, cut into fat wedges

freshly grated zest of 1 navel orange

8 tablespoons cake crumbs

2 tablespoons butter

Decoration
4 sprigs of fresh mint

In a medium-sized bowl, combine the softened vanilla ice cream with the Málaga wine. Add the figs and the orange zest and toss gently until the fig wedges are covered in ice cream. Place in the freezer until 20 minutes before you are ready to serve. (Keep in the refrigerator for the final 20 minutes.)

In the meantime, sauté the cake crumbs in the butter until lightly browned. Remove the crumbs from the pan and allow them to cool.

When ready to serve, remove the slightly softened fig and ice cream mixture from the refrigerator and spoon onto 4 chilled dessert plates. Sprinkle with browned cake crumbs and decorate with a sprig of fresh mint.

Serves 4

Postre de fresas y almendras
Strawberry almond dessert

A do-it-ahead, last-minute-assembly dessert of great charm. Chilled ripe strawberries, marinated in sugar and dessert wine, are ladled over squares of sponge cake and sprinkled with chopped (or slivered) toasted almonds – to great effect.

450 g / 1 lb ripe strawberries

3–5 tablespoons sugar

300 ml / ½ pint good sweet dessert wine, chilled

4–6 pieces sponge cake (or almond cake,
   approximately 7.5 cm / 3 inches square)

4 tablespoons chopped almonds

crème fraîche or whipped cream to serve

sprigs of fresh mint, to decorate

If the strawberries are large, slice them in half lengthwise. Combine the strawberries in a bowl with sugar to taste and the dessert wine. Cool in the refrigerator for several hours.

When ready to serve, arrange a square of sponge cake on each dessert plate, ladle berries and wine over the sponge and sprinkle with chopped almonds. Serve with crème fraîche or whipped cream, and decorate with a sprig or two of fresh mint.

Serves 4 to 6

Peras rellenas de dátiles con merengue
Date-stuffed pears in meringue

So many egg yolks are used in Spanish recipes for sweets, cakes, cookies and pastries that I became obsessed with finding out what they did with the whites. Well, it seems that the wine-makers of Spain have traditionally used great quantites of egg whites for clarifying their wines. This left fresh egg yolks freely and charitably available to Spanish nuns to create the famous galaxy of little sweets, cookies and pastries (see pages 208–9) that served to supplement their income. More rarely, the whites alone are used in recipes, such as this one for meringue. This recipe is a particular favourite of mine.

The Pears

100 g / 4 oz sugar

450 ml / ¾ pint water

6 tablespoons apricot jam

4 eating pears

8–10 fresh dates

1–2 tablespoons softened butter

½ teaspoon ground cinnamon

The Meringue

3 egg whites

1 pinch salt

100 g / 4 oz sugar

Preheat the oven to 200°C/400°F/gas 6. Make a syrup for the pears by combining the sugar, water and apricot jam. Bring to the boil and cook for 3 minutes or until reduced to one third.

Peel the pears. Cut them in half lengthwise and remove their cores with a melon ball cutter (or tea-spoon). Poach in the apricot syrup for 10 minutes. Remove the pears from the syrup and allow to cool.

Stone the dates and chop them coarsely. Mix them with 1–2 tablespoons of softened butter and the cinnamon. Fill the pear cavities with this mixture. Place the date-stuffed pears, rounded sides down, on a buttered baking tray, spacing them out evenly.

To make the meringue mixture, beat the egg whites with the salt until peaks form, then gradually beat in the sugar, a tablespoon at a time, until the egg whites are glossy. Carefully spoon the meringue mixture decoratively over each pear, mounding it to form a whole pear shape. Bake in the preheated oven for 10 minutes, or until the meringue is golden brown. Serve at once.

Serves 4

Frutas secas y del tiempo en salsa de Rioja
Fresh and dried fruits in Rioja

Sliced fresh fruits – apples, pears and oranges – make a wonderful dessert when simmered with dried fruits and nuts in a rich-tasting Rioja syrup flavoured with peppercorns, rosemary and thyme. Serve chilled and accompany with a celebratory glass of *cava*.

8 prunes or 4 dried figs

12 dried apricots

50 g / 2 oz seedless raisins

sprigs of fresh rosemary and thyme

2 ripe apples, unpeeled, cored and quartered

2 ripe pears, unpeeled, cored and quartered

2 small oranges, peeled and sliced crosswise

8 dates

The Syrup

100 g / 4 oz sugar

1 vanilla stick

2 cinnamon sticks, cut in two

4–6 peppercorns

2 strips orange peel

150 ml / 5 fl oz red Rioja wine

Decoration

cinnamon sticks (from the syrup)

sprigs of fresh rosemary and thyme (from the syrup)

16 walnut halves

To prepare the syrup, in a medium-sized saucepan, combine the sugar, spices, orange peel and red wine and bring to the boil. Then reduce the heat to medium, and simmer for 5 minutes.

Add the prunes or figs, apricots and raisins to the syrup and bring to the boil again. Then add the sprigs of fresh rosemary and thyme and the quartered apples and pears and cook over a low heat until the fruits are soft. Remove the saucepan from the heat. Add the orange slices and dates and allow the fruits to cool in the syrup. Chill.

When ready to serve, remove the chilled fruits with a slotted spoon and arrange in a glass serving dish. Decorate with the sprigs of herbs and sticks of cinnamon. Pour over the cooled syrup and garnish with halved walnuts.

Note: If the syrup is not thick enough, before letting it cool pour it off from the fruits into a clean saucepan and reduce over a medium heat to the desired consistency. Remove the pan from the heat and allow the syrup to cool. Then chill with the fruits returned to it.

Serves 4

Piña helada 'Jockey Club'
Pineapple ice 'Jockey Club'

The Jockey Club in Madrid was one of the city's most prestigious restaurants when I first published my weekly Spanish magazine *El menú de Robert Carrier*. At a superb dinner party to celebrate the magazine's launch, the Jockey Club created this splendid pineapple-shaped iced sweet in my honour. Make sure you pick a pineapple with perfect green leaves to create your own iced 'pineapple'.

1 large pineapple, about 1.4 kg / 3 lb, complete with
  green frond
225 ml / 8 fl oz milk
350 g / 12 oz sugar

250 ml / 8 fl oz water
3 tablespoons lemon juice
12 tablespoons apricot jam
24 toasted almonds, to decorate

Cut a thin slice from the top of the pineapple, to include the frond, and reserve. With a sharp kitchen knife, remove the peel. Remove the flesh from the hard core in the centre of the pineapple. Dice the flesh, purée in a food processor and press through a sieve into a large bowl. There should be 1 litre / 1¾ pints of purée. Add the milk and mix well.

Combine the sugar and water in a saucepan and heat gently, stirring, until the sugar is dissolved; then bring to the boil. Simmer, covered, for 5 minutes. Remove from the heat and allow to cool.

Combine the pineapple purée, the cooled syrup and the lemon juice. Divide this mixture equally between two 600 ml / 1 pint pudding bowls and put in the refrigerator. When cold, cover with clingfilm and put in the freezer until the mixture freezes firm 2.5 cm / 1 inch thick around the sides of the bowls. At this point, whisk the sorbet with a fork to break up the ice particles and return it to the freezer for 30 minutes.

Repeat this process twice more.

In a small saucepan, heat the apricot jam until runny. Remove from the heat and cool.

To re-form the pineapple, turn the sorbet out of the pudding bowls, by either (1) dipping the bowls for a few seconds in hot water, or (2) wrapping the base and sides of the bowls in cloths wrung out in hot water. Place one half of the sorbet (large side up) on a serving dish and brush the large, flat surface area with the apricot jam. Then invert the other half of the sorbet onto the apricot jam-covered surface. Carefully smooth the join with a palette knife dipped in hot water and return the shaped 'pineapple' to the freezer.

Before your guests are due to arrive, remove the pineapple from the freezer. Lightly score the surface of the 'pineapple' in criss-cross diagonals with a hot knife. Place a toasted almond in each diamond to resemble the pineapple skin. Return the 'pineapple' to the freezer until just before you sit down at the table. Then it is time to remove the pineapple from the freezer, replace the frond on top and place it in the refrigerator (to soften a little) until it is time to serve.

At the table, remove the leaves and cut the 'pineapple' vertically into long slices.

Serves 8

Helado de cardamomo con piña
Cardamom ice cream with pineapple

The haunting taste of cardamom seeds and finely pared orange zest infuse this fabulous ice cream. Serve paper-thin slices of fresh pineapple and a scattering of chopped pineapple, top with the ice cream and powder with ground cinnamon and icing sugar. Your guests will come back for more.

Cardamom Ice Cream
300 ml / ½ pint milk
1 tablespoon cardamom seeds removed from pods
finely grated zest of 1 large navel orange
4 egg yolks
200 g / 7 oz caster sugar
300 ml / ½ pint whipping cream
juice of 1 large navel orange, strained
1 teaspoon vanilla essence

Decoration
12 thin slices unpeeled fresh pineapple
remainder of pineapple, peeled, cored and cut into
   dice or segments
ground cardamom
icing sugar
6 sprigs fresh mint leaves

In a medium-sized saucepan, heat the milk with the cardamom seeds and orange zest until it just begins to simmer. Remove the pan from the heat and allow the spice and peel to infuse in the milk for 20 minutes. Strain through a fine sieve into a clean bowl.

In a medium-sized bowl, combine the egg yolks and sugar. With a hand-held electric beater, whisk until pale-coloured and creamy: this takes about 5 minutes. Stir a little of the warm infused milk into this mixture, then beat in the rest. Pour the mixture into the top of a double saucepan and cook, stirring constantly, over simmering water, until the custard is thick enough to coat the back of a spoon. Remove the pan from the heat. Cool to room temperature and then chill.

With the hand-held electric beater, beat the cream in a clean bowl, beating in a little of the strained orange juice and finally the vanilla essence from time to time, until the mixture forms into soft peaks. Remove the custard from the refrigerator and gradually fold in the orange-flavoured whipped cream.

Freeze the ice cream mixture according to the directions of your ice-cream maker. Or freeze in ice trays, or a loaf tin, for about 1 hour or until crystals form 1cm / ½ inch deep around the edges. Then remove the container from the freezer and beat the cream with a fork to break up the crystals. Return to the freezer.

About 20 minutes before serving, transfer the ice cream from the freezer compartment to the refrigerator to soften slightly. When ready to serve, arrange 2 thin pineapple slices, slightly overlapping, on each chilled dessert plate. Cover with pineapple segments, sprinkle with a little ground cardamom and icing sugar, and top each serving with 1 large ball of ice cream. Decorate with sprigs of fresh mint. Serve immediately.

Serves 6

Torta de naranja
Valencian orange tart with almonds

This warm, custardy orange-flavoured tart is easy to make in advance. Stud it with flaked almonds, sprinkle it with icing sugar and glaze it under a hot grill just before serving.

I baked pastry case, baked in two steps in a
    25-cm / 10-inch loose-bottomed tart tin (see
    facing page for directions)
200 ml / 7 fl oz freshly squeezed orange juice
200 g / 7 oz butter, diced
150 g / 5 oz sugar
3 whole eggs
3 egg yolks
25 g / 1 oz cornflour, dissolved in 4 tablespoons
orange-flavoured liqueur

Decoration
flaked almonds (about 12–16 flakes)
50 g / 2 oz sugar, to glaze

To make the filling, in the top of a double saucepan combine the orange juice, butter and sugar. Cook over boiling water, stirring constantly, until the mixture just comes to the boil. Then remove from the heat and reserve.

In a mixing bowl, combine the eggs and egg yolks and the cornflour dissolved in orange liqueur and beat until the mixture is light-coloured. Then gradually beat in the warm orange and sugar mixture. Return the combined mixture to the top of the double saucepan and heat over simmering water, stirring, for about 15 minutes, or until the mixture sets enough to thickly coat the back of a spoon. Pour into the pre-baked pastry case.

One hour before the guests arrive, preheat the grill. Stud the circumference of the tart with the flaked almonds, sprinkle the surface with the sugar and place the tart under the preheated grill until it is slightly glazed and golden brown: about 5 minutes.

Serves 8

Masa para torta
Pastry

Readers of my cookery columns and cookbooks will recognize this old favourite – an absolutely foolproof rich butter and egg yolk pastry perfect for all kinds of open tarts. Use it for *torta de naranja*.

225 g / 8 oz plain flour
pinch of salt
2–4 tablespoons icing sugar
150 g / 5 oz butter, at room temperature, diced
1 egg yolk
2–4 tablespoons iced water

Sieve the flour, salt and icing sugar, to taste, into a mixing bowl. Rub in the diced butter with your fingertips (or a pastry blender) until the mixture resembles fine breadcrumbs. Do this gently and lightly, or the mixture will become greasy.

Beat the egg yolk with 2 tablespoons of the iced water and sprinkle over the dough. Work in lightly with your fingers, adding a little extra water if needed. Shape the moist dough lightly into a flattened round, wrap in foil or clingfilm, and leave in the refrigerator for at least 1 hour to ripen.

If the chilled dough is too firm for handling, allow it to stand at room temperature until it softens. Then turn it onto a floured board and roll out as thinly as required to line a 23–25 cm / 9–10 inch tart tin. Press the thin dough into the (loose-bottomed) tart tin with your fingers and prick the bottom of the pastry case evenly with a fork. Chill for 20 minutes in the refrigerator.

Preheat the oven to 220°C/425°F/gas 7.

Prepare the pastry case for baking blind by covering the pastry with a piece of foil. Fill the case with a layer of dried beans (or raw rice), and bake in the preheated oven for 10 minutes. Lower the heat to 180°C/350°F/gas 4 and bake for 20 minutes more. Then remove the foil and beans (or rice) and continue cooking for 5 to 10 minutes, or until the bottom of the case is golden. If the crust becomes too brown at the edges at any time during baking, cover the edges loosely with a little crumpled foil.

Cool the tart shell in the tin on a wire cake rack.

Pastel de chocolate con piel de naranja escarchada
Chocolate cake with candied orange peel

Chocolate and orange. Orange and chocolate. Ever since I was a little boy these two flavours together have spelt delight. I remember strips of candied orange peel dipped in bitter chocolate; rich, dark, deep chocolate puddings, 'lightened', as my mother used to say, with the juice and zest of an orange; and a brilliant orange and chocolate 'heavy' cake (Cuban, I think; my family lived there for twelve years). How my mother would have loved this light-as-air Spanish version: orange-flavoured, chocolate-iced, with its brightly coloured topping of twists of candied orange.

6 free-range eggs, separated

175 g / 6 oz sugar

grated peel of 1 orange

4 tablespoons orange juice

generous pinch of salt

100 g / 4 oz flour

butter and flour for the cake tins

The Topping

100 g / 4 oz deluxe dark chocolate

6 tablespoons water

100 g / 4 oz icing sugar, sifted

2 large egg yolks

The Candied Peel

2 unwaxed navel oranges

strained juice of the oranges

100 g / 4 oz granulated sugar

Preheat the oven to 180°C/350°F/gas 4.

Beat the egg yolks, sugar. orange peel, juice and salt until light and fluffy. Sift the flour into a bowl and gradually blend in the yolk mixture. In a clean bowl, whisk the egg whites until stiff but not dry, and fold gently into the yolk mixture. Pour equal quantities of batter into 3 round 20-cm/8-inch tins, which you have buttered and lightly dusted with flour. Bake for 45 minutes. or until golden brown.

Place the tins on racks to cool, and when cool, loosen the edges of the tins and remove from the cakes.

For the topping, heat the chocolate with the water in a bowl set over a pan of simmering water. When completely melted, take the bowl off the pan (and the pan off the heat), and beat in the icing sugar and egg yolks. Leave to cool.

When ready to ice the cake, beat the icing again and, using a palette knife, sandwich together the 3 layers and then coat the sides and top. Decorate with candied orange peel.

To make the candied orange peel, scrub the oranges and score off thin strips of peel with a sharp paring knife. Cut off any white pith. In a small saucepan, combine the orange juice and sugar and add twice the amount of water (as orange juice). Bring gently to the boil. Add the strips of peel. Bring to the boil again. Lower the heat and simmer gently for 15 minutes. Remove the pan from the heat and allow to cool. Then return the pan to the heat. Add enough cold water to cover the orange strips by 7.5 cm / 3 inches, bring to the boil again, lower the heat and simmer for 20 minutes, adding a little more water, if necessary, to keep the orange strips moist. Repeat this process one more time to ensure the orange strips are very moist and tender. Allow to cool in the syrup. When cool, strain the strips through a colander. Place on a cake rack to drain excess moisture. Then roll in granulated sugar and use to decorate the cake. You will have candied strips left over: lovely to nibble with tea or coffee.

Makes 1 large cake or, if you prefer, 4 to 6 individual cakes (see picture)

Pastel de chocolate Arzak
Arzak's warm chocolate pudding

The best ever, no holds barred, chocolate pudding: so rich and runny on the inside that the warm chocolate just flows out as you cut into it with your dessert spoon. Juan Mari Arzak has been making this pudding for over twenty years.

200 g / 7 oz best-quality bitter chocolate, broken into squares

20 g / ¾ oz butter, plus extra, softened, butter to prepare the dishes

4 egg yolks

4 egg whites

50 g / 2 oz sugar

crème fraîche or fresh fruit purée

In the top of a double saucepan, combine the chocolate with the butter and cook, over simmering water, until the chocolate has melted. Remove the pan from the heat and beat the egg yolks, one by one, into the chocolate mixture using an electric hand-held beater. Set aside.

Preheat the oven to 220°C/425°F/gas 7. Butter 4 individual ramekins (or individual soufflé moulds).

With a clean hand-held beater, whisk the egg whites until soft peaks form, then add the sugar gradually and whisk until the egg whites are stiff. Fold the egg whites carefully into the chocolate mixture. Fill the ramekins (or soufflé moulds) with this mixture and cook in the preheated oven for about 6 minutes, or until the outsides of the pudding are cooked but the insides are still soft and creamy.

To serve, slip the point of a small sharp knife around each ramekin to loosen the *pastel*. Turn out the pudding carefully onto a heated dessert plate and serve with crème fraîche or a purée of fresh fruit.

Serves 4

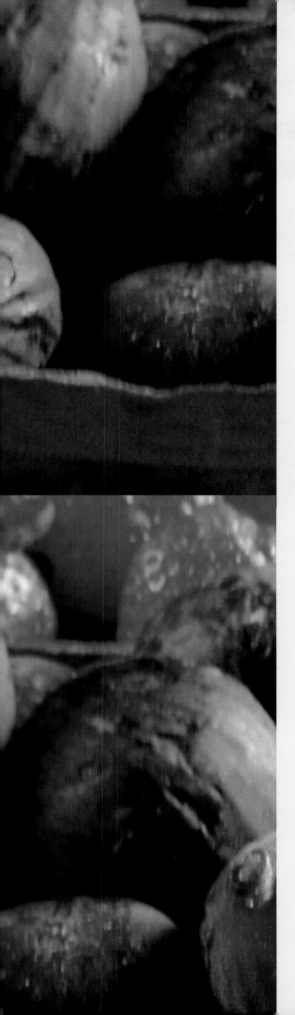

Tarta de Santiago
Almond cake with crème fraîche and fresh figs

This, one of the most famous cakes in Spain, is almond-flavoured (and textured), moist and crumbly. Serve it with purple fig 'flowers' (ripe figs, cut almost to the base, so the four quarters make petals) and a dollop of crème fraîche.

100 g / 4 oz icing sugar

100 g / 4 oz self-raising flour

50 g / 2 oz ground almonds

3 egg yolks

125 ml / 4 fl oz melted butter, cooled

finely grated zest of ½ orange

juice of 1 orange

½ teaspoon almond essence

½ teaspoon vanilla essence

4 egg whites, beaten until stiff
   (using a hand-held beater for ease)

melted butter and sifted flour for
   the cake tin

Decoration

sifted icing sugar

fresh fig 'flowers' (see introductory
   note above)

crème fraîche

6 sprigs fresh mint (optional)

Preheat the oven to 180°C/350°F/gas 4.

Sift the icing sugar and flour into a mixing bowl. Add the ground almonds and mix well. Make a well in the centre and add the egg yolks, cooled melted butter, orange zest and juice and almond and vanilla essences, and stir until all the ingredients are well mixed. Then fold in the stiffly beaten egg whites.

Brush the cake tin well with the melted butter and dust with a little sifted flour. Turn the tin upside down and tap once or twice on the work surface to remove excess flour.

With a spatula, spread the cake mixture evenly in the prepared cake tin. Tap the tin once or twice on the work surface to release any air bubbles and bake the cake in the preheated oven for 40 to 45 minutes. The cake should be cooked through but still be a little moist when tested with a skewer.

When the cake is done to your liking, remove it from the oven and leave it in the tin to relax for 5 minutes. Then remove it from the tin and allow it to cool on a wire rack before serving.

To serve, cut the cake into 6 slices and dust each slice with icing sugar. Serve on individual dessert plates accompanied by fig 'flowers' and crème fraîche. Decorate each plate, if desired, with fresh mint.

Serves 6

Brazo de gitano
Gypsy's arm

Brazo de gitano is a famous cake out of gypsy folk times; its rolled sponge shape and its tawny powdered cinnamon covering give it its name. In this version the flavours of Sevilla's orange orchards – fresh orange juice and finely grated orange zest – lend their elusive flavours to this classic gypsy cake. Make the pastry cream first and allow it to cool while you are baking the sponge. Then, at the last minute, slather the sponge with the pastry cream and gently roll up the cake as you would a swiss roll. Just before serving, dust with blended icing sugar and powdered cinnamon.

The Pastry Cream
5 egg yolks
5 tablespoons sugar
4 tablespoons plain flour
pinch of salt
400 ml / ⅔ pint milk
1 cinnamon stick
juice of ½ orange

The Cake
5 large egg yolks
225 g / 8 oz sugar
225 g / 8 oz plain flour
1 teaspoon baking powder
½ teaspoon salt
6 tablespoons icing sugar
finely grated zest of ½ orange
1 teaspoon vanilla essence
7 egg whites
1 pinch salt
½ teaspoon ground cinnamon

First make the pastry cream. In a medium-sized bowl, combine the egg yolks and sugar and whisk, using a hand-held electric beater, until light and pale lemon in colour. This takes about 5 minutes. Then whisk in the flour and salt. Reserve.

Pour the milk into a medium-sized saucepan, add the cinnamon stick and cook gently until the milk just begins to bubble. Remove the pan from the heat, stir in the orange juice, cover the pan and allow the flavours to blend for 15 minutes.

Remove the cinnamon stick from the milk and discard. Return the pan containing the milk to the heat and cook until bubbles just begin to appear again on the surface.

Gradually whisk the hot milk into the egg yolk and flour mixture. Return this mixture to the saucepan and cook, stirring constantly, until the mixture comes to the boil. Continue to cook for 2 to 3 minutes, and then remove from the heat. Transfer the pastry cream mixture to a clean bowl and allow to cool.

To prepare the cake, first preheat the oven to 190°C/375°F/gas 5. Line a swiss-roll tin with parchment paper. Brush the paper with melted butter and dust lightly with flour.

In a medium-sized mixing bowl, beat the egg yolks and three-quarters of the sugar with a hand-held electric beater until thick and pale lemon in colour.

Sift the flour, baking powder, salt and half the icing sugar into a small bowl. Add the orange zest, mix well, and then gradually beat this mixture into the egg yolk and sugar mix. Whisk in the vanilla essence and reserve.

In a separate bowl, whisk the egg whites with a pinch of salt until they form soft peaks. Then add the remaining sugar and whisk until shiny smooth: about 1 minute.

Fold one third of the beaten egg white into the flour and egg yolk mix; then fold in the remaining egg white. With a spatula, spread the cake mixture evenly in the prepared swiss roll tin. Bake in the preheated oven for 8 to 10 minutes, or until the top is golden-brown and the cake springs back when lightly pressed with the back of a teaspoon.

Dust a clean tea towel with a little sifted icing sugar. Remove the cake from the oven and turn it over on top of the sugar-dusted tea towel. Peel the parchment paper carefully from the cake and then, working from the long side, carefully roll the cake in the towel. Cool for about 30 minutes.

When the cake has cooled, unroll it. Trim the edges and spread with an even layer of the pastry cream. (If the pastry cream is too thick to spread easily, add a little more milk to the mix.) Carefully unroll the cake and arrange it (seam-side down) on an oval platter. Just before serving, mix together the remaining icing sugar and powdered cinnamon and sift it evenly over the cake.

Serves 8

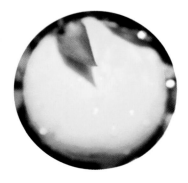  

Torrija antequerana con miel y canela 'Castillo de Monda'
Fried bread with honey and cinnamon 'Castillo de Monda'

Castillo de Monda is a high-perched hotel of great charm. Located above the sleepy little village of Monda, in the hills behind Marbella, the ancient fortress, once the site of an imposing Arab castle, has recently been reconstructed with maximum taste and flair by its English owners to become a wonderfully comfortable hotel. Each room has splendid views over the surrounding hills. Go when the almond trees are in blossom, ask for the fabulous Sirius suite, and make sure you taste the *torrija*.

500-g / ½ -lb jar liquid acacia honey

1 stick cinnamon

300ml / ½ pint milk flavoured to taste with
  cinnamon and sugar

3 free-range eggs, well beaten

8 thick slices day-old country bread, cut diagonally

4 tablespoons butter

1 tablespoon extra virgin olive oil

Decoration

1 quince, peeled and cored

juice of 1 lemon

ground cinnamon, to dust

Cut the quince for the decoration into 6-mm/¼-inch thick slices and then cut the slices into small diamond shapes. You will need at least 12. Brush with lemon juice to preserve the colour.

Combine the honey and cinnamon stick in a large frying pan. Cook over medium heat for 5 minutes. Add the quince diamonds and poach for about 3 minutes or until just tender. Allow to cool in the pan. Remove the honey-poached cinnamon stick and with a sharp knife cut into 12 thin threads. Set aside. Remove the diamonds and set aside along with the cinnamon threads. Reserve the cinnamon honey.

Pour the flavoured milk into a large flat bowl. Pour the beaten eggs into another flat bowl. Dip the bread in the milk then in the eggs. Allow the slices to drain on a cake rack over a baking sheet or swiss-roll tin. Melt the butter and olive oil in a large frying pan and sauté the bread on both sides (as you would for French toast) until golden brown. Arrange 2 slices on each individual dessert plate and spoon over the cinnamon honey. Decorate each serving with a flower of quince diamonds and thin threads of cinnamon (see picture).

Just before serving, dust the edges of the plate with cinnamon.

Serves 4

Dulces de monjas
Nun's sweets

Apart from the ubiquitous *crema catalana*, the most famous sweets in Spain are the great spreads of little egg, almond, sugar and honey fritters, cookies and meringues traditionally made by the nuns in the convents to celebrate Holy Week. Many of them are decorated in filigrees of sugar or dribbles of honey, intricately geometric in their designs.

Bizcochos de almendras y piñones
Almond butter biscuits with pine nuts

50 g / 2 oz lightly toasted almonds, ground
100 g / 4 oz caster sugar
50 g / 2 oz flour, sifted
1 teaspoon vanilla essence
2 medium sized egg whites
100 g / 4 oz butter
pine nuts
butter, for greasing

Preheat the oven to 180°C/350°F/gas 4.

In a medium sized bowl, combine the ground almonds, caster sugar, flour and vanilla essence. Beat the egg whites lightly and add them to the ground almond mixture. Mix well.

Melt the butter, taking care not to let it bubble. Gradually pour it into the almond mixture, beating vigorously with a spoon as you pour, so that it is thoroughly blended.

Spoon the mixture into a piping bag (fitted with a plain 1 cm / ½ inch nozzle) and pipe out 5 cm / 2 inch lengths onto buttered baking sheets, spacing them well apart as the biscuits spread while cooking.

Place the baking sheets in the preheated oven for 5 minutes. Remove from the oven and sprinkle with the pine nuts.

Continue to bake the biscuits for a further 5 to 10 minutes, or until they are firm and tinged golden brown around the edges.

Use a spatula to transfer the biscuits to a wire cooling rack. Allow to become quite cold and crisp before storing in an airtight container.

Makes 36

Almendrados
Little almond meringues

100 g / 4 oz blanched almonds
100 g / 4 oz caster sugar
1 egg white
1 teaspoon almond essence
butter, for greasing

Decoration
24 whole almonds

Preheat the oven to 110°C/225°F/gas ½.

In a mortar, combine the almonds, sugar, egg white and almond essence and pound until a smooth dough.

Roll out the dough and cut into 24 small rectangles or diamonds. Place them on a buttered baking sheet at intervals of 6 cm / 2½ inches. Decorate each cookie with a whole almond, and bake in the preheated oven for 15 minutes, or until golden.

Makes 24

Bizcochos de almendras
Almond cookies

75 g / 3 oz blanched almonds, coarsely chopped

100 g / 4 oz plain flour

100 g / 4 oz fine cornmeal

200 g / 7 oz sugar

200 g / 7 oz butter at room temperature, diced

1 teaspoon finely grated orange zest

3 egg yolks, well beaten

butter, for greasing

18 blanched almonds, halved

Preheat the oven to 180°C/350°F/gas 4.

Place the almonds on a baking sheet and toast under a hot grill until golden brown. Process the toasted almonds in a food processor, in short bursts, until finely ground.

Sift the flour and cornmeal into a mixing bowl. Make a well in the centre and gradually stir in the sugar, almonds, butter, grated orange zest and, finally, egg yolks. Knead all the ingredients together until a soft dough is formed.

Divide the dough into 36 little balls and place 6 cm / 2½ inches apart on a buttered baking sheet. Press half an almond in the centre of each ball and bake in the preheated oven for 15 to 20 minutes, or until golden.

Makes 36

Mostachones
Macaroons

50 g / 2 oz lightly toasted almonds, ground

75 g / 3 oz caster sugar

1–2 egg whites, as needed

1–2 teaspoons ground cinnamon

½–1 teaspoon vanilla essence

butter, for greasing

chopped almonds

Preheat the oven to 180°C/350°F/gas 4.

In a mixing bowl, combine the ground toasted almonds and sugar. Gradually stir in enough beaten egg white to form a soft dough. Flavour with the cinnamon and vanilla essence.

Drop the macaroon dough by the tablespoonful onto a buttered baking sheet at intervals of 6 cm / 2½ inches. Decorate each spoonful with a pinch of chopped almonds and bake the macaroons in the preheated oven for 10 to 12 minutes.

Makes about 10

Pastelitos de coco
Coconut puffs

4 small eggs, separated

225 g / 8 oz sugar

225 g / 8 oz shredded dried coconut

butter, for greasing

Preheat the oven to 150°C/300°F/Gas 2.

In a bowl beat the egg yolks with the sugar until light-coloured. Stir in the dried coconut.

In a clean bowl, with a clean whisk, beat the egg whites until stiff peaks form. Gently fold the egg whites into the yolk, sugar and coconut mixture. Drop the mixture, by the tablespoonful, onto a buttered baking tray at intervals of 6 cm / 2½ inches. Bake in the preheated oven for 20 minutes, or until golden.

Makes 24 to 36

Leche frita con crema de whisky
Fried cream with whisky sauce

Fried cream – sounds impossible, doesn't it? – but the Chinese and the Spanish have been doing it for centuries. Albacar's version brings the age-old sweet up to date with a creamy whisky and coffee liqueur sauce. Better still, serve it with a rich ice cream or fruit sorbet, too. Albacar serves it with honey ice cream.

Fried Cream

25 g /1 oz flour

25 g /1 oz cornflour

500 ml / 16 fl oz plus 3 tablespoons cold milk

100 g / 4 oz sugar

1 lemon slice

1 small cinnamon stick

2 eggs

1 egg yolk

Whisky and Tia Maria Sauce

120 ml / 4 fl oz caramel

7 tablespoons whisky

7 tablespoons Tia Maria

120 ml / 4 fl oz double cream

2 tablespoons sultanas, plumped up in a little whisky

flour, beaten egg and vegetable oil to fry the creams

To make the sauce, combine the liquid ingredients and whisk until well blended. Stir in the plumped-up raisins, and reserve.

To make the fried cream, in a small bowl, dissolve the flour and cornflour in a little of the cold milk. In the top of a double saucepan, over simmering water, heat the remaining milk and the sugar with the lemon and cinnamon. Stir in the flour and cornflour mixture and the eggs and egg yolk, and cook, stirring, until the custard is thick and smooth. Do not allow the mixture to come to the boil after the eggs have been added or it will curdle. Strain the custard into a rectangular swiss-roll tin and allow the mixture to cool and set. Chill in the refrigerator until ready to use.

When ready to finish the dish, take the swiss-roll tin from the refrigerator and cut the cream into even-sized squares, about 4 per serving. Dip each cream square into flour and then into beaten egg. Fry in batches in hot oil until golden brown on all sides. Transfer to kitchen paper to remove excess oil and keep warm until ready to serve.

Serve with sauce poured around the deep-fried cream squares, and with ice cream if the introduction to this recipe has so tempted you.

Serves 4 to 6

Churros
Deep-fried batter fingers

These lengths or coils of deep-fried light batter are Spanish sweet snacks personified, often eaten as a quick breakfast in the many *churrerías* or *chocolaterías* dotted throughout Spanish cities. They are delicious dipped into rich hot chocolate or coffee, and an absolute must as a late-night treat after a night on the tiles: fiesta food at its best. Similar in shape, texture and flavour to Morocco's sfenj and Marseille's famous street-stall snack, chichi fregi, they are softer in texture than the cruller to which they are often compared. Make them at home. The kids will love them.

150 g / 5 oz plain flour
150 ml / 5 fl oz water
5 tablespoons olive oil or peanut
   oil
1–2 tablespoons sugar
pinch of salt

4 eggs, beaten until frothy
1–2 tablespoons orange flower
   water (optional)
peanut oil, for frying
granulated sugar, for sifting

Sift the flour on to a sheet of aluminium foil. In a heavy-bottomed, medium-sized saucepan, combine the water, oil, sugar and salt and bring to the boil. As soon as the liquid is boiling briskly, remove the pan from the heat. Quickly pour in the flour from the foil all at once and immediately start beating vigorously with a wooden spoon. Return the pan to a lower heat and continue to beat the paste until it attaches itself around the spoon in a smooth ball, leaving the bottom and sides of the pan clean. This takes about 2 minutes.

Remove the pan from the heat once more. Add the eggs, a little at a time, beating vigorously with the spoon after each addition. Then add the orange-flower water, if using, and continue beating until the paste is glossy. Fill a pastry bag (ideally, with a star-shaped nozzle) with the dough.

Heat a big saucepan (or deep-fat fryer) two-thirds full with peanut oil. When it is hot, squeeze 4 thin lengths of dough, about 12 cm / 5 inches long, into the hot oil and deep-fry until puffed and golden-brown. Remove the *churros* from the hot fat with a skimmer and leave to drain off any excess oil on kitchen paper while you continue to fry the remaining dough. Serve hot.

Makes about 16

Index

Albóndigas de cordero 20
Alcachofas 172
Alcachofas a la granadina 173
Alioli 86, 93
Alioli al azafrán 93
Alioli a la naranja 93
Almejas finas en salsa verde 26
Almendrados 208
almonds:
    Almond butter biscuits with pine nuts 208
    Almond cake with crème fraîche and fresh figs 203
    Almond cookies 209
    Almond soup 83
    Chicken in almond sauce 154
    Little almond meringues 208
    Macaroons 209
    Picada 84, 88
    Strawberry almond dessert 192
    Valencian orange tart with almonds 198
Andalusian baked eggs 72
Andalusian salad 39
Andalusian vegetable hotpot 'Castillo de Monda' 166
Angulas 117
apples: Fresh and dried fruits in Rioja 194
apricots, dried: Fresh and dried fruits in Rioja 194
Arabo-Andaluz marinade 115
Arroz a banda 103
Arroz al azafrán 111
Arroz al horno con chorizo 102
Arroz con leche y pétalos de rosa 189
Arroz con pasas y piñones 109
Arroz negro 105
artichokes 172
    Artichokes Granada-style 173
    Vegetables with serrano ham 171
Arzak's warm chocolate pudding 202
asparagus:
    Baked asparagus with pimiento 176
    Sautéed asparagus 174
Atún escabeche 24
aubergines:
    Charred vegetable salad 52
    Pan-fried aubergine slices 178
    Samfaina 95
    Stewed vegetables from La Mancha 167

bacalao 54
Bacalao al pil-pil 62
Bacalao con ostras 57
Bacalao con pasas, buñuelos de queso y picata con tomate 56–7
Bacalao vasco con pimientos choriceros 61
bacon:
    Garlic and tomato toasts 13
    Roast lamb with honey, rosemary, *migas* and *foie gras*, 'Albacar' 142–3
Banderillas de gambas y jamón con vinagreta 22
Basque chicken 150
Basque piperade 71

Basque salt cod with dried red peppers 61
batter:
    Deep-fried batter fingers 211
    Light frying batter 114, 183
beans:
    Braised white beans 23
    Classic *cocido* Madrid-style 132–3
    Don Rafael's Valencian *paella* 98
    Green beans with *pimiento* 182
    Pan-grilled lamb with baby broad beans 137
    Tolosa red bean soup 79
    Tuna and white bean salad 43
    Vegetables with serrano ham 171
beef:
    Classic *cocido* Madrid-style 132–3
    A simpler *cocido* 134
Berenjena frita 178
Besugo a la sal 129
biscuits:
    Almond butter biscuits with pine nuts 208
    Almond cookies 209
Bizcochos de almendras 209
Bizcochos de almendras y piñones 208
Boniatos a la plancha 178
Brandada 54, 128
Brandade de morue 86
brandy: Oranges with Spanish brandy 190
Braseado de ternera con ajillo 155
Brazo de gitano 204–5
bread:
    Fried bread with honey and cinnamon 'Castillo de Monda' 207
    Garlic and tomato toasts 14
    Pan-browned bread with garlic 14
Buñuelos 34
Buñuelos de chorizo y queso manchego 35
Buñuelos de espinacas 34

cakes:
    Almond cake with crème fraîche and fresh figs 203
    Chocolate cake with candied orange peel 200–1
    Gypsy's arm 204–5
Calabacines con pimientos rojos 181
Calabaza 'El Molino' 184
Calamares a la plancha 18
Calamares al pil-pil 19
Calamares fritos 116
Caldereta de cordero a la malagueña 140
Candied peel 200–1
capers: Saffron caper sauce 123
Cardamom ice cream with pineapple 197
carrots: Vegetables with serrano ham 171
Catalan coca pastry 33
cauliflower: Deep-fried cauliflower 183
Cazuelitas 17
Cebollitas en adobo 32
Cerdo con salsa de pimentón 21
champagne: Scallops with a sauce of Spanish champagne 120

Champiñones al ajillo con jamón 29
Champiñones al horno 28
cheese:
    Cheese puffs 56
    Chorizo and cheese fritters 35
    Manchego cheese and quince paste salad 44
chicken:
    Basque chicken 150
    Chicken in almond sauce 154
    Chicken with tomato and red peppers 152
    Classic *cocido* Madrid-style 132–3
    Don Rafael's Valencian *paella* 98
    Roast chicken with red peppers 151
    A simpler *cocido* 134
chickpeas:
    Chickpea and spinach hot pot 80
    Quick chickpeas Sevilla-style 185
chillies:
    Baby squid with chilli and garlic 19
    Poached dried salt cod with garlic and dried chillies 62
    Spanish omelette with chilli and onion 67
    Tuna in chilli-lime dressing 24
chives: Herb dressing 47
chocolate:
    Arzak's warm chocolate pudding 202
    Chocolate cake with candied orange peel 200–1
    Partridge cooked in chocolate 160
chorizo:
    Chorizo and cheese fritters 35
    Fideuá with *chorizo* and mussels 108
    Frazzled *chorizo* 15
    Oven-baked saffron rice with *chorizo* 102
    Prawn, *chorizo*, new potato and rocket salad 47
    Saffron rice and tuna salad 45
    Scrambled eggs with *chorizo* 74
    Spanish omelette with *chorizo* and saffron 67
Chorizo a la plancha 15
Churros 211
cinnamon: Fried bread with honey and cinnamon 'Castillo de Monda' 207
citrus fruit:
    see also limes; oranges, etc
    Citrus marinade 124
    Citrus marinade with thin wedges of lime and orange 91
clams:
    'Catalan' seafood *paella* 100–1
    Hake with clams in green sauce 118
    Seafood salad 48
    Small clams in spicy green sauce 26
Coca pastry 33
Cocas de verduras 33
Cocido 131
Cocido madrileño 132

Cocido sencillo 134
Coconut puffs 209
cod, dried salt (*bacalao*) 54, 86
    Basque salt cod with dried red peppers 61
    Brandada 128
    Poached dried salt cod with garlic and dried chillies 62
    Salt cod with fresh oysters 57
    Salt cod with raisins, cheese puffs and tomato *picata* sauce 56–7
    Salt cod and saffron fritters 60
    Salt cod salad 59
Coliflor frita 183
Conejo con ajo y limones en conserva 148
Conejo relleno de setas 146–7
cookies, Almond 209
Cordero asado con miel, romero, migas y foie gras, 'Albacar' 142–3
Cordero a la plancha con habas 137
corn on the cob, Roasted 165
courgettes:
    Courgettes with red peppers 181
    Stewed vegetables from La Mancha 167
    Summer vegetables with saffron rice 170
Crema catalana 186, 188
crème fraîche: Almond cake with crème fraîche and fresh figs 203
Croquetas de bacalao con azafrán 60
cucumber: *Gazpacho* salad 40
cumin: Grilled lamb sausages with cumin and paprika 138
custard cream, Catalan 186, 188

dates:
    Date-stuffed pears in meringue 193
    Fresh and dried fruits in Rioja 194
desserts *see* sweets and puddings
dough *see* pastry
dressings:
    Chilli-lime dressing 24
    Green dressing 43
    Herb dressing 47
    Honey and lime dressing 44
    Mediterranean dressing 48
    Picada salad dressing 51
    Saffron *vinagreta* 45, 53
    Sherry *vinagreta* 22
    Vinagreta 38, 40, 53, 59
Dulces de monjas 208

eels:
    Baby eels 117
    Don Rafael's Valencian *paella* 98
eggs:
    Andalusian baked eggs 72
    Basque piperade 71
    Catalan custard cream 186, 188
    Coconut puffs 209
    Deep-fried batter fingers 211
    Fried cream with whisky sauce 210
    Light frying batter 114
    Little almond meringues 208

eggs: (cont)
Mayonnaise 92
Meringue 193
Pastry cream 204
Picada salad dressing 51
Potato saffron omelette 70
Scrambled eggs with *chorizo* 74
Sea scramble of grilled tuna and eggs 75
Spanish omelette with chilli and onion 67
Spanish omelette with *chorizo* and saffron 67
Spanish potato omelette 66
Wild mushroom omelette 69
Ensalada al gazpacho 40
Ensalada andaluza de pimientos 39
Ensalada de arroz al azafrán 53
Ensalada de arroz al azafrán con atún 45
Ensalada de atún y alubias blancas 43
Ensalada de gambas, chorizo, patatas y roqueta 47
Ensalada de naranja y pomelo con pimiento rojo 49
Ensalada de queso manchego y dulce de membrillo 44
Ensalada marinera 48
Ensalada mixta con foie gras 42
Ensalada verde con cebolletas y aceitunas 38
Ensaladas de verano con picada 51
Escabeche 161
Escalivada 52
Espárragos asados con pimiento 176
Espárragos salteados 174
Espinacas con piñones y pasas 177
Esqueixada 57

Fideuá con chorizo y mejillones 108
Fideuá con gambas y calamares 106
figs:
Almond cake with crème fraîche and fresh figs 203
Fresh and dried fruits in Rioja 194
Fresh figs in syrup with cardamom ice cream 191
Grilled figs wrapped in *serrano* ham strips 50
Pigeon *escabeche* with ripe fig salad 161
Purple figs with Málaga wine and ice cream 191
fish 112
see also hake; salmon, etc
Fish stew 84
Rice and fish served apart 103
Spanish fish casserole 125
foie gras:
Mixed salad with sizzled fresh *foie gras* 42
Roast lamb with honey, rosemary, *migas* and *foie gras*, 'Albacar' 142–3
Frazzled *chorizo* 15
Fritter dough 35
Fritters 34
Salt cod and saffron fritters 60
Spinach fritters 34
fruit:
see also apples; pineapple, etc

fruit: (cont)
Fresh and dried fruits in Rioja 194
Fruit salad 190
Frutas secas y del tiempo en salsa de Rioja 194

gammon: A simpler *cocido* 134
Garbanzos a la sevillana 185
garlic:
Alioli 86, 93
Baby squid with chilli and garlic 19
Braised veal steak with garlic 155
Brandada 54, 128
Garlic soup 82
Garlic and tomato toasts 13
Mushrooms with garlic and ham 29
Pan-browned bread with garlic 14
Picada 88
Picada salad dressing 51
Poached dried salt cod with garlic and dried chillies 62
Rabbit with garlic and preserved lemons 148
Salmorejo 89
Sherry *vinagreta* 22
Sherry vinegar and oil marinade with garlic and watercress 91
Small clams in spicy green sauce 26
Sofrito 72, 88
Gazpacho 76
Andalusian *gazpacho* 78
Gazpacho andaluz 78
Gazpacho salad 40
gherkins: *Picada* salad dressing 51
goose barnacles 112
Goose with pears 158–9
grapefruit: Orange and grapefruit salad with red peppers 49
Green dressing 43
Gypsy's arm 204–5

haddock: Seafood salad 48
Hake with clams in green sauce 118
ham:
Classic *cocido* Madrid-style 132–3
cured (*Jamón serrano*) 15
Grilled figs wrapped in *serrano* ham strips 50
Mushrooms with garlic and ham 29
Roasted corn on the cob 165
A simpler *cocido* 134
Vegetables with serrano ham 171
hazelnuts: *Picada* 88
Helado de cardamomo con piña 197
Herb dressing 47
Hervido de verduras 168
Higos con helado y vino malagueño 191
Higos en almíbar con helado de cardamomo 191
honey:
Andalusian monkfish with honey and saffron 127
Fried bread with honey and cinnamon 'Castillo de Monda' 207

honey (cont)
Honey and lime dressing 44
Roast lamb with honey, rosemary, *migas* and *foie gras*, 'Albacar' 142–3
Huevos a la flamenca 72
Huevos revueltos con atún 75
Huevos revueltos con chorizo 74

ice cream: Cardamom ice cream with pineapple 197
ices: Pineapple ice 'Jockey Club' 196

Jamón serrano 15
John Dory: Spanish fish casserole 125
Judías verdes con pimiento 182

lamb:
Grilled lamb sausages with cumin and paprika 138–9
Lamb meatballs 20–1
Málaga lamb stew 149
Pan-grilled lamb with baby broad beans 137
Roast lamb with honey, rosemary, *migas* and *foie gras*, 'Albacar' 142–3
langoustines:
'Catalan' seafood *paella* 100–1
Fish stew 84
Spanish fish casserole 125
Leche frita con crema de whisky 210
lemons:
Preserved lemons 149
Rabbit with garlic and preserved lemons 148
limes:
Citrus marinade 124
Citrus marinade with thin wedges of lime and orange 91
Honey and lime dressing 44
Red mullet with orange and lime 124
Tuna in chilli-lime dressing 24
Limones en conserva 149
Lubina con brandada de bacalao 128
Lubina hervida con salsa de alcaparras y azafrán 123

Macaroons 209
Macedonia de frutas 190
Maíz asado 165
Marinada con lima y naranja 91
Marinada de azafrán y pimiento 91
Marinada de jerez y aceite con ajo y berros 91
marinades 91
Aromatic marinades for seafood 115
Citrus marinade 124
Citrus marinade with thin wedges of lime and orange 91
Cooked saffron and pepper marinade 91
Sherry vinegar and oil marinade with garlic and watercress 91
Masa para buñuelos 35
Masa para torta 199
Mayonesa 92
Mayonesa catalana 92
Mayonesa con pimiento 92

Mayonnaise 92
Mediterranean dressing 48
Meringue 193
Little almond meringues 208
Merluza con almejas en salsa verde 118
Migas 14
milk:
Fried cream with whisky sauce 210
Rose-petal rice pudding 189
monkfish:
Andalusian monkfish with honey and saffron 127
'Catalan' seafood *paella* 100–1
Mostachones 209
mushrooms:
Baked mushrooms 28
Leg of rabbit stuffed with wild mushrooms 146–7
Mushrooms with garlic and ham 29
Wild mushroom omelette 69
mussels:
'Catalan' seafood *paella* 100–1
Fideuá with chorizo and mussels 108
Fish stew 84
Seafood salad 48
Spanish fish casserole 125

Naranjas al coñac 190
Naranjas al Rioja 190
noodles: *Fideuá* with tiger prawns and ribbons of baby squid 106
Fideuá con chorizo y mejillones 108
Nun's sweets 208–9

Oca con peras 158–9
olive oil 10–11
olives 10
Saffron rice and tuna salad 45
Simple Spanish salad 38
Stuffed red peppers 180
Olla podrida 131
omelettes:
Potato saffron omelette 70
Spanish omelette with chilli and onion 67
Spanish omelette with *chorizo* and saffron 67
Spanish potato omelette 66
Wild mushroom omelette 69
onions:
Gazpacho salad 40
Marinated button onions in a sweet and sour Andalusian sauce 32
Mediterranean dressing 48
Onion and red pepper sauce 61
Samfaina 95
Sherry *vinagreta* 22
Sofrito 72, 88
Spanish omelette with chilli and onion 67
Stewed vegetables 167
Summer salad 51
Summer vegetables with saffron rice 170
onions, salad: Vegetables with serrano ham 171
oranges:
Alioli a la naranja 93
Candied peel 200–1
Chocolate cake with candied orange peel 200–1

oranges: (cont)
 Citrus marinade 124
 Citrus marinade with thin
  wedges of lime and orange
  91
 Fresh and dried fruits in Rioja
  194
 Fruit salad 190
 Orange and grapefruit salad
  with red peppers 49
 Oranges in Rioja 190
 Oranges with Spanish brandy
  190
 Red mullet with orange and
  lime 124
 Valencian orange tart with
  almonds 198
oxtail: Bullfighter's oxtail stew 145
oysters: Salt cod with fresh oysters
 57

Pa amb tomàquet 13
Paella 96–7
 'Catalan' seafood paella 100–1
 Don Rafael's Valencian paella
  98
Paella 'catalana' 100–1
Paella valenciana di Don Rafael
 98
palourdes:
 'Catalan' seafood paella 100–1
 Fish stew 84
 Hake with clams in green sauce
  118
 Seafood salad 48
paprika:
 Grilled lamb sausages with
  cumin and paprika 138
 Grilled scallops with paprika
  and sherry 119
 Paprika sauce 179
 Pork strips in paprika sauce 21
 Potatoes with paprika sauce
  179
parsley:
 Grilled stuffed sardines 31
 Hake with clams in green sauce
  118
 Picada salad dressing 51
 Small clams in spicy green
  sauce 26
 Sofrito 72, 88
Partridge cooked in chocolate
 160
Pastel de chocolate Arzak 202
Pastel de chocolate con piel de
 naranja escarchada 200–1
Pastelitos de coco 209
pastry:
 Catalan coca pastry 33
 Fritter dough 35
 Tart pastry 199
Pastry cream 204
Patatas a la plancha con alioli 27
Patatas al alioli 27
Patatas bravas 179
peaches: Fruit salad 190
pears:
 Date-stuffed pears in meringue
  193
 Fresh and dried fruits in Rioja
  194
 Goose with pears 158–9
peppers:
 Andalusian gazpacho 78
 Andalusian salad 39
 Basque chicken 150

peppers: (cont)
 Basque piperade 71
 Basque salt cod with dried red
  peppers 61
 'Catalan' seafood paella 100–1
 Charred vegetable salad 52
 Chicken with tomato and red
  peppers 152
 Cooked saffron and pepper
  marinade 91
 Courgettes with red peppers
  181
 Onion and red pepper sauce 61
 Orange and grapefruit salad
  with red peppers 49
 Oven-baked saffron rice with
  chorizo 102
 Red peppers stuffed with quail
  and saffron rice 156–7
 Roast chicken with red peppers
  151
 Roasted red peppers 165
 Romesco 94
 Saffron rice and tuna salad 45
 Salt cod salad 59
 Samfaina 95
 Stewed vegetables from La
  Mancha 167
 Stuffed red peppers 180
 Summer salad 51
 Summer vegetables with
  saffron rice 170
 Tuna in chilli-lime dressing 24
 Vegetables with serrano ham
  171
Peras rellenas de dátiles con
 merengue 193
Percebes 112
Perdiz con chocolate 160
Pescado frito 114
Picada 84, 88
Picada con huevo 51
Picada salad dressing 51
Pichón en escabeche con ensalada
 de higos 161
Pigeon escabeche with ripe fig
 salad 161
pimentón see paprika
pimiento:
 Baked asparagus with pimiento
  176
 Green beans with pimiento 182
Pimientos rellenos 180
Pimientos rellenos de codorniz y
 arroz de azafrán 156–7
Pimientos rojos asados 165
Piña helada 'Jockey Club' 196
pine nuts:
 Almond butter biscuits with
  pine nuts 208
 Rice with raisins and pine nuts
  109
 Spinach with pine nuts and
  raisins 177
pineapple:
 Cardamom ice cream with
  pineapple 197
 Pineapple ice 'Jockey Club' 196
Piparrada 71
Piperade, Basque 71
Pisto manchego 167
pistou 86
Pollo al chilindrón 152
Pollo asado con pimientos rojos
 151
Pollo en salsa de almendras 154
Pollo vasco 150

pork:
 Grilled lamb sausages with
  cumin and paprika 138–9
 Pork strips in paprika sauce 21
 Stuffed red peppers 180
Postre de fresas y almendras 192
Potaje andaluz 'Castillo de Monda'
 166
Potaje de alubias blancas 23
Potaje de espinacas y garbanzos 80
potatoes:
 Grilled potatoes with alioli 27
 Grilled sweet potatoes 178
 Potato saffron omelette 70
 Potato salad 138–9
 Potatoes with alioli 27
 Potatoes with paprika sauce 179
 Prawn, chorizo, new potato
  and rocket salad 47
 Spanish potato omelette 66
 Vegetables with serrano ham 171
prawns:
 Banderillas (picador's sticks) of
  grilled prawns and ham in a
  sherry vinegar dressing 22
 Fideuá with tiger prawns and
  ribbons of baby squid 106
 Prawn, chorizo, new potato
  and rocket salad 47
 Seafood salad 48
prunes: Fresh and dried fruits in
 Rioja 194
puddings see sweets and puddings
pumpkin: Puréed 184
 Samfaina 95

quail: Red peppers stuffed with
 quail and saffron rice 156–7
quince paste: Manchego cheese
 and quince paste salad 44

rabbit:
 Don Rafael's Valencian paella 98
 Leg of rabbit stuffed with wild
  mushrooms 146–7
 Rabbit with garlic and
  preserved lemons 148
Rabo de toro 145
Ragu de mariscos y pescados 125
raisins:
 Fresh and dried fruits in Rioja
  194
 Rice with raisins and pine nuts
  109
 Salt cod with raisins, cheese
  puffs and tomato picata
  sauce 56–7
 Spinach with pine nuts and
  raisins 177
Rape andaluz con miel y azafrán
 127
Rebozado a la romana 114
Red mullet with orange and lime
 124
red snapper: Spanish fish casserole
 125
rice:
 'Catalan' seafood paella 100–1
 Don Rafael's Valencian paella 98
 Oven-baked saffron rice with
  chorizo 102
 Paella 96–7
 Red peppers stuffed with quail
  and saffron rice 156–7
 Rice and fish served apart 103
 Rice with raisins and pine nuts
  190

rice: (cont)
 Rice with squid and squid ink 105
 Rose-petal rice pudding 189
 Saffron rice and tuna salad 45
 Stuffed red peppers 180
 Virgin paella 111
Rioja:
 Bullfighter's oxtail stew 145
 Fresh and dried fruits in Rioja
  194
 Oranges in Rioja 190
rocket: Prawn, chorizo, new potato
 and rocket salad 47
Rollitos de jamón rellenos de higos
 50
Romesco 94
Rose-petal rice pudding 189
rosemary: Roast lamb with honey,
 rosemary, migas and foie gras,
 'Albacar' 142–3

saffron:
 Alioli al azafrán 93
 Andalusian monkfish with
  honey and saffron 127
 Cooked saffron and pepper
  marinade 91
 Oven-baked saffron rice with
  chorizo 102
 Potato saffron omelette 70
 Saffron caper sauce 123
 Saffron rice salad 53
 Saffron vinagreta 45, 53
 Salt cod and saffron fritters 60
 Spanish omelette with chorizo
  and saffron 67
 Virgin paella 111
salads:
 Andalusian salad 39
 Charred vegetable salad 52
 Gazpacho salad 40
 Grilled figs wrapped in serrano
  ham strips 50
 Manchego cheese and quince
  paste salad 44
 Mixed salad with sizzled fresh
  foie gras 42
 Orange and grapefruit salad
  with red peppers 49
 Pigeon escabeche with ripe fig
  salad 161
 Potato salad 138–9
 Prawn, chorizo, new potato
  and rocket salad 47
 Saffron rice salad 53
 Saffron rice and tuna salad 45
 Salt cod salad 59
 Seafood salad 48
 Simple Spanish salad 38
 Summer salads with picada
  dressing 51
 Tuna and white bean salad 43
Salchichas de cordero con comino
 y pimentón 138–9
Salmonete con naranja y lima 124
Salmorejo 89
Samfaina 95
Sardinas a la plancha 31
Sardinas al horno 122
Sardinas rellenas a la plancha 31
sardines:
 Grilled sardines 31
 Grilled stuffed sardines 31
 Oven-baked sardines 122
sauces:
 Alioli 86, 93
 Fresh tomato sauce 183

sauces: (cont)
  Mayonnaise 92
  Onion and red pepper sauce 61
  Paprika sauce 179
  Romesco 94
  Saffron caper sauce 123
  Salmorejo 89
  Samfaina 95
  Sherry tomato sauce for *Albóndigas* 20
  Tomato *picata* sauce 56
  Tomato sauce 156, 180, 183
  Whisky and Tia Maria sauce 210
sausages:
  Chorizo and cheese fritters 35
  Fideuá with *chorizo* and mussels 108
  Frazzled *chorizo* 15
  Grilled lamb sausages with cumin and paprika 138–9
  Oven-baked saffron rice with chorizo 102
  Prawn, *chorizo*, new potato and rocket salad 47
  Saffron rice and tuna salad 45
  Scrambled eggs with *chorizo* 74
  Spanish omelette with *chorizo* and saffron 67
  Tolosa red bean soup 79
scallops:
  Grilled scallops with paprika and sherry 119
  Scallops with a sauce of Spanish champagne 120
scampi: 'Catalan' seafood *paella* 100–1
sea bass:
  Poached sea bass with saffron caper sauce 123
  Sea bass with *brandada* 128
  Spanish fish casserole 125
Sea bream baked in sea salt 129
Sea scramble of grilled tuna and eggs 75
seafood 112
  see also prawns; squid, etc
  Deep-fried seafood 114
  marinades for 115
  Seafood salad 48
shellfish 112
sherry:
  Grilled scallops with paprika and sherry 119
  Sherry tomato sauce 20–1
  Sherry *vinagreta* 22
sherry vinegar:
  Sherry vinegar marinade 115
  Sherry vinegar and oil marinade with garlic and watercress 91
snails: Don Rafael's Valencian *paella* 98
Sofrito 72, 88
Sopa de ajo 82
Sopa de almendras 83
Sopa de alubias rojas de Tolosa 79
sorbet: Pineapple ice 'Jockey Club' 196
soups:
  Almond soup 83
  Andalusian *gazpacho* 78
  Chickpea and spinach hot pot 80
  Garlic soup 82
  Gazpacho 76
  Salmorejo 89
  Tolosa red bean soup 79
Spanish fish casserole 125

Spanish omelette with *chorizo* and saffron 67
Spanish potato omelette 66
Spanish salad, simple 38
spinach:
  Chickpea and spinach hot pot 80
  Spinach fritters 34
  Spinach with pine nuts and raisins 177
squid:
  Baby squid with chilli and garlic 19
  Deep-fried squid rings 116
  Fideuá with tiger prawns and ribbons of baby squid 106
  Grilled baby squid 18
  Rice and fish served apart 103
  Rice with squid and squid ink 105
stock, Vegetable 168
strawberries:
  Fruit salad 190
  Strawberry almond dessert 192
Summer salads with *picada* dressing 51
sweet potatoes, Grilled 178
sweets and puddings:
  see also cakes
  Arzak's warm chocolate pudding 202
  Cardamom ice cream with pineapple 197
  Catalan custard cream 186, 188
  Date-stuffed pears in meringue 193
  Fresh and dried fruits in Rioja 194
  Fresh figs in syrup with cardamom ice cream 191
  Fried bread with honey and cinnamon 'Castillo de Monda' 207
  Fried cream with whisky sauce 210
  Fruit salad 190
  Nun's sweets 208
  Oranges in Rioja 190
  Oranges with Spanish brandy 190
  Pineapple ice 'Jockey Club' 196
  Purple figs with Málaga wine and ice cream 191
  Rose-petal rice pudding 189
  Strawberry almond dessert 192
  Valencian orange tart with almonds 197

tapas:
  Albóndigas de cordero (Lamb meatballs) 20–1
  Almejas finas en salsa verde (Small clams in spicy green sauce) 26
  Atún escabeche (Tuna in chilli-lime dressing) 24
  Banderillas de gambas y jamón con vinagreta (Banderillas (picador's sticks) of grilled prawns and ham in a sherry vinegar dressing) 22
  Buñuelos de chorizo y queso manchego (*Chorizo* and cheese fritters) 35
  Buñuelos de espinacas (Spinach fritters) 34

tapas: (cont)
  Buñuelos (Fritters) 34
  Calamares al pil-pil (Baby squid with chilli and garlic) 19
  Calamares fritos (Deep-fried squid rings) 116
  Calamares a la plancha (Grilled baby squid) 18
  Cebollitas en adobo (Marinated button onions in a sweet and sour Andalusian sauce) 32
  Cerdo con salsa de pimentón (Pork strips in paprika sauce) 21
  Champiñones al ajillo con jamón (Mushrooms with garlic and ham) 29
  Champiñones al horno (Baked mushrooms) 28
  Chorizo a la plancha (Frazzled chorizo) 15
  Cocas de verduras (Vegetable croustades) 33
  cold 12
  Ensalada de arroz al azafrán (Saffron rice salad) 53
  Escalivada (Charred vegetable salad) 52
  hot dishes 16–35
  Jamón serrano 15
  Masa para buñuelos (Fritter dough) 35
  Migas (Pan-browned bread with garlic) 14
  Pa amb tomàquet (Garlic and tomato toasts) 13
  Paella 'catalana' ('Catalan' seafood paella) 100–1
  Patatas a la plancha con alioli (Grilled potatoes with *alioli*) 27
  Patatas al alioli (Potatoes with *alioli*) 27
  Potaje de alubias blancas (Braised white beans) 23
  Sardinas a la plancha (Grilled sardines) 31
  Sardinas rellenas a la plancha (Grilled stuffed sardines) 31
  simple 12–15
Tarta de Santiago 203
tarts: Valencian orange tart with almonds 198
Tia Maria: Whisky and Tia Maria sauce 210
toasts: Garlic and tomato toasts 13
Tolosa red bean soup 79
Tomates asados 165
tomato purée: Lamb meatballs 20–1
tomatoes 162
  Andalusian *gazpacho* 78
  Andalusian salad 39
  Basque chicken 150
  Chicken with tomato and red peppers 152
  Don Rafael's Valencian *paella* 98
  Fresh tomato sauce 183
  Garlic and tomato toasts 13
  Gazpacho salad 40
  Quick chickpeas Sevilla-style 185
  Roasted tomatoes 165
  Romesco 94
  Salmorejo 89
  Samfaina 95
  Simple Spanish salad 38

tomatoes: (cont)
  Sofrito 72, 88
  Stewed vegetables from La Mancha 167
  Summer salad 51
  Summer vegetables with saffron rice 170
  Tomato *picata* sauce 56
  Tomato sauce 156, 180
Torrija antequerana con miel y canela 'Castillo de Monda' 207
Torta de naranja 198
Tortilla 64
Tortilla con chile y cebolla 67
Tortilla de chorizo con azafrán 67
Tortilla de setas 69
Tortilla española 66
Tortilla española de azafrán 70
tuna:
  Saffron rice and tuna salad 45
  Sea scramble of grilled tuna and eggs 75
  Tuna in chilli-lime dressing 24
  Tuna and white bean salad 43

Valencian boiled vegetables 168
Valencian orange tart with almonds 198
veal: Braised veal steak with garlic 155
vegetables 162
  see also beans; potatoes, etc
  Andalusian vegetable hotpot 'Castillo de Monda' 166
  Charred vegetable salad 52
  Roasted vegetables 165
  Stewed vegetables from La Mancha 167
  Summer vegetables with saffron rice 170
  Valencian boiled vegetables 168
  Vegetable croustades 33
  Vegetable stock 168
  Vegetables with serrano ham 171
Verduras asadas 165
Verduras con jamón serrano 171
Verduras de verano con arroz al azafrán 170
Vieiras con cava 120
Vieiras a la plancha con pimentón y jerez 119
Vinagreta 38, 40, 53, 59
  Saffron *vinagreta* 45, 53
  Sherry *vinagreta* 22

watercress:
  Sherry vinegar and oil marinade with garlic and watercress 91
  Summer salad 51
Whisky and Tia Maria sauce 210
wine:
  Bullfighter's oxtail stew 145
  Fresh and dried fruits in Rioja 194
  Marinated button onions in a sweet and sour Andalusian sauce 32
  Oranges in Rioja 190
  Purple figs with Málaga wine and ice cream 191
  Small clams in spicy green sauce 26
  Strawberry almond dessert 192

Zarzuela 84

Acknowledgements

So many people have helped with this book. First of all my publishers, Boxtree at Macmillan, who joined with me so wholeheartedly when I first mentioned Spain as the subject for my next book.

My old friend Mohamed Bari travelled selflessly with me for two months, planning the itinerary, driving the car, acting as translator when my rudimentary Spanish, or my French or Italian, just didn't get across, and was the perfect photographer's assistant when I took the thousands of variables for the many photographs in this book. I especially want to thank him.

I also want to thank the Málaga office of tourism who first introduced me to the gastronomic delights of Andalusia and patiently took me to restaurants and *bodegas* in Málaga. They hosted one of the greatest luncheons of my life: a trip through Andalusia's gastronomic history in one great meal.

And then there are the wonderful meals I enjoyed wherever I went on my travels. I would like to thank Don Rafael Vidal, king of *paella del país*, who taught me just what a true wood-fired countryman's *paella* could be in his restaurant Levante at Benissanó just outside Valencia; the brothers Albacar, Tito and Salvador, whose elegant restaurant, Albacar, in Valencia itself, became one of my favourite restaurants in Spain; Picata, on the seafront in Valencia, where I finally understood what all the fuss was about when it came to a magnificent *arroz a banda*; La Barceloneta and Ca L'Isidre in Barcelona; José Luis Capo and Dominique Fourny, chef and proprietor of Maricel in Sitges; and Manolo and Javier Carrillo-Diaz in their restaurant/museum El Molino in the little town of Dúrcal in the Alpujarras, who so unquestioningly and patiently let me photograph the foods I ate as they arrived at the table. And a special thank you to Bruce Freeman and John Morris, my English friends, the proprietors of El Castillo de Monda, in the almond-blossom-covered hillsides above Málaga, where I stayed one perfect spring weekend that seemed to bring into focus the many pleasures of Spain.

I missed, I am afraid, Pedro Subijana of Akelare in San Sebastián and Ferran Adrià of El Bulli in Roses – their restaurants were closed on two of my visits – but I did get to know Juan Mari Arzak, the third of the famous triumvirate, the instigators of Spain's modern *cocina*, in his brilliant restaurant high on the hill over-looking San Sebastián, where he and his beautiful daughter Elena overwhelmed me with their generosity, their talents and their charm.

Great Dishes of Spain has been one long series of fabulous adventures. I am almost sorry that I cannot do it all over again. Maybe I will …